HANDBOOK OF PSYCHOLOGICAL TERMS

by

PHILIP L. HARRIMAN

About the Author

PHILIP L. HARRIMAN was professor of psychology at Bucknell University, visiting professor of psychology at Susquehanna University and advisory editor for the *Encyclopedia Americana*. He contributed many articles to scientific journals and is the author of *Modern Psychology,* Littlefield, Adams & Co. 1969.

About the Book

THE PURPOSE of this handbook is to give concise definitions of the technical terms which appear in the literature of psychology. Variant forms of the terms have been omitted in order to conserve space.

Though this book was prepared with the undergraduate student in mind, it will serve a purpose for the general reader who studies psychological literature.

HANDBOOK OF
PSYCHOLOGICAL TERMS

by
PHILIP L. HARRIMAN

Professor of Psychology, Emeritus
Bucknell University

Visiting Professor
Susquehanna University

A HELIX BOOK

ROWMAN & ALLANHELD
Totowa, New Jersey

First Edition, 1959

Reprinted, 1961, 1963, 1966, 1968, 1969,
1971, 1974, 1975, 1977, 1980

Library of Congress Catalog No. 58-12753

PRINTED IN THE UNITED STATES OF AMERICA

FOREWORD

This *Handbook* is designed to be an inexpensive, convenient reference on terms and concepts which have technical meanings in, or which are peculiar to, psychology and cognate fields.

For more complete definitions, etymologies, and variant usages, the student must consult such references as the following:

Baldwin's *Dictionary of Philosophy and Psychology;*
Dorland's *American Illustrated Medical Dictionary;*
Drever's *Dictionary of Psychology;*
English and English's *Psychological and Psychoanalytical Terms;* and especially
Webster's New International Dictionary.

Here the purpose is to speed the reader on the way through the maze of technical vocabulary in scientific psychology. The definitions are terse and often tautological, but they suggest the meanings when they are referred to the contexts in which they temporarily halted the reader.

Though this little book was prepared with the undergraduate and first-year graduate student in mind, it will serve a purpose for the general reader who studies psychological literature.

HANDBOOK OF
PSYCHOLOGICAL TERMS

a-, an-: (Greek prefix) *lack* or *loss of.*

a posteriori reasoning: that which is inductive and empirical; that which proceeds from observed data to a general conclusion.

a priori reasoning: that which proceeds from assumptions, established premises, authoritative or intuitive propositions, to another conclusion.

ab-: Latin prefix meaning *away from.*

abalienated: psychotic.

abarognosis: inability to perceive differences in lifted weights.

abasia: incoordination in walking.

abaxial: located away from the lateral or the horizontal axis of the body.

ABC method: the procedure in which the child is taught to read by initial drills on the alphabet, then on combinations, and next on words.

abdomen: that part of the body, or the cavity, situated between the thorax and the pelvis. The middle area is divided from the top down into the following regions: epigastric, umbilical, and hypogastric; on the lateral sides the parts from top down are, respectively, hypochondriac, lumbar, and inguinal sections.

abducent nerve: the 6th cranial nerve, reaching out to the external rectus muscle of the eyeball.

abductor muscle: one which, when contracted, pulls a member of the body away from the normal axis.

ABEPP: American Board of Examiners in Professional Psychology.

aberrant behavior: that which deviates from psychological or social norms.

aberration: a disorder not grave enough to be a psychosis.

abient behavior: an avoidance reaction.

ability: proficiency in any type of general or specific behavior.

abiotrophy: deterioration of tissues.

ablation experiment: an empirical investigation of the abilities of an animal from the brain of which certain areas have been excised.

ablepsia: blindness.

ablutomania: compulsive bathing.

1

abnormal: deviating from the normal; those cases lying outside the first standard deviation from the mean; the subnormal and the supranormal as distinguished from the average.

aborigine: one of the earliest inhabitants of a region.

abortive jump: the leap of a rat from a Lashley jumping stand that does not bring the animal through the window to the reward.

aboulia (abulia): chronic indecision.

abreaction: in psychoanalysis, the revival of repressed memories accompanied by the full expression of the associated pent-up affects, usually occurring in the analysand-analyst relationship.

abscissa: the x or horizontal axis of rectilinear coördinates.

absence: temporary loss of consciousness.

absenteeism: in business and industry, repeated failures to report for work.

absolute pitch: ability to identify the pitch of an isolated sound.

absolute threshold: the minimal energy necessary to arouse a sensation.

absolute zero: the ultimate reference point at which a scale may, in theory, start.

absorption: undistracted attention.

abstract intelligence: the ability to reason symbolically and to form broad concepts.

abstraction: the reasoning process in which common elements are found among concrete data and in which general concepts are achieved; loosely, a condition in which the individual ignores stimuli immediately present and concentrates upon other matters.

absurdities test: a psychological examination in which the testee is required to point out illogical, irrelevant, or improbable aspects of pictured situations or in verbal items.

academic aptitude: ability to succeed in traditional liberal-arts studies.

acalculia: inability to solve even the simplest arithmetic problems.

acatalepsia: inability to comprehend because of mental deficiency.

acatamesthesia: inability to understand spoken language because of a cerebral lesion.

acceleration: in educational psychology, more rapid promotion than is customary; in statistics, the positive gain, or the negative decrement, shown when test scores are plotted in a cumulative frequency curve.

acceptance: in counseling, a nonjudgmental attitude by the therapist.

accessible: lacking resistance to the therapist's help.

accessory apparatus: all parts which make up a sense organ and facilitate the function of the receptor cells.

accident proneness: the tendency to incur many accidents because of mental conflicts, sensory deficits, or lack of aptitude for the performance.

accommodation: adjustments in a sense organ which facilitate maximum stimulation of receptor cells; alterations in shape of the lens for near and distant vision; adjustments among groups whereby they live peacefully together.

accompanying movements: synkinesis; the muscular activities which are by-products of a directed series of motor actions or which arise during periods of intense concentration.

accomplishment: any performance measured by a standard of reference.

accomplishment quotient: educational age over mental age as a ratio between actual and expected achievement.

accomplishment test: a measure of achievement, usually of individual subjects in the curriculum or a sampling of the curriculum as a whole.

accretion: that which is additive, as in rote acquisitions of details.

acculturation: the process of a newly arrived immigrant in learning the customs of the adopted country; the imposition of a foreign culture upon the subject group.

ACE: the American Council on Education.

acedia: a condition of melancholia and apathy.

acetycholine: a substance believed to mediate the synaptic function in some reflex systems.

acheiria (achiria): congenital absence of one or both hands.

achievement test: a measure of what has been learned.

achloropsia: deuteranopia or green blindness.

achromate: a color-blind person.

achromatic: the hues from black through gray to white.

achromatism: a condition in which all hues appear as whites-grays-blacks.

achondroplasia: a form of dwarfism resulting from abnormal development at the ends of long bones.

acmesthesia: a pathological response in which stimuli normally painful are experienced as pressures only.

aconative: an act involving no intent or voluntary direction.

aconuresis: involuntary voidance of the bladder in states of strong emotion.

acouasm (acoasm, akoasm):   a subjective noise caused by disturbances in the middle ear or the inner ear, not by sound waves impinging upon the eardrum.

acoumeter: an audiometer; an instrument for measuring auditory acuity.

acoustic: pertaining to the sense of hearing.

acoustic nerve: auditory nerve; the 8th cranial nerve.

acoustics: that branch of psychophysics which is concerned with the stimuli and the sensory mechanisms involved in audition.

acquired character: a trait or alteration in body structure which is developed or incurred during the life history of the individual and which, according to Lamarck, may be transmitted through heredity.

acquisition: that which is gained through environmental opportunity.

acquisitiveness: hoarding; by older theorists said to be an instinct.

acrasia: neurotic intemperance.

acratia: extreme weakness.

acrid: harsh, bitter, irritating to skin or mucous membranes.

acro-:   Greek combining form meaning *extremity*.

acro-agnosia: inability to respond to proprioceptive stimulation, especially in neck, feet, or hands.

acroamatic teachings: in folklore, those instructions which are esoteric in nature and not to be divulged to the uninitiated.

acro-esthesia: hypersensitivity to discomfort or pain in extremities.

acromegaly: a deformation of the physique, usually with large feet and hands and a prognathous jaw, caused by pituitary dysfunction after the process of ossification has ceased.

acromicria: abnormally small head, hands, and feet.

acroparesthesia: feelings of numbness in hands or feet.

acrophobia: morbid fear of high places.

Act Psychology: a theory upheld by Brentano, which states that mental functions, not, as Wundt was then teaching, mental contents, should be the concern of psychologists.

ACTH: adrenocorticotropic hormone (produced in the pituitary gland).

acting out: the direct expression of conflictual tensions in annoying or antisocial behavior or in fantasies.

action theory: the doctrine that consciousness is basically a sequence of motor responses.

action time: the interval which is required for a stimulus to act upon a sense organ before the nervous impulse is elicited in the sensory nerve.

active therapy: in psychiatry, the use of directive methods in order to hasten the expression of unconscious conflictual tensions; techniques which are designed by the psychoanalyst to overcome the resistances of the patient.

activity quotient: an index obtained by dividing the total number of spoken or written verbs by the total number of adjectives (said by Buseman to reflect alternating periods of emotional instability, 1925).

activity wheel: an apparatus like the squirrel cage, with a counter to record the laboratory animal's rate of activity.

actual neurosis: in psychoanalysis, anxiety resulting from impairment of the anatomy or the physiology of the sex organs.

acuity: keenness of the sense organs in effecting discriminations among stimuli.

acynoblepsia: blue blindness.

ad- : Latin prefix meaning *toward, adjacent to.*

adaptation: modifications resulting from the processes of evolution which facilitate adjustment to the environment; the adjustment to the environment; the adjustment of a sense organ, particularly the eye, for intensity and quality of a stimulus.

adaptation syndrome: (Selye) physical pathologies resulting from prolonged exposure to stress.

adaptive behavior: that which facilitates adjustment to the environment and promotes wholesome psychological growth.

adaptometer: an instrument for recording changes in the lens and the pupil of the eye under varying conditions of light.

addict: one who, without expert help, is unlikely ever to break the habit of using drugs.

Addison's disease: a disorder marked by progressive emaciation and weakness, digestive troubles, and a bronze-colored skin, caused by an underfunctioning of the cortex of the adrenal glands.

adductor: a muscle which pulls towards a major axis of the body.

adequate stimulus: one which normally elicits a response.

adiadokinesis: inability to make rapid alternating movements with arms or legs.

adient reaction: behavior which brings the organism towards the source of stimulation.

adiposogenital disorder: syn. *Frölich's disease;* a condition of stunted growth, obesity, undeveloped genitals, and, usually, dullness.

adipsia: absence of thirst.

adjustment: those responses which relate to a harmonious, effective adjustment to the situation and which are likely to promote psychological growth.

akinesis: motor paralysis.

adrenal (suprarenal) gland: an endocrine gland adjacent to the kidney, the outer portion being called the cortex of the adrenal and the inner portion, the medulla.

adrenalin (epinephrin): secretion from the adrenal gland.

adult: one who has reached maturity; a person who is 21 years of age or older; an emotionally mature, socially responsible person.

adymia: lack of strength.

aerophagia: compulsive swallowing of air, as in hysteria.

aesthetics: in psychology, an analysis of the pleasantness-unpleasantness feelings aroused by an object or situation and an experimental inquiry into the reasons therefor.

affect: the totality of feeling-emotion, with reference to the pleasantness-unpleasantness quality.

affect hunger: (Levy) the small child's desire for love and emotional security.

affectation: a pretentious, unnatural role, often symptomatic of underlying feelings of insecurity.

affections: feelings and emotions, as differentiated from the cognitive and the conative aspects of personality.

affective disorder: a psychosis in which profound depressions and unjustified feelings of elation are predominant symptoms; manic-depressive psychosis.

affectivity: the totality of moods, temperament, feelings, and emotions.

afferent neuron or fiber: one which leads inwards away from a receptor.

affirmation: a judgment expressing a positive attitude toward a situation.

affliction: any disorder, mental or physical, temporary or long-enduring, or handicap which prevents the individual from making effective adjustments to the normal demands of life.

aftereffect: any result which, after a time interval, follows a necessary cause.

after-movement: the spontaneous elevation of the arm after a prolonged and numbing down-pressure.

afterimage (after-sensation): the persistence of the effects of stimulation after the stimulus itself has ceased.

age: the interval between the present date and the start of postnatal life.

age, basal: top level at which all test items are passed when test items are graded for average age levels.

age, carpal (skeletal age): the age equivalents as determined by ossification of cartilege and growth of bones.

age, chronological (C.A.): interval since birth to present.

age, educational (E.A.): school accomplishment as compared to the average pupils at various levels of chronological age.

age, mental: test performance evaluated in terms of the performances of average testees at various chronological ages.

age, psychological: a vague determination usually given by reference to puberty.

age, true: interval from conception to the present *(conceptual age).*

age norms: an array of data indicating the performance levels of average persons at various chronological ages.

age scale: a series of test items graded in difficulty for the average individual at successive chronological ages.

agenesia: a condition of sterility or impotence.

ageusia: impairment or absence of taste sensitivity.

aggregation: a grouping which depends solely upon mere physical proximity.

aggression: hostility resulting from underlying frustration.

aggressiveness: proneness to attack that which is perceived as a frustrating situation.

agitated melancholia: depression of affects with restlessness and compulsive motor activities.

agitation: mental disturbance with accompanying physical excitement.

agitographia: incoherent writing as a result of great excitement.

agitolalia: rapid, incoherent speech.

agitophasia: speech or writing marked by omissions of words, by general incoherence, and other indicators of flight of ideas.

aglaucopsia: green blindness.

aglossia: congenital absence of tongue; mutism.

agnosia: inability to perceive familiar objects and situations.

agnosticism: the doctrine that all knowledge is merely relative, and hence that absolute knowledge is unattainable.

agony: extreme pain, mental or physical.

agoraphobia: morbid fear of open spaces.

agrammatica: the form of aphasia in which the victim is unable to use the word sequences and sentence structures employed in normal spoken or written communications.

agraphia: loss of ability to write.

agromania: psychotic impulse to wander off into the countryside.

agrypnia (ahypnia): insomnia.

"ah-hah" experience: a sudden insight.

Ahlfeld's sign: uterine contractions occurring after the third month of pregnancy (possibly related to onset of fetal behavior).

Ahlfeld's breathing movements: rhythmical contractions of the fetal thorax.

aichmophobia: morbid fear of sharp-pointed objects.

ailurophobia: morbid fear of cats.

aim: a symbolically represented goal which sustains and directs a sequence of purposeful activities.

akinesia: a condition of paralysis.

akoasm (acoasm): a subjective noise within the ear.

alalia: mutism.

albedo: the whiteness of a surface; percentage of light reflected from a surface.

albedo perception: perceptual constancy in responding to the albedo of a surface regardless of the degree of illumination.

albinism: a condition, not pathological, of deficiency of pigmentation in skin, hair, and iris.

alcoholism: compulsive drinking, as a grave symptom of mental disorder.

Alcoholics Anonymous (AA): a loosely organized movement, founded in 1935 in Akron, Ohio, "to help the sick alcoholic to recover if he wishes."

alertness: speed and efficiency in learning or in making decisions.

alertness test: a time-limit measure of the speed and the accuracy with which test items are completed.

alexia: inability to read.

alg- (algo-): Greek combining form meaning *pain.*

algedonic: feelings of pleasure-pain.

algesia: sensitivity to painful stimuli.

algolagnia: active algolagnia or sadism—sexual pleasure in inflicting pain; passive algolagnia or masochism—sexual pleasure in suffering pain.

algometer (algesimeter, algesiometer): apparatus for measuring the threshold for sensitivity to cutaneous pain.

algophobia: morbid fear of pain.

alienation: in legal psychology, a condition of grave mental disorder.

alienation coefficient: a statistic indicating the lack of association between two arrays of scores; $(1 - r^2)$ ½.

alienist: a psychiatrist who presents testimony in a court of law.

allachesthesia (allesthesia): inability to locate the point where a tactual stimulus is applied.

alliaceous: resembling the odor of garlic.

allesthesia: mislocation of the point at which the skin is stimulated.

allo-: Greek prefix meaning *other; differing from the norm.*

allobriophagy: syn. *pica;* abnormal cravings for food substances.

allocheira (allochiria): the reference of a tactual stimulus to the opposite side of the body.

allo-erotism: libidinal attachments to other persons.

allopsychic delusion: projection of a delusion upon other persons.

alogia: speechlessness.

algophilia: sexual gratification from suffering pain.

alpha rhythm: syn. *Berger rhythm;* a brain wave occurring normally at the rate of about ten a second.

alter ego: a relationship so close that the other person is a "second self."

altitude test: a series of test items graded in difficulty, from easy to hard, the score being the level of difficulty the testee is able to cope with.

altrigendristic association: a relationship between members of opposite sexes which involves no erotic behavior whatsoever.

Alzheimer's psychosis: unusually early onset of senile dementia.

amathophobia: morbid fear of dust and germs.

amaurotic family idiocy (Tay-Sach's disease): congenital blindness coupled with mental deficiency.

ambi-: Latin prefix meaning *both, either.*

ambivalence: contradictory unconscious emotions toward the same situation; in psychoanalysis, unconscious love-hate toward the same person, a characteristic normal among small children but neurotic if found in adults.

ambiversion: the condition of being neither extraverted nor introverted.

amblyopia: reduced visual acuity.

ambrosiac: a musk-like odor.

amentia: mental deficiency.

ametropia: failure of retinal images properly to come to a focus.

amnesia: loss of memory.

amnion: membraneous sac enclosing the fetus and containing the amniotic fluid.

amplitude: the height of a light wave.

ampulla: an enlargement at the end of each semicircular canal.

ampullar sense: vestibular sensibility; cues from the ampulla for static and dynamic adjustments relative to gravity.

amuck: frenzied, often homicidal behavior.

amusia: inability to perceive tones and melodies.

ana-: Greek prefix meaning *up.*

anabolism: constructive metabolism; building up of cells.

anaclisis: emotional dependence upon another person.

anaclitic object-choice: in psychoanalysis, dependence upon some love object (e.g., mother or father) associated with infantile needs.

anacusia: deafness.

anaglyptoscope: apparatus for demonstrating visual depth perception by means of shadows.

anagogic: in Jung's theory, the constructive impulses of the collective unconscious.

anal character: in psychoanalysis, a personality marked by orderliness, miserliness, and obstinacy.

anal erotic: in psychoanalysis, an individual whose personality is organized around retention and/or expulsion of feces.

analgesia: insensitivity to pain.

analogies test: items consisting of pictures or words having some logical relationship, the testee then to apply this principle in selection among suggested possibilities.

analysand: one undergoing psychoanalysis.

analysis: judgment about the logical subdivisions of a situation; psychoanalysis.

analyst: an accredited practitioner of Freud's theory.

Analytical Psychology: principles and theories proposed by Jung.

anamnesis: case history up to the time of the disorder or to the start of the treatment.

ananabasia: inability to climb stairs or steep inclines.

anaphia: insensitivity to touch.

anarthria: inability to articulate words.

anatomical age: development of the body relative to the average body at a comparable level of chronological age.

anatomy: science of the structure of the body and its parts.

anecdotal method: unverified, fragmentary, often dramatic tales which support questionable generalizations.

anesthesia: arrest of the sensory functions; lack of sensitivity.

anhedonia: absence of happiness in life.

anima: in Jung's theory, the feminine archetype in the collective unconscious of man.

animal magnetism: a force allegedly possessed by Mesmer and his followers which could be used to induce trances and to cure ailments.

animal psychology: the empirical investigation of the behavior of lower animals.

animism: the primitive belief that all objects and forces of nature have psychological aspects which motivate them.

animus: in Jung's theory, the masculine archetype in the collective unconscious of woman.

aniscocoria: unequal size of pupils of the eyes.

aniseikonia: inequalities in retinal images.

anisometropia: inequalities in the refractive powers of the eyes.

anoia: mental deficiency.

anomaly: an irregularity.

anomalous trichromatism: a color weakness which necessitates unusual admixtures of the three Young-Halmholtz primaries to obtain the various hues.

anomia: inability to name familiar objects.

anomie: without norms, absence of rules for a social group; hence, a disordered society.

anorexia: loss of hunger, without aversion to food.

anosmia: absence of olfactory sensitivity.

anosmic: odorless.

anoxia. deprivation of oxygen.

antagonistic muscle groups: those which pull in opposite directions and among which, when the one is contracted, the other must relax.

ante-: Latin prefix meaning *before*.

anterograde amnesia: failure of events to register in memory.

anthropology: a broad term signifying the study of man in his historical, geographical, physical, and cultural aspects.

anthropometry: the scientific measurement of the human body, its parts, and their functions.

anthropomorphism: the conception of natural objects and events and of animals in terms of those psychological processes which occur among human beings.

anthroponomy: the science of human behavior.

anti-: Latin prefix meaning *opposed to*.

anticathexis: in psychoanalysis, the inhibitory forces exerted by the ego to restrain the primitive impulses of the id.

antispasmodic: a sedative preventing or reducing a convulsive seizure.

antonym test: a measure of abstract intelligence requiring the discrimination of words, or sometimes of pictures, opposite in meaning.

anvil: the incus, or one of the ossicles in the middle ear.

anxiety: in psychoanalysis, a pervasive apprehension of threat of danger—reality anxiety being a fear of external danger; neurotic anxiety, of instinctual promptings to engage in acts which will be punished; and moral anxiety, that which results from a disapproving superego.

anxiety hysteria: an affective disorganization resulting from a failure of the defense mechanisms to hold the unconscious fears and forebodings in check.

anxiety neurosis: chronic worry.

anypnia: sleeplessness.

APA: American Psychological Association.

apareunia: impotency.

apastia: refusal to eat.

apathy: neurotic or psychotic indifference.

apepsia: indigestion.

apesthesia: insensibility in leg or arm.

aphasia: any disturbance in the ability to use or understand language.

aphemia (motor aphasia): inability to speak intelligibly.

aphilantropy: dislike of social occasions or of other persons.

aphonia: inability to speak above a whisper.

aphrasia: inability to talk or to write coherently.

aphrodisia: a condition of abnormal sexual excitement.

aphromia: inability to make logical judgments.

aplasia: a failure in the processes of biological maturation.

apo-: Greek prefix meaning *deviation* or *separation from.*

apocleisis (apositia): morbid aversion to eating.

aphthongia: spasms of muscles involved in articulation of language.

apodia: congenital absence of a foot or of both feet.

apodictic belief: one which may be clearly and unambiguously demonstrated as being valid.

Apollonian culture: in cultural anthropology, a society which is peaceful, nonaggressive, cooperative, and hence mentally healthy (e.g., Pueblo Indian culture).

aponeurosis: the integument covering portions of certain muscles.

aponia: absence of pain.

apopathetic: exhibitionistic.

apoplexy: a sudden stroke which affects brain functions.

aposia: absence of thirst.

apparatus: any instrument or contrivance which facilitates empirical observations; in physiology any group of organs which unite in a common function (e.g., the digestive apparatus).

apparent movement: syn. *phi-phenomenon;* the illusion that movement occurs between stimuli which are separated by a certain temporal interval (e.g., motion pictures).

apparition: ghost; visual hallucination of a person or strange creature.

appeal: that which instigates action; an incentive.

appendix cerebri: the pituitary gland.

apperception: the process of integrating new material into the learner's background of experience; clearness in consciousness.

apperceptive mass: in Herbart's psychology, the totality of ideas already present in the mind into which the new material is integrated.

appersonation: a deluded person's assumption of the role of an eminent individual.

appetite: desire; craving.

apprehension: the act of comprehending data; the simplest form of understanding.

apprehension test: a measure of the span for a series of digits, words, pictures, or symbols presented but once.

apprehensiveness: anticipative dread.

approach-approach conflict: a rivalry between equally attractive goals.

approach-avoidance conflict: a rivalry between a wish to attain a certain goal and a wish to avoid it.

approximation method: the reinforcing of a response which is somewhat like that eventually to be learned through patient conditioning of the animal.

apraxia: loss of ability for habits requiring muscular coordination.

aprosexia: inability to maintain a mental set; defective ability to maintain attention.

apselaphesia: insensitivity to touch.

aptitude: the likelihood for future success, usually after instruction, in some given field of endeavor.

aptitude test: a predictive measure of a person's likelihood of benefit from instruction or experience in a given field, such as art, music, clerical work, mechanical tasks, or academic studies.

aqueous humor: the fluid which fills the space between the lens and the cornea of the eye.

arachnoid membrane: the membrane covering brain and spinal cord, lying between the dura mater and the pia mater.

Arapesh: a preliterate New Guinea society in which aggressive impulses are not overtly displayed.

arborization: the branchings of the axon of the neuron.

archetype: in Jung's psychology, the basic structural component of the racial unconscious; a phylogenetic acquisition in the collective unconscious.

archipallium: the olfactory area, located in the roof of the foremost brain vesicle and, in evolution, an old part of the cerebral cortex.

ardanesthesia: insensitivity to hot objects.

Argyll-Robertson pupil: one not accommodating to light but adjusting for near-far fixations, symptom of a grave brain lesion.

Aristotle's illusion: the illusion of twoness when a small round object is held between crossed finger tips of the same hand.

arithmetic mean (average): sum of scores divided by number of scores.

arithmomania: compulsion to count objects.

"armchair psychology":   a term of derision for nonempirical speculations.

Army Alpha: a group measure of general intelligence used in the classification of soldiers of the Army in World War I.

Army Beta: a group measure of general intelligence used in the classification of illiterate and non-English-speaking soldiers in World War I.

Army General Classification Test (AGCT):   a measure of general intelligence administered to about ten million inductees in World War II.

aromatic: an odor resembling nutmeg or anise.

array: classification of scores in order of magnitude.

art judgment test: usually, a measure of ability to select a reproduction of a standard work of art from among reproductions which violate an accepted canon of art.

arteriosclerosis: a hardening and thickening of the inner muscular walls of arteries (intima) which may occur in advanced age.

Arthur Scale: a performance (formboard) test of intelligence (1930).

articular sensitivity: sensations from joints and ligaments.

articulation: the juncture between bones; the production of intelligible speech.

artifact: a product made by primitive groups; a product caused by extraneous factors.

artless: ignorant; unskilled.

as-if behavior: vicarious trial-and-error responses.

ascendance-submission test: a measure which distributes along the continuum from assertiveness to deference to others in social relations.

ascetic: aggressive in self-denial.

asceticism: rigorous abstention from physical gratifications.

aseity: (William James) great self-sufficiency.

aselgea: lascivious behavior.

asexual: lacking, or indifferent to, sex drive.

asita: intense aversion towards food.

asocial: indifferent to the customs and values of the social group.

asonia: inability to discriminate among pitches.

asopholalia: mumbling; indistinct speech.

aspiration level: (Hoppe) alterations in expectations and goal formations for future performance as a result of an experience of success or failure.

assertion: an opinion declared with great assurance.

assimilation: in Herbart's psychology, the process of integrating the new experience into the apperceptive mass or background of relevant experiences; the absorption of one culture by another.

association: the establishment of relationships among ideas which, in Aristotle's psychology, occur at the same, are similar in nature, or are contrasting.

association test: a list of stimuli, such as words, inkblots, pictures and the like, to which the individual must respond with the first association that occurs to him.

associationism: the doctrine that sensations, revivals of past experiences, and a tendency of ideas to become linked together are the major aspects of mental life.

assumption: a proposition tentatively taken for granted without empirical proof.

astasia: inability to hold an erect posture sitting or standing.

astasia-abasia: inability to stand or walk in coordinated manner.

astereognosis: inability to perceive the shapes of objects by handling them.

asthenia: physical weakness.

asthenic build: in Kretschmer's typology, long limbs and short, concave trunk.

asthenopia: weak eyes.

astigmatism: a defect in the refractive system of the eye.

astrology: a pseudo-science of planetary influences upon personality.

astrophobia (brontephobia):   morbid fear of lightning and thunder.

asylum: an outmoded term applied to a place of shelter for abnormal persons.

asymbolia: inability to recognize signs and written materials which were formerly known by the patient.

asymmetry: lack of correspondence between two parts; skewness in an array of scores.

asynergia: lack of muscular coordination.

ataraxia: serenity, according to the Greeks to be achieved by philosophy or religion and now, possibly, by certain drugs.

atavism: recurrence of a trait or an organ that has outlived its biological purpose in the evolution of normal persons; a reversion or throwback.

ataxlaphasla: inability to speak coherently in sentences.

ataxiagraph: apparatus for measuring steadiness or involuntary movement.

athetosis (athetoid movements): weaving movements of the arms and the legs and facial grimaces, usually as a result of a brain lesion.

athletic build: in Kretschmer's typology, a well-proportioned physique.

atomistic point of view: a system of psychology which reduces mental functions to elements or simple, indivisible units.

atonicity: loss of contractions in muscles which maintain posture.

atrophy: a wasting away of tissues; progressive debility.

atropine: a potent drug that relaxes the smooth muscles.

attachment: a fixation.

attack: a sudden lapse of consciousness or a muscular spasm.

attensity: the quality of being clear in consciousness or in the focus of attention; sensory clearness.

attention: the adjustment of posture and of sensory mechanisms in order to obtain maximum responsiveness to a situation; the degree of clearness in consciousness, from a periphery to a focus.

attention span: the number of separate items or objects which, during a brief exposure, may be apprehended by the observer.

attenuation: the decreased reliability of a coefficient of correlation between two arrays of scores because of the inexactness of the measuring instruments or other undependable factors, to be corrected by some statistical formula.

attitude: a readiness to respond in a certain way when the appropriate situation occurs; a mental set.

attitude scale: a measure furnishing a quantified indicator of a person's relative status along a unidimensional continuum, usually ranging from strong agreement, through neutrality, to strong dissent.

attribute: the manner in which psychological experiences—particularly sensations, images, and feelings—differ in intensity, clearness, duration, and quality from one another.

atypical: deviating from the norm.

audience: an assemblage whose attention is directed towards a person or an object.

audile: one who learns better by hearing than by silent reading.

audiogenic seizure: a convulsion produced by an intense noise.

audiogram: a graphic record of a person's auditory acuity in various pitch ranges.

audiometer: an instrument for measuring sensitivity to various pitch ranges.

audition: the sense of hearing.

Aufgabe: the mental set induced by instructions before a task is undertaken.

aura: a premonitory symptom which occurs before some patients have a convulsive seizure.

auricular: pertaining to the ear.

Aussage test: a measure of ability to observe and accurately report a series of events or of objects.

authoritarian personality: one greatly concerned with power relationships, conventionality, religiosity, and exploitation of others; a rigid stereotyped, prejudiced individual.

autism: a fantasy.

autistic thinking: syn. dieristic thinking; that which satisfies unconscious wishes and which is not tested by reference to reality.

auto-:   Greek prefix meaning *self*.

autochthonous factors: those which, in the perceptual activities, are independent of all subjective determinants and which are derived from the structural properties of the situation itself.

autoerotism: sexual gratifications not dependent upon the presence of another person or persons.

autognosis: self-knowledge, usually as a result of treatment by a clinical psychologist or a psychiatrist.

autokinetic effect: the apparent movement of a pinpoint of light observed in a dark room.

automatic behavior: that which is done without conscious direction or intention.

automatograph: apparatus for recording unintentional movements of the hand and forearm normally used in writing.

automatisms: those activities which are performed without conscious intent or direction.

automaton theory: the point of view that all behavior is machine-like and, conversely, that mentalistic explanations are invalid and unnecessary.

autonomic nervous system: that portion which regulates the smooth (unstriated) muscles and the glands; by some authorities, all nerves and nerve ganglia not included in the cerebrospinal nervous system.

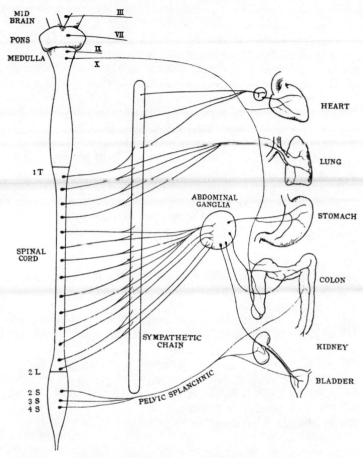

Figure 1. A schematic drawing of the autonomic nervous system.

autonomy: by reason of psychosocial maturity, having full direction of one's own life.

autophysic delusion: a false belief which relates to the patient, not to the environment.

autosuggestion: self-suggestion.

autothaumaturgist: one who neurotically strives to be mysterious or outstanding.

avalanche theory: the view that convulsive seizures may result from sudden outflow of motor impulses.

average: the ordinary; in statistics, a typical value which sums up the whole array of data and points to the location of central tendency (commonly, the arithmetic mean, the median, the mode, the geometric mean, or the quadratic mean.)

average deviation: syn. mean deviation; a statistic indicating the average amount by which individual statistics deviate from a measure of central tendency: $MD = \Sigma X/N$, where $X =$ the sum of each score from the arithmetic mean, signs ignored.

aversion: a dislike, with a strong impulse to avoid.

avoidance behavior: in anthropology, that which impells a person to flee from a taboo or to keep from forbidden actions; an abient response.

avoidance learning: through punishments (shocks), training the animal to avoid wrong responses and, hence, through this treatment to hasten the proper learning.

axilemma: the sheath covering the axis cylinder of a medullated nerve fiber.

axiology: in philosophy, the study of values and value systems.

axiom: a proposition which is taken for granted as a basis for further inquiry; a universally accepted, though unproved, assumption.

axis: a line of reference, as the cephalocaudal (head-tail), dextrosinistral (right-left), or dorsoventral (back-front) axis of the body; in a graph, usually the abscissa, or x axis, and the ordinate, or y axis, as coordinates of reference.

axon (e): the process of the neuron which transmits the nervous impulse away from the cell body and towards the dendrite of the next neuron in the chain.

Aztec idiocy: microcephaly.

babbling: inarticulate, meaningless speech sounds.

Babinski reflex: upward extension of the great toes when the sole of the foot is scratched, indicating a lesion in the cord or the brain (Babinski sign).

baby: commonly, a child under a year of age.

baby talk: an imitation of childish speech by a maladjusted adult.

backward conditioning: an inefficient but workable method in conditioned-response training in which the unconditioned stimulus is presented before the conditioned stimulus.

Bacon's method: inductive reasoning.

Baldwin's hypothesis: the view that the small child's vocal responses to speech arise from adult intervention into the child's babblings.

ball-and-field test: a measure of ability to form a plan of search to locate a ball in a circular field, used in the 1916 Stanford Revision of the Binet-Simon Scale as a test of common sense.

ballism: muscular spasms.

balneotherapy: use of continuous baths and prolonged immersion or showers in calming excited patients.

bar graph: vertical or horizontal bars to represent frequencies in an array of scores.

Barany chair: a rotating chair used in studies of nystagmus, the head of the person being held successively in three planes to stimulate the three semicircular canals.

barbitalism: a condition of ataxia or loss of consciousness as the result of excessive use of a barbiturate.

baresthesia: pressure sense.

baro-agnosis (barognosis): perception of weight by means of pressure on the skin or by prioceptors.

barrier: anything which prevents the motivated individual from progressing towards a goal.

baryecoia: reduced auditory acuity.

baryencephalia: borderline or dull in intelligence.

baryesthesia: sensitivity within the body; interoceptive sensation.

barylalia: thick, heavy speech.

basal age: in an intelligence test, the age level at which all test items are successfully passed.

basal metabolic rate (BMR): the rate at which body heat is given off while the body is at rest and while only enough energy is being used to maintain circulation, respiration, and vital cellular functions.

basal metabolism: the metabolism when resting and having fasted and when just enough energy is used to maintain basic physiological functions.

Basedow's disease: exophthalmic goiter.

basilar membrane: located in the cochlea, the membrane which includes the organ of Corti, the receptor for hearing.

basophobia: morbid fear of being unable to walk.

bathophobia: morbid fear of deep places or of an impulse to jump from high places.

bathyhyperesthesia: heightened sensitivity to visceral stimulation.

batophobia: morbid fear of passing near high objects.

battarism: stammering or stuttering.

battery: a group of psychological tests and measures, all of which contribute to a better understanding of achievement or to a personality diagnosis.

Beard's disease: neurasthenia.

beat: the fluctuations between two sound waves of slightly different frequencies.

behavior: a broad term to connote all the responses, overt or implicit, muscular or glandular, of an organism.

behavioral rigidity: inability to cope effectively with new situations.

Behaviorism: a point of view, usually identified with John Broadus Watson, which is a revolt against mentalistic concepts and which takes an objective point of view (1913 et seq.).

bel: a unit in measurement of sound intensities; a decibel.

belief: a proposition accepted with unquestioning confidence, often the result of a strong wish for credence in the belief and of a dislike to evaluate it empirically.

Bell's paralysis: palsy on one side of the face.

Bell-Magendie law: the teaching that the ventral (anterior) roots of the spinal cord contain motor fibers and that the dorsal (posterior) roots contain sensory fibers.

belonephobia: morbid fear of objects like sharp needles or pins.

Bender Visual-Motor Gestalt Test: a measure of intellectual deterioration consisting of nine figures adapted from Wertheimer, the designs to be copied by the testee.

beneceptor: a receptor initiating behavior that is pleasant or beneficial for the individual.

benign disorder: one for which a favorable outcome may be predicted.

berdache: a transvesite; one who adopts the role of the opposite sex.

Bernreuter Personality Inventory (BPI): a list of 125 questions, to be answered Yes-No-?, to appraise neuroticism, self-sufficiency, introversion, and dominance, and found by Flanagan to appraise confidence and sociability.

berserk: a state of frenzied, uncontrollable rage.

bestiality: sexual play with animals.

beta hypothesis: syn. *negative practice;* Dunlap's suggestion that, to break up a well-established inefficient habit, the learner should become conscious of the error through deliberate practices of it while knowing what ought to be done.

beta rhythm: brain waves occurring at the rate of about 25 a second.

bias: a prejudgment, pro or con, toward a proposition or concept.

bibliophobia: a morbid dislike for books.

bibliotherapy: the use of reading materials to palliate or cure a neurosis or psychosis.

biconvex: a lens convex on both sides.

bicron: one billionth of a meter.

Bidwell's ghosts: the after-effect of prolonged or intense stimulation of the retina by a beam of moving light, the subject reporting sensations of bluish semicircles moving against a whitish circle.

bifurcation: a division into two branches, as of blood vessels or nerve fibers.

bifurcation theory: in traditional psychology, the view that mind and the external world are two distinct entities.

bilateral: occuring on two sides.

bilateral transfer: the extent to which motor dexterity of a member is affected by training of a member on the opposite side of the body.

bilingual: a person who uses two different languages.

bilious: choleric.

bimanual: a task requiring use of both hands.

bimodal: a frequency distribution or curve having two modes or peaks.

binaural: pertaining to both ears.

Binet-Simon Scale: an individual measure of complex intellectual functions, first published in 1905 and revised in 1908 and 1911, the scores being expressed as mental ages.

binocular: pertaining to both eyes.

binocular parallax: the disparity in retinal images which furnishes a cue to depth perception.

binocular rivalry: the alternation of sensations when each eye is stimulated simultaneously by a different color or design, as contrasted with the fusion of retinal images normally taking place.

biochemistry: that branch of chemistry which investigates physiological functions.

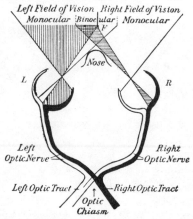

Figure 2. A schematic diagram of the decussation of the optic nerve at the chiasm.

biogenesis: the view that living organisms can be generated by preexisting organisms or parents.

biography: a case history.

biology: the science of life; the investigation of the origin, development, structure, functions, distribution, and reproduction of organisms.

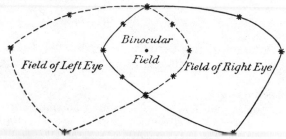

Figure 3. Monocular and binocular fields of vision.

biopsychology: that systematic view of psychological facts and principles which is based wholly upon the broad science of biology.

biostatistics: vital statistics.

birthmark: a congenital blemish on the skin.

birth order: in Adler's view, an important determinant of personality organization, the first-born sometimes becoming maladjusted, the second-born being ambitious, and the youngest being a spoiled child and a maladjusted adult.

birth rate: the number born in any given year divided by the number in the total population times 1,000.

birth trauma: in Rank's system, a shock which is the prototype of all anxieties and longings for Nirvana.

biserial r: a coefficient of correlation between a dichotomous variable and a continuous variable.

black-out: loss of consciousness.

Blacky Pictures: a projective technique consisting of a series of pictures of dogs in various situations, the child's stories being interpreted from a psychoanalytic point of view.

blend: a fusion of separate elements in taste (e.g., sour-sweet, as in lemonade), or in cutaneous sensitivity (e.g., stimulation of cold-warmth-pain receptors, as in heat).

blepharism: spasms in eyelids.

blind: visual acuity of 20/200 or less in the better eye, even with corrective lenses.

blind alley: in a Thorndike maze, a turn which brings no reward and thus serves as an annoyer; behavior in a maze which is not reinforced.

blind diagnosis: a procedure based upon data about the person, the diagnostician not seeing or talking with the person himself.

blind spot (Mariotte's blind spot): the point where the optic nerve emerges through the inner membrane of the eye and where there are no cones or rods.

blocking: an arrest of associational sequences, usually caused by the arousal of unconscious conflictual tensions.

body-mind problem: in traditional psychology, the doctrines about the relationships between mentalistic and physiological events.

bond: in Thorndike's connectionistic theory, the link between a stimulus and a response—a S-R bond.

borderline defective: in Terman's view, a person whose IQ lies between 70 and 80; one who has more intelligence than a moron but less than a dull normal.

Brace Test: measures of muscular coördination and strength.

brachycephaly: round skull; a skull that in side-side and front-back has a ratio of 8/10 to 10.

bradyarthia: painfully slow manner of articulation in speech.

bradylalia: abnormally slow manner of speech.

Braidism: hypnotism.

Braille: a system of writing or printing characters which the blind may be taught to read by touch or to reproduce by means of a template (devised by Louis Braille, 1829).

brain: the large mass of gray and white matter in the skull; the encephalon.

brain-spot theory: the view that psychoses have an organic basis and are not functionally produced.

brain waves: the recorded electrical impulses from the cortex of the cerebrum (Hans Berger), the normal voltages ranging be-

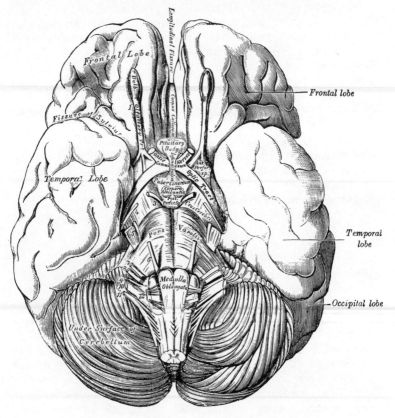

Figure 4.   The under part of the brain, with the representation of where the cranial nerves are situated.

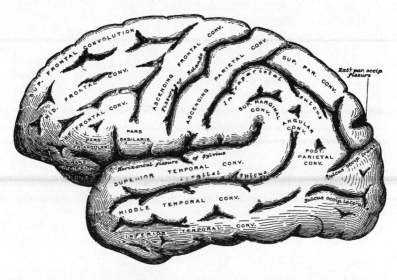

Figure 5. The external surface of the left hemisphere of the cerebrum, showing the convolutions, or gyri, and the depressions, or sulci.

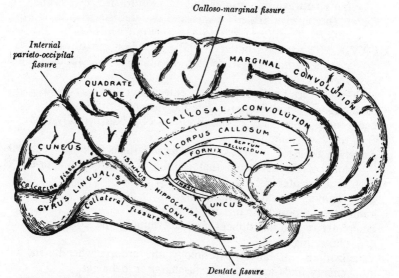

Figure 6. The medial aspect of the left hemisphere of the cerebrum.

tween 100 and 1,000 microvolts and the procedure being known as electroencephalography (EEG).

brilliance: the relative position of a hue on the scale of grays, ranging from white to black.

Broca's area: the posterior area of the inferior frontal gyrus of the left cerebral hemisphere (discovered in 1861 by Paul Broca).

brontephobia: morbid fear of thunder and lightning.

buccal: pertaining to the cheek.

bulb: the medulla oblongata.

bulimia (boulimia): morbid hunger.

Brudzinski phenomenon: in the neonate, a drawing up of the legs when the head is bent forwards.

bruxism: grinding the teeth in sleep.

burnt: syn. *empyreumatic;* a tarry or smoky odor.

CA: chronological age.

California First Year Mental Scale: a test of intelligence for infants between one month and 18 months of age (1933).

Cattell Intelligence Scale: a measure of intelligence designed for children from 2 months to 4½ years of age (1947).

CAVD: Thorndike's battery (1926) including measures of completion, arithmetic reasoning, vocabulary, and following directions.

cachexia: serious ill-health, with emaciation and debility.

cachination: loud, inappropriate laughter of a psychotic.

cacogenics: the study of the ill effects of a bad heredity (e.g., of the Jukes family).

calcarine fissure: a sulcus in the mesial surface of the occipital lobe of the cerebrum that is said to function as a primary visual center.

calligraphy: beautiful handwriting.

camisole: a popular name for strait jacket.

campimeter: an instrument for determining the color zones of the retina.

canalization: in Janet's psychology, the process whereby mental energy finds an outlet for discharge in behavior.

cancellation test: a measure of speed and accuracy in crossing out letters or numbers in a pied series, and used in tests of clerical aptitude.

canabis americana (canabis indica): marijuana smoked in "reefers."

canchasmus: loud, psychotic laughter.

canon: an arbitrary, or normative, principle used in empirical investigations (e.g., Occam's razor—choose the simplest explanation to fit all the facts.)

capacity: the limit, as determined by heredity, of a person's improvability in any learned function.

capacity: the limit, as determined by heredity, of a person's improvability in any learned function.

cardiac: pertaining to the heart.

card-sorting test: a measure of proficiency in placing cards in assigned boxes and of demonstrating habit interference.

carpal bones: wrist bones, the ossification of which is an index of the age or the nutritional status of an individual.

Cartesian coordinates: the familiar axes (x and y) of a graph; abscissa and ordinate.

case-history method: an intensive study of a single case, with all available genetic data, test results, opinions cited about the individual, usually an autobiography, results from projective techniques, and any other data including medical and psychiatric appraisals.

caste status: a class position determined by hereditary tradition and precluding any possibility of upward mobility.

castration anxiety: in psychoanalysis, unconscious anxieties causing a repression of sexual wish for the mother and a hostility towards the father.

castration complex: in psychoanalysis, the girl's penis envy.

cata- (kata-): Greek prefix meaning *downward*.

catabolism: destructive processes of metabolism.

catagelophobia: morbid fear of being ridiculed.

catalepsy: a condition of muscular rigidity, as in hysteria or in catatonia.

catamnesis: that part of the case history which is concerned with the effects of therapy and with the patient's rehabilitation.

cataphasia: meaningless repetition of words or phrases in the catatonic form of schizophrenia.

cataplexy: muscular rigidity induced hypnotically or by a fright.

catastrophe: a calamitous event; a devastating psychic trauma.

catathymia: a condition of disruptice emotions.

catatonia: that form of schizophrenia (dementia praecox) in which motor symptoms are important manisfestations of the disorder.

categorical imperative: Kant's dictum: "Act only on that maxim whereby you can at the same time will that it should become a universal law."

category: historically, Aristotle's ultimate concepts of action, passivity, time, position, possession, place, relation, quality, quantity, and substance; any basic concept.

catharsis: in psychoanalysis, Freud's early view that therapy could be achieved by having the analysand react with adequate emotionality to forgotten (repressed) experiences; abreaction.

cathexis: in psychoanalysis, the concentration of psychic energy into one channel or outlet which may be only remotely connected with the original object of an instinct.

caudate nucleus: the inner of the two nuclei of the corpus striatum, touching anteriorly the thalamus and projecting into the third ventricle.

causalgia: an intense burning sensation; thermalgia.

causation: J. S. Mill: "The law of causation, the recognition of which is the main pillar of inductive science, is but the familiar truth that invariability of succession is found by observation to obtain between every fact in nature and some fact which has preceded it."

cause: a necessary antecedent for any given consequent.

CAVD: (Thorndike) a test of completion, arithmetic, vocabulary, and directions.

CEEB: College Entrance Examination Board.

ceiling: the upper limit of performance measured by a test.

cell: the structural and the functional unit of organisms, consisting of a nucleus, cytoplasm, and a semlpermeable membrano.

cenophobia: morbid fear of barren, empty spaces; agoraphobia.

censor: in psychoanalysis, the repressive function of the ego which prevents unconscious instincts from direct expression.

center: any portion of the cortex of the cerebrum where, supposedly, some function is located; any point at which afferent impulses are transmitted to efferent fibers of the nervous system.

centile: any point indicating a variable fitted into a group of 100 intervals (e.g., the 60%-ile indicates a score exceeded by 40% of the total distribution of scores.)

centimeter: 0.3937 inch.

central fissure: the fissure of Rolando.

central nervous system: the brain and the spinal cord.

central tendency: a representative score for a frequency distribution, such as mean, median, geometric mean, harmonic mean, or mode.

centrifugal swing: likelihood of the animal to continue in the general line of travel throughout the entire maze.

cephalagra (cephalgia): headache.

cephalic index: the ratio of the skull measured for length and breadth and multiplied by 100.

cephalization: the evolutionary tendency towards dominance of behavior by the brain.

cephalocaudal axis: in man, the vertical axis of the body (head to base of spine); in lower animals, the head-tail axis.

cerebellum: that part of the brain lying below and to the rear of the cerebrum and partly overlapping the medulla.

cerebral: pertaining to the cerebrum.

cerebral arteriosclerosis: hardening of the arteries of the brain.

cerebral localization: the doctrine that different areas of the cortex of the cerebrum are concerned with various specific or general aspects of voluntary, conscious acts.

cerebralism: the speculative doctrine that consciousness is an epiphenomenon or a by-product of brain physiology.

cerebration: reflective or purposeful thinking.

cerebrospinal system: brain, spinal cord, cranial nerves, and spinal nerves.

cerebrotonia: (Sheldon) a temperament marked by restraint, secretiveness, and introversion, and correlated with an ectomorphic body build.

cerebrum: popular, the whole brain (encephalon); the rhinencephalon (olfactory lobe), the corpus striatum, and the neopallium (cortex of the cerebrum) in man.

ceremonial: in anthropology, a traditional and standard procedure in religio-magical activities.

ceremony: a ritualistic observance, usually carried on in a manner set by tradition.

cerephobia: morbid concern about inability to control urination.

certifiable: legally committed, as by reason of mental deficiency, psychosis, or other cause ruled upon by a court of law.

chain reflex: an integrated sequence of reflexes in which one response acts as a stimulus for another response.

chalone: an inhibitory secretion from an endocrine gland.

chance error (chance factor): an error occurring without bias or poor experimental design and not materially affecting the results in a large distribution of scores.

character: personality evaluated from the standpoint of an ethical code; in biology, the observable effect of genes.

character neurosis: in psychoanalysis, a compulsive-obsessive repetition of behavior which leads to suffering and disappointment.

characterology: the investigation of unique constellations of traits or of Gestalten which differentiate one individual from another, usually from the standpoint of depth psychology.

charisma: a high degree of wisdom, sanctity, or authority attributed by the followers to their leader.

Cheyne-Strokes breathing: the erratic respiratory rhythm of the newborn.

chiascuro response: a response in terms of lights and shades represented in an inkblot or a dimly reproduced picture in a projective technique.

chiasm: a crossing over: a decussation.

child: loosely, a human being below the stage of puberty.

child psychology: the scientific investigation of growth and development from birth to adolescence.

child study: a practical inquiry into appropriate ways of guiding children towards desirable growth and development.

Children's Apperception Test (CAT): a projective technique in which children interpret pictures of animals in human roles (Bellak and Bellak, 1950).

chirognomy (chiromancy): palmistry.

chi-square: a statistic indicating the relationship between the obtained and the expected distributions of scores; written usually as x^2.

chlor: green-yellow hue.

choc: a shock; a strong response evoked by a situation for which the laboratory animal has no prepared reaction.

choice point: in a maze or similar type of apparatus, the point at which two or more responses may be made, only one of which is correct.

choleric: in ancient physiology, a temperament caused by relative excess of yellow bile; irascible.

chorea: syn. *Sydenham's disease;* spasmodic twitchings and tremors.

choreoathetosis: jerky movements.

chorioid (choroid): the vascular membrane of the eye, lying between the sclerotic membrane and the retina.

choromania: syn. *corybantism;* the dancing mania which started in Germany in the late 14th century; epidemic chorea.

chroma: the degree of saturation of a hue; any hue except black, grays, white.

chroma-blind: totally color blind.

chromatic cards: the Rorschach cards which contain hues other than, or in addition to, grays, whites, blacks.

chromatism: syn. *photism, synesthesia;* an image of color when some sense organ is stimulated (e.g., colored hearing).

chromesthesia: image of a color when a sense organ is stimulated (e.g., colors associated with words or numbers).

chromosome: a small body in the nucleus of the cell at the time of mitotic division.

chronaxie: an index of the time of excitability of tissue.

chronic: long-continuing; progressively more severe symptoms.

chron(o): Greek combining form meaning *time.*

chronograph: apparatus for recording small intervals of time in an experiment; a chronoscope.

cibophobia (sitophobia): morbid aversion to food.

ciliary muscle: a nonstriated muscle which mediates the accommodation of the lens.

cinanesthesia: absence of sensitivity to visceral stimulation.

cinesia: car or sea sickness.

circular behavior: a sequence of activities in which the response for one activity is the stimulus for the next.

circumstantiality: talk which is directed towards a goal but which is repeatedly interrupted to speak of irrelevant associations and minor details.

circumvallate papilla: a V-shaped area on the dorsal surface of the tongue and containing many taste buds.

cittosis: syn. *pica;* abnormal food cravings.

clairvoyance: in occultism, the ability to perceive without the mediation of any known sense organs.

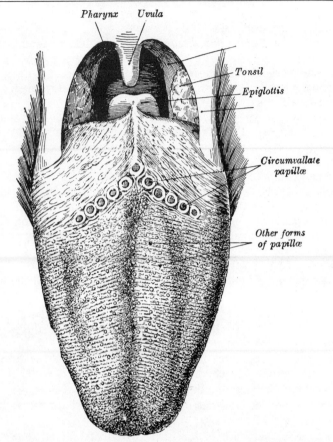

Pharynx   *Uvula*

Tonsil

Epiglottis

Circumvallate papillæ

Other forms of papillæ

Figure 7. The tongue as an organ of taste. Note the irregular distribution of taste buds (papillae).

clan: a group of persons who are descended from common ancestors.

clang association: in an association test, repeating a word of similar sound regardless of its meaning or status in the language.

class: in social psychology, a grouping based upon ancestry, economic position, social recognition and acceptability, and usually divided into three major categories: upper, middle, and lower.

class interval: the distance between the lowest and the highest limits of a step in a grouped frequency distribution of scores.

classical conditioning (Pavlonian conditioning): the learning situation in which one stimulus is repeatedly paired with another stimulus, until the second stimulus elicits the response originally attached only to the other (e.g., buzzer-food-salivation, and then buzzer-salivation).

classification batteries: groups of tests designed to measure aptitudes for various tasks in a military setting (e.g., Army General Classification Test, AGCT); in educational psychology, placement tests used in assignments to grades or curricula.

claudication: spasms of excruciating pain.

claustrophobia: morbid fear of small enclosed places.

clearness: syn. *attensity;* the condition of vividness in awareness.

client: in nondirective psychotherapy, the person who seeks or needs help.

climacophobia: morbid fear of using stairs.

climacterium: alterations in glandular balance attendant upon aging; the menopause; the male climacterium.

clinic: a place for ideographic analyses of individual problems, assets, liabilities, and personality diagnosis.

clinical psychology: that major branch of general psychology which applies facts and principles in individual diagnoses and remedial programs.

clique: a small, tightly-knit social group determined to exclude others from membership.

clitoris: the female analogue of the penis.

cloaca birth theory: in psychoanalysis, the belief of some children that infants are expelled through the anus.

clonus: an alteration of muscular contractions and sudden relaxations.

closure: in *Gestaltteorie,* the organization of a configuration into a whole or a closed system.

clouded consciousness: disorientation; confusion.

coaching effect: the spuriously high scores on a psychological test as a result of previous experiences with similar types of tests.

coarctated: inhibited.

coarctative: on the Rorschach, neither strongly introversive nor extratensive.

cocainism: mental confusion and physical deterioration as a result of prolonged addiction to cocaine.

cochlea: a snail-shaped structure in the inner ear containing receptors for hearing.

coccyx: termination of the spinal column.

coefficient of alienation: an index of the lack of correspondence between two sets of scores: $k = (1 - r^2)^{1/2}$,where k is the alienation coefficient and r is the coefficient of correlation.

coefficient of correlation: a statistic expressing the degree of association between two or more arrays of scores, usually expressed as plus 1 through 0 to minus 1;

$$r = \Sigma XY/N - MxMy$$
$$XY = \sigma x\ \sigma y$$

coefficient of reliability: an index between a series of scores and a set of equivalent data, such as observations or another set of scores obtained from the same individuals.

coefficient of validity: an index as to the dependability of the scores, usually obtained by comparing the scores with some criterion.

coenesthesia: the mass of interoceptive stimulations.

cogitate: to plan; to reflect.

cognition: the intellective functions; knowledge.

cognitive dissonance: conflicts among a person's attitudes, beliefs, and opinions.

cognitive theory: that which views the learning process as a reorganization of perceptions.

cohabit: to live together as man and wife.

coherence theory: the doctrine that, for theory to be valid, all its parts must be in harmony with the whole and with the experience of qualified observers.

coherent: that which is logically consistent.

cohesian: the tendency of successive or simultaneous acts to become associated; in *Gestalttheorie,* the condition of being brought together by closure.

cold spot: any small point on the surface of the body which gives rise to a sensation of cold.

colitis: inflammation of the large intestine.

collateral fissure: a sulcus which extends from the under side of the occipital lobe of the cerebrum towards the temporal pole.

collaterals: fibers which branch off the axon.

collective unconscious: in Jung's theory, the racial or phylogenetic unconscious determinants of behavior; the archetypes out of which the individual unconscious is developed.

colon: that part of the large intestine extending from the caecum to the rectum.

color: that quality of visual experience which is differentiated from saturation and brilliance; a generic name for chromatic hues (red, violet, green, etc.) and for achromatic hues (e.g., white, black, and intermediate grays).

color blindness: inability to differentiate certain hues.

color theory: (1) Young-Helmholz primaries: red, yellow-green (chlor), and blue; (2) Hering primaries: white-black, yellow-blue and red-green; and many other explanations from chemical, physical, or psychological standpoints.

color solid (pyramid): a figure drawing of all possible relationships among colors from the point of view of chroma, saturation, and brilliance.

color wheel: a device for rotating disks of colors to display cancellations, fusions, tints, shades, and other phenomena.

color zones: areas of the retina which when stimulated cause different sensations, such as gray on the periphery, blue-yellow next, and red-green on the central section.

colorimeter: apparatus for identifying colors in numerical symbols.

coma: a state of insensibility.

commissures: nerve fibers which connect the lateral halves of the brain and of the spinal cord.

common elements: similarities between two or more tasks or performances, which, according to Thorndike, account for what appears to be transfer of training.

common sense: in philosophical psychology, intuitions or judgments which are generally accepted without need for further proof.

comparative psychology: the science dealing with the behavior of lower animals from an evolutionary point of view.

compensation: in Jung's theory, the procedure in which system within the personality may make up for weakness in another; according to Adler, an attempt to deal with an inferiority attitude by achieving a sense of superiority.

complaint: the patient's own report of the symptoms of a disorder.

completion test: (Ebbinghaus) one requiring a word or phrase to be filled in.

complex: in Jung's theory, a group of attitudes, feelings, and memories existing in the personal unconscious and drawing into it various other experiences.

component: in psychoanalysis, a part of the libido which makes up one of the instinctual drives (e.g., masochism is a component of the sexual instinct).

compos mentis: legally sane.

compulsion: a sense of being compelled to perform an action (e.g., stepping on lines, touching objects).

compulsion neurosis: an attempt to relieve conflictual tensions by ritualistic, stereotyped purposeless actions (e.g., Lady Macbeth's handwashing mania).

conarium: the pineal gland.

conation: that part of the mind which includes impulses, motives, wishes, drives, and appetites, as distinguished from the cognitive and the affective parts of the mind.

concatenation: a hierarchy of reflexes, unlearned and conditioned, which are involved in behavior.

concave: curving in.

concentrate: to bring into the focus of attention.

concept: an idea including many separate percepts; a mental image of an event, a quality, or a quantity.

conception: an abstract, cognitive interpretation.

concha auriculae: the hollow portion of the external ear.

concrete response: in Goldstein's theory, a direct, fairly simple reaction to a situation, usually in an automatic fashion.

condensation: in psychoanalysis, a fusion of many unconscious elements into a small dream image.

conditioned reflex or response (CR): a response to a stimulus originally inadequate to elicit it.

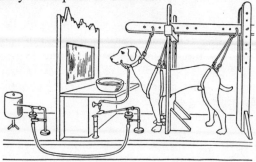

Figure 8. Pavlov's procedure in classical conditioning.

conduct disorder: antisocial behavior resulting from mental conflicts.

cone: a receptor mediating day vision and color vision.

confabulation: the process of filling in gaps in memory (as in Korsakoff's psychosis) or in comprehension by talking glibly or by chatter.

configuration: a Gestalt; any organized whole.

conflict: in Lewin's theory, a rivalry between approach-approach, approach-avoidance, or avoidance-avoidance motives; in psychoanalysis, tensions arising from incompatible unconscious wishes simultaneously operative.

confusional state: psychotic disorientation; distorted mental functions.

congenital: existing from birth, usually attributable to heredity but sometimes to prenatal pathologies.

congruence: in *Gestalttheorie,* with increasing maturity, the individual's choices made in terms of environmental opportunities and the psychological factors already differentiated within the mind.

Connectionism: E. L. Thorndike's system, in which all behavior is reduced to stimulus-response bonds, native and learned.

connector: neurons or nerve fibers which link afferent and efferent tracts.

consciousness: awareness.

constancy: the tendency of perceptual responses to remain about the same regardless of distance, degree of illumination, or position.

constitutional psychology: Sheldon's theory of somatotypes, which describes the ectomorphic build with associated cerebrotonic temperament; the mesomorphic, with somatotonic temperament; and the endomorphic, with viscerotonic temperament.

constitutional psychopath inferior: (Prichard, 1835) an outmoded term to denote a person who is lacking in self-government; hence, a moral imbecile.

constriction: a limitation in speed and number of free associations, as on a Rorschach test.

constrictor: a muscle fiber, such as a sphincter, which contracts an opening, such as the pupil of the eye.

contiguity: experiences occurring simultaneously or in the same place, the recurrence of the one tending to revive memory of the other (Aristotle).

contrast: tendency of unlike experiences to be associated.

contrectation: psychotic impulse to embrace a stranger of the opposite sex.

control: a procedure used to check the validity of a similar observation in which an experimental factor has been introduced.

controlled association test: one in which the response is determined by the instructions (e.g., an opposites test).

convergence: the coordinations of both eyeballs toward the point of fixation.

conversion: in psychoanalysis, the hysterical expression of an unconscious conflict in some physical sympton (e.g., hysterical paralysis or blindness).

convex: curved as viewed from the front (opposite of concave).

convolution: gyrus; a ridge on the surface of the brain.

convulsion: spasmodic contractions of the muscles; a seizure.

coördination: the functioning of groups of muscles in proper interrelationships and sequences.

coprolagnia: abnormal and obsessive interest in feces.

coprolalia: filthy language.

coprophilia: a perversion in which the act or the products of defecation are enjoyed; pathological joy in feces.

copulation: sexual intercourse.

cord: that part of the nervous system which lies encased in the vertebral column; a tendon or a nerve.

corda tympani: a branch of the 7th cranial nerve which is distributed to the front of the tongue and to the submaxillary and the sublingual glands.

corium: the layer of skin directly underneath the epidermis.

cornea: the transparent covering of the eyeball lying before the iris and the lens.

corneal reflex: blinking and experiencing pain when the cornea is touched with sterile cotton.

cornu ammonis (horn of Ammon): the hippocampus major.

corpora quadrigemina: four small elevations on the rear surface of the midbrain, the upper pair of which mediate optic reflexes; the lower pair, auditory reflexes.

corporeal: pertaining to the body.

corpus callosum: the large band of transverse fibers connecting the cerebral hemispheres.

corpus striatum: a part of the base of each hemisphere of the cerebrum.

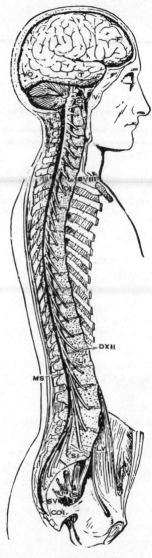

Figure 9. A schematic view of the cerebrospinal axis. O. T. F. indicate the cerebral hemisphere; C is the cerebellum; P, pons Varolii; C I to C VIII, cervical nerves; D I to D XII, thoracic nerves; L I to L V, lumbar nerves; S I to S V, sacral nerves; and Co I, the coccygeal nerve.

correlation: in statistics, the tendency of certain arrays of frequency distributions to be positively, negatively, or not at all associated, so that predictions may be inferred from one array to another.

corrugator: a muscle that causes wrinkles when it contracts.

cortex: the outer portion.

cortex of the cerebrum (neopallium): the layer of gray matter forming the outer covering of the cerebral hemispheres (a similar layer covering the cerebellum).

cortin: a hormone secreted by the cortex of the adrenals, which also secrete cortisone.

Couéism: a procedure of self-suggestions as a means of achieving good health (popularized by Coué, 1900 et seq.).

counseling psychology: that branch of psychology which is designed to help persons who are in difficulties. (The counselor may be directive or nondirective.)

counter transference: in psychoanalysis, the transference by the analyst upon the patient (analysand) of his own unconscious repressions and wishes.

covert: hidden; not overtly expressed.

CPI: constitutional psychopath inferior.

cramp: a tonic muscle spasm.

cranial nerves: those arising from the brain or the upper part of the cord—namely, olfactory, optic, oculomotor, trochlear, trigeminal, abducent, facial, auditory or acoustic, glossopharyngeal, vagus or pneumogastric, accessory, and hypoglossal.

craniology: phrenology.

craniometry: measurements of the skull.

cranium: the skull.

craving: a tissue lack which initiates behavior.

craze: a fashion or mode of behavior that is irrationally followed for a time with great enthusiasm, and then suddenly dropped.

creative thinking: purposeful imaginative activity which (Wallas) typically proceeds from preparation, incubation, and illumination to verification.

credulous: inclined to accept opinions with slight evidence to justify them.

cremnophobia: morbid fear of precipices.

creasomania: delusions of vast wealth.

Crespi effect: alteration in a performance that is not proportional to the strength of reinforcement used in the training period.

cretinism: mental deficiency caused by hypothyroidism, resulting in dry, scaly skin, a stunted physique, and a protruding abdomen.

criterion: the standard used to validate a psychological test or measure.

critical flicker frequency (CFF): in visual perception, the point at which successive stimuli fuse.

critical incident: an observation which is said to be typical of the total behavior of the person or the group being described.

critical ratio (CR): the difference between the means of two comparable distributions of scores divided by the standard error or the probable error of the difference.

critical score: on a distribution, the score which divides those likely to succeed from those likely to fail.

cross-cultural method: comparisons of behavior typical in one geographical area or ethnic group with that in another.

cross education: transfer of a skill gained by one part of the body to the opposite side (e.g., skill in writing with the right hand to some skill with the left hand).

crowd: a large assemblage, often united in a common endeavor.

crush: intense, but usually brief, fixation of a child or adolescent upon an older person.

crypt-, crypto-: Greek combining form meaning *secret, hidden.*

cryptesthesia: in occultism, perceptions without mediation by known sense organs.

cryptodynamic: in occultism, having secret powers.

cryptogenic: having obscure, undeterminable origins.

cryptology: a secret language, such as used by some psychotics.

crystal gazing: syn. *scrying;* in occultism, determining the course of future events by looking into a glass ball.

cue: a stimulus which guides the response.

cul-de-sac: a blind alley in a maze.

cultural lag: the tendency of modes of behavior to persist even after better modes of behavior are known.

cultural relativism: the doctrine that there are no absolute ethical standards.

culture: the totality of customs differentiating one social group from another; the totality of behavior patterns, attitudes and values shared and transmitted by a social group.

culture-epochs theory: (G. S. Hall) the notion that the child recapitulates all the developmental stages of the race.

cumulative frequency curve or table: a representation of the summation of scores at each successive level in the distribution.

cumulative-record folder: in educational practice, the accumulation of data about a pupil as he progresses from grade to grade.

cunnilingus: application of the mouth to the female genitalia.

cunnus: female genitalia.

custom: any pattern of habits prevalent in a social group and, usually, transmitted by elders to children.

cutaneous: pertaining to the skin.

cutaneous sensitivities: responses of cold, warmth, pressure, or pain when appropriate stimuli are applied to the surface of the body.

cybernetics: (Wiener) the science dealing with the mechanisms of control, whether of human behavior or the action of machines.

cycloid: one who has extreme shifts in mood.

cyclopean eye: localization of objects observed with both eyes simultaneously at a single mid-point.

cyclothymia: alternations between elation and depression.

cynophobia: morbid fear of dogs.

Cyrenaicism: an ancient doctrine in ethics to the effect that behavior is motivated by a quest for pleasure and an avoidance of pain.

cynorexia: syn. *bulimia;* excessive eating.

cyto-: Greek combining form meaning a *cell*.

cytology: a division of biology dealing with the structure and the function of cells.

cytoplasm: the content of a cell, excepting the nucleus.

dactology: the science of teaching the deaf to communicate by the fingers.

Daltonism: color blindness.

damp: to reduce the vibrations of a tuning fork.

dancing mania: in states of religious ectasy, uncontrollable urge to dance until exhausted; a form of mass hysteria occurring in the 14th century.

danger situation: any circumstance which induces unconscious or conscious states of anxiety, the situation being either real or imaginary.

dark adaptation: adjustment of the eye for vision under low intensities of light.

Darwinian tubercle: a small projection on the pinna, once thought to be a stigma indicating atavistic tendencies.

Darwinism: the theory of organic evolution introduced by Darwin in 1859.

data: factual items collected by experiment or clinical methods.

datum: a factual item or observation.

day blindness: inability of the retina to become accommodated to high intensities of light waves.

daydream: a revery said to be motivated by unconscious and frustrated wishes.

daymare: an acute fright induced by fantasies.

de-: a Latin prefix meaning *from, away.*

deaf-mute: one who can neither hear nor speak intelligibly.

death instinct: syn. *thanatos instinct;* in psychoanalysis, the unconscious wish to destroy, to be aggressive.

debility: general physical weakness.

decephalization: deterioration of the brain.

deception test: in the Character Education Inquiry (1929), a measure of certain abstract virtues by keeping the testee ignorant of the true purpose of the test.

decerebration: removal of the brain or severance between brain and cord (as in a laboratory animal for experimental purposes.

decibel: 1/10th of a bel (used as a convenient measure of an auditory stimulus).

decile: every 10th percentile of a distribution of scores or measures.

decompensation: (Adler) inability to make up for one's inferiorities by compensatory activities.

decussation: a chiasma or crossing of nerve fibers.

deduction: that form of inference which proceeds from a general premise to a specific conclusion.

deep reflex: a response elicited in a muscle located beneath the surface of outlying skeletal musculature.

defecation: voidance of feces.

defective: one who is low in the scale of intelligence by reason of an inherent disability; an ament.

defense mechanism: in psychoanalysis, an unconscious resolution of a conflict, whereby the ego is somewhat protected from anxieties.

deflection: in psychoanalysis, an unconsciously determined way of directing attention from an unwelcome motive or unpleasant idea.

defusion: in psychoanalysis, a result of regression to the level where the Eros and the Thanatos instincts were separate and distinct.

degenerate: in popular usage, one who resorts to perversions of sex outlets.

degree of freedom (d.f.): the number of theoretical frequences that may be assigned arbitrarily.

déjà entendu: the illusion that a strange sound or voice has been previously heard.

déjà pensée: the illusion that a new idea really had been experienced in the past.

déjà vu: the illusion that a strange place is actually familiar to the viewer.

delayed reaction experiment: one in which the subject must respond after the stimulus has been removed.

delayed response: a conditioned reflex in which a time interval is interposed between the conditioned stimulus and the response.

delinquent: one who commits a misdemeanor, usually the offender being under legal age to be held fully accountable (e.g., 16 or 18 years of age or under).

delirium: a feverous state affecting the physiology of the nervous system.

delirium tremens: a condition of physical disorder and terrifying hallucinations caused by excessive and prolonged consumption of alcohol.

delusion: a fallacious idea held in spite of all evidence to demonstrate its error.

dementia: psychosis.

dementia praecocissima: (Kraepelin) a grave personality disorder occurring in early childhood; childhood schizophrenia.

dementia praecox: Kraepelin's term for a grave mental disorder characterized by blunting of the affective life, withdrawal, and incoherent delusions and occurring in late adolescence or early adulthood.

demography: the study of regional and national groups from the standpoint of their vital statistics.

demology: the science of collective behavior of social groups.

demon-possession theory: the ancient superstition that disorders are due to the invasion of evil spirits into the body or the mind of the victim.

demonology: the study of popular superstitions, ancient and modern, about evil spirits and their alleged influence upon human beings and natural events.

demonstration: a classroom presentation, for instructional purposes, of a scientific procedure normally carried out in the laboratory.

demophobia: morbid fear of large crowds.

dendrite: that part of a nerve cell which transmits the impulse to the axon (e) of the nerve cell.

denial: (Anna Freud) a primary defensive process whereby the individual tries unsuccessfully to ignore the unconscious mental conflict.

density: (Titchener) the awareness of solidity or compactness in a tone.

dentate nucleus: syn. *corpus dentatum;* a sheet of gray matter, wavy in shape, lying in capsule form within the white matter of the cerebral hemispheres.

dependency: that state of needing economic or psychological support (in the latter instance, implying a want of ego strength or a state of immaturity).

dependent variable: in an experiment, the factor which according to the hypothesis may change with changes in the independent variable; the observed result from the effect of the independent variable or cause.

depersonalization: (Janet) a sense of unreality about one's own body, associates, or the environment in general; hence, a common symptom in psychasthenia.

depression: psychotic or neurotic melancholia.

depth psychology: any systematic formulation which emphasizes the unconscious mind (e.g., psychoanalysis).

dereistic thinking: syn. *autistic thinking;* fantasy, unconsciously motivated imaginative processes.

derivative reaction: in psychoanalysis, an unconsciously determined activity whereby the id may be given expression with a minimum of arousal of anxieties.

dermographia (dermatographia): a form of urticaria (inflammatory sensitivity of the skin) whereby wheals are produced by drawing a stylus over the skin.

desensitization: in clinical treatments, lessening the client's anxiety about defects or inferiorities.

design: the general and specific plans for an experiment or piece of research.

desire: a longing which leads to some form of actual behavior or which builds up some tensions within the individual.

destrudo: in psychoanalysis, any expression of the Thanatos (death) instinct.

deterioration: a progressive loss of a function or an organ.

deterioration index: (Wechsler) the comparison on "hold" vs. "don't hold" tests.

determinism: in philosophical psychology, the doctrine that nothing occurs by free will or choice or by chance, but that every effect has a necessary and adequate cause.

detour problem: one which requires the animal (or human being) to reach the goal by a concealed and circuitous pathway in an experiment.

detumescence: subsidance of swelling, especially in the genitals after an orgasm.

deuteranopia: green blindness.

development: syn. *growth;* progressive changes resulting from maturation and experience.

developmental psychology: that special branch of psychology which is concerned with characteristic modes of behavior at successive age levels, from infancy to maturity.

deviate (deviant): one who differs from the average; in popular usage, one who is a mental defective.

deviation: the amount by which a score deviates from the measure of central tendency.

dextrality: preference for use of the right hand.

dextrosinistral: one who has been changed from left-handed to right-handed.

di-: Greek prefix meaning *twofold, double.*

diadokineses: alternating contractions and extensions of large muscle groups in a limb at a normal rate of speed and with normal vigor.

diagnosis: the analysis of a disorder or a maladjustment from the pattern of symptoms.

diagnostic test: one which indicates specific areas of weakness in the pupil's achievement in any given subject and which, therefore, suggests appropriate remedial instructions (e.g., Iowa Silent Reading Tests, 1943).

diastole: the phase in which the cavities of the heart are expanded.

dicho-: Greek prefix meaning *separated into two parts.*

dichotic stimulation: stimuli which affect each ear simultaneously but differently.

dichotomy: division of a class (e.g., test scores) into two distinct subclasses.

dichromatism: the condition of one wholly red-green blind (hence, seeing only yellow and green).

didactic analysis: psychoanalysis of an analysand who is in training for certification as an analyst, the purpose being educational, not primarily therapeutic.

diencephalon: the posterior section of the prosencephalon (forebrain), which includes the thalamus, the epithalamus (consisting of the habenular trigone, the pineal body, and the posterior commisure), and the hypothalamus.

difforonoo limon (differential limen or DL): the threshold of just noticeable difference between stimuli.

difference tone: syn. *Tartini tone;* a tone occasionally heard when two tones are simultaneously made.

Differential Aptitude Tests (DAT): a battery of educational-vocational tests for high school pupils.

differential psychology: that branch of general psychology which studies individual differences and likenesses in behavior and especially on test performances.

differentiation: in Lewin's field theory, the increase of the number of parts of a whole (e.g., the increase of the number of differentiated tension systems as the individual grows towards maturity).

diffuse reaction: a poorly coordinated, inefficient response.

diffusion of culture: in sociology, the transplantation of customs, from one social group to another (e.g., the diffusion of Greek culture to ancient Rome).

digit-span: the number of unrelated digits correctly reproduced after a single presentation.

digit-symbol test: a measure of speed of learning in which associations between numbers and geometrical designs must be established.

dilapidation: mental deterioration: psychosis.

dilation (dilatation): enlargement of an organ of the body.

dimensions of consciousness: (Wundt and Titchener) the attributes of attensity or clearness, extensity, intensity, protensity, and quality of the experience.

Dionysian culture: one in which exuberant, frenzied, uninhibited behavior prevails.

diotic stimuli: those affecting both ears.

diplegia: paralysis affecting both sides of the body (as both legs or both arms).

diplomate: one who holds a certificate granted by a board controlling a specialty.

diploneural: supplied by two systems of nerve fibers.

diplopia: double vision of a single object.

dipsia: syn. *diposia;* thirst.

dipsomania: irresistible craving for alcohol.

direct analysis: a variant of psychoanalysis in which the analyst takes the dominant role and bluntly explains the reasons for the analysand's symptoms (Rosen).

directions test: measure of ability correctly and quickly to execute orders of varying levels of difficulty (Army Alpha subtest).

directive counseling: the procedure in which the client is advised or persuaded to undertake constructive actions by the counselor.

dirhinic: a stimulus affecting both nostrils.

dis-: Greek prefix meaning *a separation from or deprivation of, a negation of.*

disarranged-sentences test: a measure of ability to rearrange jumbled words into a meaningful statement.

discipline: a means of social control in which one individual exercises authority over the behavior of another (e.g., as by a teacher over a pupil).

discomfort-relief quotient (DRQ): (Dollard and Mower) the ratio between initial tensions and the condition eventuating from a series of psychotherapeutic interviews; discomfort units/discomfort units plus relief units times 100.

discontinuous variables: numbers which proceed by discrete steps, as from 1 to 2, 2 to 3, and so on; variables which lack intermediate values.

discrete data: those which do not shade imperceptibly one into another but which are separate and distinct (e.g., each person in a grade considered as a unique individual).

discrimination: judgments about likenesses or differences between stimuli presented simultaneously or sequentially.

discrimination learning: the acquisition of responses based upon small cues or minor differences among stimuli.

disinhibition: (Pavlov) the inhibition of an inhibition, as by an extraneous stimulus or by disorganization of inhibitory controls.

disorder: a pathological condition of the organism; any physical or mental illness.

disorientation: the condition of being unable to recognize normal temporal, spatial, or locality relations and to identify persons normally familiar to the individual.

dispersion: the manner in which the scores within the range are distributed about the mid-point.

displacement: in psychoanalysis, the unconscious mechanism whereby one repression surrenders its affective component to another; the shift of sexual energy from one outlet to another.

disposition: (McDougall) the sum total of all the propensities of a person; the characteristic behavior of an individual observed under many diverse circumstances.

dissociation: (Charcot) the severance of one or more psychological functions from voluntary control by the patient; a "logic-tight compartment."

dissonance: a sensation aroused by tones which do not blend to form a chord.

distal: away from the midline of the body.

distractor: a misleading item in an objective test, especially one of the multiple-choice type.

distortion: in psychoanalysis, the alteration of unconscious materials before they may be permitted in consciousness, as in the manifest content of a dream.

distributed practice: spaced periods in learning, especially in committing to rote memory or in mastering a motor skill.

disuse: Thorndike's law stating that if a stimulus-response bond goes unexercised because it results in annoyance, it gradually loses strength.

divigation: psychotic incoherence in speech.

dizygotic twins: fraternal, not identical, twins, who may be of the same or the opposite sex.

dolichocephaly: long, narrow head.

dolichomorphy: a body build characterized by long bones, stringy muscles, and thinness.

dominance: a trait indicated by a zeal to control the behavior of others.

dominant character: in heredity, one which suppresses the appearance of a recessive character.

dorsal: pertaining to the posterior or back of the body or of an organ.

dorsal column: that portion of the spinal cord that receives the roots of the sensory nerves.

dorsal nerve: the thoracic nerve; any of the nerve fibers emerging from the area below a thoracic vertebra.

dorsicollar: related to back and neck region.

dorso-: Latin combining form meaning *back*.

dorsum: the back.

DOT: Dictionary of Occupational Titles.

dotage: senility.

double-aspect theory: one of the classical explanations of the so-called body-mind problem which states that a single entity underlies body and mind and that basically they are one and the same.

Draw-a-Man Test: Goodenough's psychometric technique for estimating mental age by scoring the details in a drawing (1926).

Draw-a-Person Test: Machover's technique for personality diagnosis from interpretations of drawings of male and female figures as projections of mental conflicts and tensions (1949).

dream: a sequence of images or other items of experience occurring in sleep or in sleep-like conditions.

dream work: in psychoanalysis, the processes whereby latent (unconscious) parts of the dream are transformed into imagery or other items of experience.

drill: repetition of a skill or a series of items which must be learned by rote.

drive: any impetus, physiological or psychological, for behavior.

dromomania: impulse to wander.

dual personality: (Janet) one in which there is dissociation between two distinct personalities, the one often having amnesia for the other.

dualism: in philosophical psychology, the point of view that mind and body are separate entities.

duct gland: one which secretes externally or internally, but not directly into the blood stream.

ductless gland: syn. *endocrine;* a gland which secretes hormones directly into the blood stream (e.g., kidneys, salivary glands).

duodenal ulcer: a lesion in that part of the intestine which is directly joined to the stomach.

duplicity theory: (von Kries) the view that cones mediate chromatic vision and rods, achromatic vision.

dura mater: the outermost covering of the brain and the spinal cord.

dynamic psychology: any systematic theory of psychology which emphasizes drives, wishes, motives, and the like, whether unconscious or conscious, as the primary determinants of behavior.

dynamism: any habitual way of easing or eliminating psychic tensions; any persisting mode of behavior, particularly when obstacles are encountered.

dynamometer: an apparatus for measuring the strength of a muscle group.

dys-: Greek prefix meaning *faulty*.

dysacousia: abnormal (neurotic) inability to endure noise.

dysaphia: faulty sense of touch.

dysarthria: inability to articulate words clearly or intelligibly.

dysbulia: inability to give sustained attention or to make decisions.

dyschromatopsia: color blindness of any type or degree.

dysergia: faulty coordination of muscles.

dysesthesia: disorder or impairment of a sense organ.

dysfunction: impairment of the functioning of any organ or of the body as a whole.

dysgenics: the study of the results of bad heredity; cacogenics.

dyskinesia: impairment in a voluntary action.

dyslalia: impairment of organs used in articulation of speech.

dyslogia: faulty ability to speak logically or coherently.

dyslexia: inability to learn to read by normal methods of instruction.

dyspepsia: indigestion.

dysphasia: inability to comprehend language.

dysphemia: stuttering or stammering.

dysphonia: difficulty in pronouncing words.

dysplastic: a body type that cannot be classified as athletic, asthenic, or pyknic; misshaped.

dyspnoea (dyspnea): difficulty in breathing.
dyssynergia: impairment in muscular coördinations.
dystrophy: faulty nutrition; wasting of tissues.

EA: educational age.
ear: the sense organ responsive to auditory stimuli and including receptors (utricle and saccule) for static and dynamic sensitivity as well.

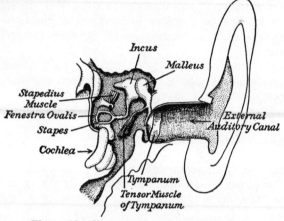

Figure 10. The structure of the human ear.

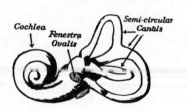

Figure 11. The inner ear.

eccentric: one who is odd, likely to be schizophrenic (e.g., Timothy Dexter, the New England eccentric).
ecdoderm: the outer layer of the embryo.

echolalia: repeating words and phrases over and over without intent to convey meaning.

echopraxia: compulsive imitation of the actions of other persons.

eclampsia: convulsions during pregnancy or parturition.

eclectic psychology: that which brings together different theoretical positions and places special emphasis upon no one set of axioms or concepts.

ecmnesia: inability to remember occurrences of recent data but retention for occurrences in the earlier life history of the patient.

ecology: the distribution of a group with reference to the geographical situation and its effect upon their lives.

ecomania: intense zeal to dominate other persons.

economics: the doctrine that the individual expends the least possible amount of energy in attaining a goal.

ecstasy: a state of exaltation, usually reached by an emotional frenzy, but also attainable through quietistic contemplation.

ecto-: Greek prefix meaning *outside*.

ectoderm: outermost layer of the skin.

ectomorphy: in Sheldon's typology, a body build characterized by flatness of chest, fragile physique, and relatively large brain and central nervous system.

ectoplasm: in occultism, an emanation from mediums which enables them to perform paranormal feats; in biology, the wall surrounding the protoplasm of a cell.

ectoretina: the outer, pigmented layer of the retina of the eye.

edea: the external genitals.

Epidal situation (Oedipal situation): in psychoanalysis, a pathological fixation upon the parent of the opposite sex.

educability: capacity to profit from instruction.

educational age: a pupil's average standing in various branches of the curriculum expressed in terms of the chronological age of the average pupil who makes an equivalent score or scores.

educational psychology: originally, the study of the learning process as it is related to mastery of the curriculum; later, an application of all pertinent facts and principles of psychology as they relate to the educative process defined in a wide sense.

eduction: the process of analysis whereby a form or a general principle is brought out.

effect: in Thorndike's theory of learning, the third major law, which states that annoyance gradually eliminates, and satisfaction gradually establishes, a connection or stimulus-response bond.

effector: a muscle or a gland.

efficiency: the maximum of output or achievement with the minimum output in time or energy.

efficiency index: a measure of deterioration in cases of organic psychoses, the score usually being the ratio between a measure of vocabulary and tests of abstract reasoning (e.g., adaptations of the Vigotsky test or the "Hold" vs. "Don't Hold" subtests on the Wechsler).

egersis: the condition of alert wakefulness.

ego: in psychoanalysis, that part of the psyche which is shaped by the reality principle and which, largely, is the product of interactions with the environment; the self, the personality.

ego cathexis: in psychoanalysis, the process of identifying with external objects and acquiring subjective images of these objects, whereas at an earlier level these were object-choices of the unconscious instinctual drives in the id.

ego dynamics: a study of the master motives, which are considered to be mainly conscious and to be available to investigations by direct methods.

ego ideal: in psychoanalysis, the superego; the introjection of high standards and values for conduct and a permanent expression of parental influences.

ego psychology: a point of view hinted at in Freud's later discussions in which some psychic energy is attributed directly to the ego motives, whereas in the earlier writings the energy was said to be derived from the id.

egoism: intense narcissism or self-love.

ego-strength: self-reliance; determination; self-confidence.

egocentric: narcissistic; self-centered.

egotism: self-exaltation or self-praise.

egregorsis: insomnia.

eidetic image: an unusually vivid image, usually a revival of a visual experience.

eidoptometry: measurement of visual form perception.

eighth cranial nerve: the auditory, or acoustic, nerve.

Einstellung: a mental set or attitude which predisposes the individual to attend to certain situations and to make certain responses to them.

eisoptrophobia: morbid fear of seeing one's own reflection in a mirror.

élan vital: (Bergson) the creative impulse.

elation: pathological gaiety.

Electra complex: in early psychoanalysis, the possessive love of a daughter for her father (now replaced by the term *Oedipus complex,* designating a fixation upon the parent of the opposite sex or a parent surrogate).

electroencephalography (EEG): the investigation of electrical impulses connected with the physiology of the brain (Berger); study of brain waves picked up on the surface of the skull, ranging from about 100 to 1,000 microvolts.

elementarism: the procedure of reductive analysis in the study of mental contents; the reduction of all psychological data to sensations, images, and feelings.

emasculation: castration.

embolalia: the psychotic introduction of meaningless words and phrases into spoken language.

embryo: in the human species, the organism from about the second to the eighth week of prenatal life, known as the ovum stage or germinal period.

emergent evolution: the doctrine that at each new level in phylogeny there are new qualities added, such as awareness, consciousness, and mind (C. L. Morgan).

emetomania: hysterical vomiting.

emission: involuntary male orgasm, usually in sleep but also in erotic fantasies; ejaculation of semen.

Emmanuel movement: the treatment of neuroses and some types of physical ailments by physicians and clergymen working in coöperation (Boston, 1906 et seq., by Worcester and Mc-Comb).

Emmert's law: the tendency of a visual after-image to increase in size with the distance to which it is projected.

emmetropia: normal refractive condition of the eye.

emotion: according to the emergency theory (Cannon), a stirred up condition in which the body is prepared for a strenuous effort; in Jamesian psychology, the awareness of such physiological conditions as ensue upon certain perceptions; popularly, any departure from the calm and normal condition of the organism.

emotional: prone to strong emotional reactions rather than to cognitive responses.

empathy: the imaginative projection of one's own psychological behavior into an object, event, or other person; the ability to identify intelligently with the problems and difficulties of another person.

empirical me: according to James, the sum total of all that a person can call his; the material, the social, and the spiritual selves, as distinguished from the pure ego.

empirical validity: in mental testing, the agreement of the test score with some criterion.

empiricism: the point of view that all knowledge arises in human experience, as opposed to the doctrine of nativism.

empyreumatic: having a tarry or smoky odor.

en-: Greek prefix meaning *in*.

encephalitis: inflammation of the brain due to infections.

encephalitis lethargica: a grave inflammation of the brain which is caused by some nonfilterable virus and which may result in destruction of neurons, great weakness, apathy, and somnolence.

encephalomalacia: softening of the brain.

encephalomyelitis: inflammation of both brain and cord.

encephalon: the brain.

encephalopathy: any organic brain disorder.

enclave: a residence or a residential district set apart from the larger society.

encoding test: a measure of ability to translate quickly and accurately ordinary language into a code.

encopresis: uncontrolled excretion of feces.

end brush: the terminal arborization of a motor nerve fiber or of the axon of a neuron.

end bulb: the bulb-like ending of a sensory nerve in the skin (e.g., the bulbs of Krause).

endo-: Greek prefix meaning *internal*.

endocrine: syn. ductless gland; a gland which secretes some specific hormone into the bloodstream (e.g., thyroids, pituitary, adrenals, gonads).

endocrinology: the science dealing with the ductless glands and their physiological or psychological effects.

endogamy: marriage within the tribe or the caste; inbreeding.

endoderm: the innermost layer of the embryo.

endogenous motivs: one which originates within the individual's own psychological make-up; one which is not urged upon the individual by another person.

endomorphy: a physique characterized by excess of fatty tissue and viscera; in Sheldon's typology, the body build predisposing to slothful ease or viscerotonia.

endowment: native capacities; special aptitudes or talents.

engram: a lasting trace left in memory.

entelechy: in Aristotle's psychology, self-realization; self-actualization.

entropy: in Jung's psychology, the tendency of psychic energy to pass from a stronger value to a weaker value until both are equal and equilibrium is restored.

enuresis: bed-wetting; involuntary discharge of urine.

environment: the sum total of all that stimulates the organism, whether from within or from without.

environmentalism: the doctrine which emphasizes the influence of formative determinants in an individual's life history and which discounts hereditary factors.

eonism: transvestitism; assuming the behavior and dress of the opposite sex.

epi-: Greek prefix meaning *upon*.

epicanthus: a long fold of the upper eyelid, common in Mongolians and found also in mongolian mental defectives.

epicritic sensitivity: responsiveness to cutaneous stimulation (such as heat, cold, pain, and pressure).

epidermis: the outer layer of the skin.

epigastrium: loosely, the stomach.

epigenesis: the appearance of secondary or accessory symptoms in a disorder.

epilepsy: convulsive seizure.

epileptoid make-up: irritable, impulsive, asocial.

epiphenomenonalism: the doctrine that consciousness is a mere by-product of nervous impulses in the brain (Hobbes).

epiphysis: the pineal gland.

epistemology: that branch of speculative thought which studies the limits and the validity of knowledge.

epithelium: the covering of the surfaces of the body and of its exposed cavities.

equilibrium: balance; stability; freedom from conflictual tensions.

equipotentiality: the capacity of an undamaged part of the brain to carry on the functions of a damaged or excised part of the brain.

equivalence: in Jung's psychology, the doctrine that energy removed from one part of the psyche will make its appearance in another part.

erethism: excessive irritability; senseless fits of anger.

ereutophobia (erythrophobia):   fear of blushing.

ergasia: (A. Meyer) the totality of all functions, mental and physical, of the organism.

ergograph: apparatus for measuring the amount of work done by a muscle group (e.g., pulling a weight repeatedly by the forefinger).

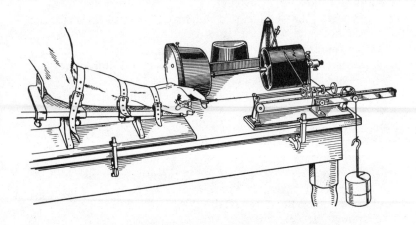

Figure 12. The Mosso ergograph. The record of the strength of pulls, registered on the kymograph, is called an ergogram.

ergomania: ceaseless toil by a psychotic individual.

ergophobia: morbid aversion to work.

erogenous zones: those which arouse sex feelings when stroked.

eros impulse: in psychoanalysis, the life instincts, which lead to gratifications necessary for survival and for parenthood.

erotic: pertaining to sexual desire.

erotomania: pathological affection for a person of the opposite sex.

error: a mistake; that which is invalid or which mars an empirical study; the deviation of a score from the true or theoretical score value.

eructation: belching, as caused by a stomach disorder or in hysteria.

erythopsia: a condition in which the visual field is tinged with red, as in snowblindness.

escape mechanism: in psychoanalysis, an unconsciously adopted way of evading unpleasant reality.

escapism: retreat from responsibilities; neurotic withdrawal from reality.

esophagus: the tube which passes from the pharynx to the stomach.

esotropia: cross-eyedness.

essential epilepsy: syn *idiopathic epilepsy;* convulsive seizures, the cause or causes being unknown.

essential hypertension: high blood pressure without any determinable organic cause, the condition being presumably due to prolonged emotional conflicts.

esthesiometer: an instrument for measuring the just-noticeable-difference threshold in tactual stimulation.

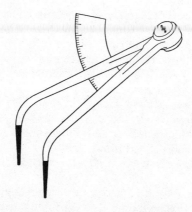

Figure 12a. One of the earliest types of esthesiometers, used in determinations of the two-point thresholds in cutaneous sensitivity.

esthetics (aesthetics): that branch of psychology which is concerned with the beauty-ugliness, or the pleasantness-unpleasantness, of objects.

estromania: inordinate sexual desire in a woman.

estrus (oestrous, oestrus) cycle: the recurrent physiological changes from quiescence to the mating period in animals.

ethics: the normative study of the principles of moral conduct; a code of approved practices to be followed by a psycho-clinician.

ethnic: pertaining to the physical and the psychological traits characterizing a racial group.

ethnocentricism: an attitude whereby evaluations of other racial groups are made from the standpoint of one's racial group as the normative standard.

ethnogeography: the study of the geographical distribution of various races and of the effects of environment upon their physical and psychological traits.

ethnology: the study of the differentiating characteristics of the races of mankind from a descriptive point of view.

ethology: the objective (non-anecdotal) study of the behavior of animals in their native habitats.

ethos: the characteristic outlook or spirit of a social group; the value systems which lie behind the mores and the folkways of a group.

etiology: that branch of psychodiagnostics which deals with the predisposing and precipitating factors of a disorder.

eu-: Greek prefix meaning *good or healthy.*

eugenics: the study, or the practice, of determining fitness for healthy, well-adjusted children; improvement of the race by restricting parentage to the superior.

eunuchoidism: absence of sexual drive in the male; hypogenitalism in the male.

euphoria: pathological gaiety and optimism.

eupraxia: well-coordinated motor behavior.

eupsychics: emphasis upon desirable practices in child training and education.

Eustachian tube: a cartilaginous tube connecting the middle ear with the nasopharynx and serving to equalize air pressure on each side of the tympanic membrane.

euthanasia: a popular term for the alleged practice of hastening the demise of the hopelessly afflicted.

euthenics: improvement of the race through desirable medical, educational, and social opportunities, as opposed to eugenics, which emphasizes heredity as the major hope for racial progress.

evolution: syn. *phylogeny;* the processes whereby a species has acquired the physical and physiological traits which characterize its members; the descent (or ascent) of man from some remote, relatively simple species, through chance alterations in the germplasm.

ex-: Latin prefix meaning *out from.*

examination: a procedure of appraising the assets-deficits of an individual or a group by means of psychological tests and measures, the purpose being to predict chances of success-failure.

exceptional child: one who deviates markedly from the norm, and, hence, needs special treatment in home and school; either a gifted or a retarded child; one with pronounced sensory or physical handicaps.

excitant: usually, a biochemical irritant affecting receptors.

excitant: the nervous impulse initiated by stimulation of a sense organ or receptor.

exercise: Thorndike's law of learning which states that repeated use of a stimulus-response bond strengthens, and that disuse weakens, the connection.

exhaustion psychosis: a disorder, often temporary, caused by prolonged stress, malnutrition, or intense physical effort.

exhibitionism: in psychoanalysis, the expression of the infantile sexual aim, or autoerotic impulse, to display the genitalia; in a loose sense, childish efforts to attract favorable attention by self-display.

existential proposition: a statement of fact, upon which all qualified persons can agree; one which is derived from empirical or demonstrated data.

existential psychology: syn. *Titchenerism;* the point of view which emphasizes demonstrable factual data (e.g., elements of sensations, images, or feelings), as identified by a scientific introspectionist, to be the proper subject matter of psychology.

exit interview: in industrial psychology, the attempt to find out why the employee left the job and to gather data for reducing job turnover.

exocrine gland: one that secretes outside the body or through a duct to an internal organ.

exorcism: in the history of psychopathology, the process of expelling evil spirits from the mentally disturbed patient.

exophthalmia: abnormal protrusion of the eyeballs as a result of a thyroid disorder.

experience: in functional psychology, the totality of all mental processes involved in any given activity which, as a result, determine the course and the quality of subsequent experience.

experiment: a controlled application of the empirical method of inquiry in which the investigator varies but one factor at a time for the purposes of testing an hypothesis.

experimental extinction: the process whereby a conditioned response is lost because of a lack of reinforcement of the adequate stimulus by the conditioned stimulus (e.g., as in the "wolf, wolf" tale).

experimental neurosis: a disorganized condition produced in a laboratory animal by subjecting it to prolonged stress or to discriminations beyond its capacity to learn.

experimental psychology: the empirical science based upon the experimental method exclusively.

expressive behavior: that which reveals, to a qualified clinical psychologist, the psychodynamics of the individual; those behavioral data which may be used to make inferences about the personality organization of an individual.

extensity: the spatial quality or the voluminousness of a sensation (Titchener).

exteroceptor: a sense organ, or receptor cell, which is normally stimulated only by stimuli from outside the body.

extirpation experiment: the removal of some organ (e.g., the adrenals of the rat or a portion of the brain) to observe the effects upon postoperative behavior of an animal.

extrapolation: the estimation of values of a function which lie beyond the available scores in the distribution.

extrasensory perception (ESP): awareness without mediation of known sense organs.

extraversion (extroversion): in Jung's psychology, the dominant psychic attitude of being oriented to the objective world of reality, while the personal unconscious is oriented in the opposite direction.

extrinsic motivation: that which is initiated by some artificial or educational technique and which would not normally arise of itself, as in the case of an intrinsic motive.

eye: the sense organ for vision, consisting of all the accessory apparatus and the rods and cones of the retina.

eye ground: the fundus or back of the eyeball viewed through an opthalmoscope.

eye muscles: the three pairs of muscles which move the eyeball,

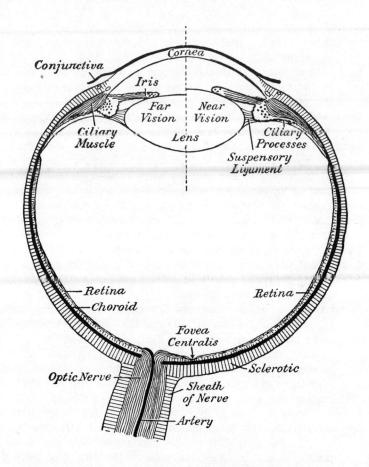

Figure 13. Schematic diagram of the structure of the human eye.

namely, the external and the internal rectus muscles, the superior and the inferior rectus muscles, and the superior and the inferior oblique muscles.

eyedness: the tendency of the right or the left eye to be used in sighting a rifle or in pointing to an object.

eyespan: the amount which can be apprehended during a brief exposure with the point of regard being stationary.

fables test: a Binet-type test in which the subject is asked to tell the meaning of a short fable (e.g., of Hercules and the Wagoner).

fabrication: syn. *confabulation;* the inappropriate response to test materials given by a disordered person.

face-to-face group: a primary group in which the members are in direct personal relationship to one another; a primary social group (Cooley).

facial vision: the sensitivity of the blind to air pressures, whereby they avoid collisions with objects in their pathways.

facilitation: the increase of coordinations in response patterns as the learned eliminates delays and mistakes; the summation of all physiological mechanisms in the well-organized performance of an act, overt or implicit.

facioplegia: the condition of paralysis of facial muscles.

factitious: that which is artificially produced and that would not normally arise in ontogenetic life history.

factor: any constituent element of a pattern.

factor analysis: a procedure for analyzing the intercorrelations among arrays of scores in order to determine those factors, real or hypothetical, involved.

factor theory of intelligence: in Spearman's theory, the g-factor (found in tests of abstraction) and the s-factors (specific abilities) measured in intelligence tests; in Thurstone's report, the primary mental abilities: verbal meaning, spatial relations, reasoning, number fluency, word fluency, perceptual speed, associative memory, each correlating more or less with the others.

factorial analysis: the analysis of test scores for the purpose of determining the least possible number of elements which underlie the total findings; the analysis of basic mental processes (usually by the Thurstone of the Hotelling method) which produced any given test results.

faculty: historically, a mental power, such as memory, reason, perception, or imagination.

faculty psychology: the point of view (developed by Wolff) which considers the mind to be composed of separate areas of power, each of which may be strengthened by exercise and each of which is relatively independent of the other faculties.

fad: any temporary enthusiasm of the individual or the public which meets no major need but which for a brief time is zealously pursued.

faint: syn. *syncope;* loss of consciousness due to a circulatory disturbance.

faith healing: the cure, partial or complete, of an ailment through the use of nonrational but sincere beliefs.

fallacy: incorrect reasoning.

falling sickness: traditional and popular label for grand mal convulsive seizures.

fames: hunger.

fantasy (phantasy):   popularly, imagination or daydreaming; in psychoanalysis, the process, usually unconscious, whereby repressed wishes are gratified indirectly.

fashion: a system of habits or preferences which are more enduring than a fad but briefer-lasting than a custom.

father-fixation: a possessive, abnormal attachment of a daughter to her father continued long after the Oedipal situation has normally been outgrown.

fatigue: objectively defined, a diminishing return in quantity and (often) quality of output as time limits are extended.

fear: an intense, primitive response to danger; a condition during which, according to the emergency theory, the body is being prepared to run, to elude detection by "freezing," or to fight; in Watsonism, a basic emotion elicited by loud noise or loss of support but, through conditioning, attached to many other stimuli.

feces: excrement.

Fechner's law: "A change in sensation occurs when the stimulus is increased or decreased by any given proportion of itself, this proportion being constant for any given sense."

feeblemindedness: syn. *oligophrenia, mental deficiency, amentia;* according to Terman, having an IQ below 70; the condition of an idiot, an imbecile, or a moron.

feedback: by analogy from electronics, the sensory component of a perceptual function; the response becoming the stimulus to further responses.

feeling tone: the pleasantness-indifference-unpleasantness component of a perceptual function.

Feleky pictures: posed representations of various emotions, the investigator to label each picture as to the emotion represented; the prototype of many tests of ability to label emotions from facial expressions.

felt-need: a conscious awareness that a wish or need must be gratfiied.

female: the sex designated by the symbol † in a family chart (e.g., in the chart of the Kallikak family).

feminism: the social movement for equality of opportunity regardless of sex; the adoption of feminine mannerisms by a male.

femur: the thigh bone (largest and longest bone in the human body).

fenestra ovalis (the oval window): an opening in the bone between the middle ear and the inner ear through the membrane covering of which the stapes transmits the vibrations.

fenestra rotunda (round window): an opening in the bone between the middle and the inner ear, the membrane cover of which acts to reduce pressure in the perilymph.

feral child: one who, reputedly, was discovered after a period during which the child was reared by wild animals (e.g., Amala and Kamala or the so-called Wild Boy of Aveyron).

fetich (fetish): in cultural anthropology, an object endowed with miraculous powers.

fetishism: an erotic attachment to some unusual object, such as a part of the body or an article of wearing apparel.

fetus: the prenatal human organism from about the 8th week to birth.

fever therapy: historically, the treatment of paresis by the induction of malaria or some other fever-producing agent.

fictional finalism: in Adler's psychology, the high and unattainable ultimate goals which spur the person on to purposive endeavor.

fiducial limits (confidence limits): in statistics, an index of the limits within which a given statistic would vary according to probability theory; the degree of confidence with which a judgment may be given about a datum.

field theory: a holistic, or global, point of view taught by Lewin and emphasizing the idea that behavior is a function of the total field of forces operative at any given time, a field being "the totality of coexisting facts which are conceived of as mutually interdependent."

figure-ground relationship: the characteristic relationships among the parts of a total perceptual response whereby there is an organization, as the melody and the harmony of a musical selection or the foreground and the background in a drawing.

filial regression: Galton's principle that nature tends towards a norm, the offspring of tall parents being less tall and those of short parents less short until finally there is a return to the average, and so with other deviations from the norm.

filiform papillae: minute protrusions on the tongue, perhaps the receptors for touch sensitivity to food and other substances.

finger talk: communication by means of a manual system of letters and symbols used by the deaf.

fissure: a deep groove in the brain, such as the fissure of Rolando or the fissure of Sylvius.

fistula: a slit as in the check of a Pavlovian dog in order to expose a part of the salivary gland.

fit: a loose term for a grand mal convulsive seizure.

fixation: in psychoanalysis, a remnant of an infantile libidinal cathexis, or the arrest of some part of the libido in the course of its development, thus impeding growth towards maturity.

fixed idea: an obsession.

flagellation: in psychopathology, the achievement of an orgasm by self-inflicted whippings.

flat affects: little or no emotionality; a blunted capacity for feeling and emotion.

flexibilitas cerea (waxy flexibility): a symptom occurring in the catatonic form of schizophrenia, perhaps also in some forms of hysteria, in which an imposed posture may be retained for a long time.

flexor muscle: one which bends a jointed member of the body.

flicker phenomenon: the effect produced when sequential visual images do not fuse into an impression of smooth and continuous movement.

flight of ideas: the rapid sequence of associations usually characteristic of a patient in a mania psychosis.

fluctuating figure-ground relationships: the alternation in visual perceptions of the Necker cube or the Schröder staircase, for instance, which appear to move from one Gestalt to another.

folie: a psychotic condition.

folie à deux: mental disorders found in two closely associated persons, the delusional content, the disordered emotions, and the motivational patterns being strikingly alike.

folk psychology (Volkpsychologie): Wundt's theories about mental processes which mark off one racial group from another.

folklore: primitive customs, practices, and beliefs which persist into modern times.

folkways: in Sumner's account, those conventional modes of thought and action which prevail in any given culture or subculture and which are not normally evaluated by reference to normative or ethical standards (as mores are).

follicle: a small depression, such as a hair follicle.

fontanel (fontanelle): one of the unossified areas observed in the skull of the newborn infant.

foramen: a small opening, usually referring to a perforation in the bony structure (e.g., the optic foramen).

force: in Lewin's psychology, a vector, which has the properties of direction, strength, and point of application, which may have a positive or a negative valence.

forced choice: a measure, such as a. rating scale or an inventory, in which arbitrary choices have to be made, even though they do not wholly suit the rater's or testee's opinion.

forced movement: in Loeb's theory, a tropism or necessary reaction to a situation (e.g., the heliotropism of the sunflower).

forcing: attempting to push the school child to levels of performance beyond the child's capacity; a futile effort to make the child a prodigy.

forebrain: the telencephalon (prosencephalon) and the diencephalon.

foreconscious: (preconscious) mental processes and contents which are not immediately in the focus of attention but which may readily be brought into full consciousness.

fore-exercise: practice materials used to introduce the testee to the procedures used in the examination itself.

fore-pleasure: in psychoanalysis, preliminary stimulation of erogenous zones in order to heighten libidinal drive.

forensic psychiatry: that branch which is applied in courts of law when questions of responsibility and mental competence are involved.

foresight: pertaining to actions prudently oriented towards the future.

forgetting: inability to recall or recognize what was learned at an earlier time.

form: a Gestalt or configuration.

formal discipline: historically, the strengthening of the mental faculties through the study of certain branches of the curriculum, mastered not for their content but for their mind-training value.

formboard: usually, a board with a number of recessions, variously shaped, into which blocks are to be fitted, the score being taken as a measure of nonverbal intelligence.

formication: a paresthesia sometimes associated with drug addiction, in which the patient feels as if bugs were crawling over the skin.

formula: any fact, principle, or rule expressed in mathematical symbols for clarity and brevity in communication.

fornication: sexual intercourse by an unmarried person.

fornix: longitudinal medullated nerve fibers which lie below the corpus callosum in front and join it posteriorily.

fossa: a pit, depression, or fissure (e.g., fossa Rolando).

foster-child fantasy: the childish belief that the "real" parents are important personages.

fovea: a depression on the retina where sharpest vision occurs.

fractionate: to break up an experience into separate parts for special investigation and verbal report.

fragrant: of a flowery odor (e.g., violet).

frame of reference: any standard that influences perceptual organization.

fraternal twins: dizogotic twins; those developing from two ova.

free association: a sequence of associations unimpeded by the imposition of any instructions; in psychoanalysis, those associations which appear to be "free wandering but which are directed by the unconscious instinctual drives and the repressions."

free will: the choices which are said to have no necessary determination from the nervous system or from any other physical cause.

frenum: the connecting membrane which holds down the tongue.

frequency: in psychophysics, the number of light waves or sound waves per second; in statistics, the number of times any score occurs in a class interval.

frequency curve: the graphic representation of the number of scores in each interval of the distribution.

frequency distribution: an array of scores showing the number which occur at each interval listed from high to low or from low to high.

frequency polygon: a graphic representation in silhouette of the distribution of scores in each of the intervals.

Freudism (Freudianism): psychoanalysis.

fringe of consciousness: (Prince) the peripheral aspects of whatever is in the focus of consciousness at any given time.

Frölich's disease: hypopituitary function, resulting in arrest of physical and mental development.

frontal lobe: that part of the brain which lies above the fissure of Sylvius and in front of the fissure of Rolando.

frontal pole: the point at the very anterior surface of the brain.

frotteur: one who achieves an orgasm by rubbing against a person of the opposite sex.

fugue: a brief lapse of consciousness during which behavior is carried out for which there is no subsequent recollection.

functional ailment: one for which no known organic cause can be assigned.

functional psychology: a systematic point of view which emphasizes the instrumental role of mental activities in directing activities leading toward adjustment to the environment and which deals with mental processes rather than contents or experience.

functional psychosis: a grave mental disorder for which no physical cause can be found but which appears to have been caused by mental conflicts.

fusion: the combination of two or more stimuli into a single sensation or perception (e.g. fusion of retinal images).

g factor (general factor): in Spearman's two-factor of intelligence a general ability which accounts for all correlations of scores for the same testee.

gag reflex: retching induced by depressing the back of the tongue, a response Charcot found to be absent in major hysteria.

gait: manner of walking, various abnormalities of which may be symptomatic of different physical or mental disorders.

Galenic: pertaining to the theories taught by Galen (c. 175 A.D.).

galeophilia: abnormal affection for cats.

galeropia: hyperacute vision.

Galton bar: apparatus for determining the differential limen for matching a movable line to the length of a standard line.

Galton whistle: apparatus for determining the upper threshold for auditory acuity by means of a whistle at high frequencies.

Galton's law: the law of inheritance which states that parents contribute ½, grandparents ¼, and so on, of the heredity of an individual.

galvanic skin reflex: an alteration in skin resistance to a small amount of electrical current as emotional states are aroused and subside; *Féré or Tarchanoff phenomenon.*

gamete: a mature sex cell; an ovum or a spermatozoön.

Gamin: in the Guilford Inventory of Factors, general drive (energy), ascendance (social boldness), masculinity (of emotions and interests), confidence vs. inferiority feelings, composure (calmness vs. nervousness).

gammacism: difficulty in articulating words with the letter g.

gang: a group of adolescents united temporarily by common interests and enthusiasms.

ganglion: a mass of nerve tissue containing cell bodies.

Ganser syndrome: absurd, irrelevant answers given by an hysterical patient.

gargalanesthesia: absence of responsiveness to tickling.

gargalhyperesthesia: abnormally responsive to tickling.

gargoylism (apochondrodystrophy): stunted physique and distorted face associated with gross mental deficiency.

gastric ulcer: a peptic ulcer of the inner lining of the stomach.

gastrodynia: stomachache.

gatophobia (galeophobia): morbid fear of cats.

Gaussian curve: a normal curve of distribution.

gene: the bearer of heredity, a minute unit in the chromosome.

genealogy: the study of family histories or lineages.

general adaptation syndrome: alarm reaction; resistance to stress; and final exhaustion.

general intelligence: the complex pattern of various abilities or capacities measured by the Binet-Simon Scale of Intelligence and other tests based upon this pattern.

general paresis (dementia paralytica or general paralysis): a mental disorder recognized in early times but discovered to be a result of syphilitic infection in 1913 (Moore and Noguchi).

general psychology: a broad exposition of psychological facts, principles, and theories pertaining to man in general.

generalization: the process of extending learned stimulus-response patterns to a wide variety of situations and complex reactions.

genetic psychology: the study of growth and development from conception to death.

genetics: the branch of biology which deals with all phases of inheritance, evolution, and variation.

geniculate bodies: the four oval prominences of the diencephalon.

genitals: the external or visible parts of the reproductive organs.

genius: a person with outstanding ability; one whose IQ is above 140 (Terman).

genotype: a type determined by the common hereditary factors of a group.

genu: any knee-shaped organ or part of an organ.

genus: a class between the family and the species, given as the first word of the technical designation of a species or its subdivisions.

geophagia: the eating of clay or dirt.

geriatrics: the branch of medicine dealing with the aged.

germinal: pertaining to the early stages in the development of an embryo.

geromarasmus: the condition of emaciation in very advanced age.

geromorphism: having the appearance and the characteristics of a person in advanced years.

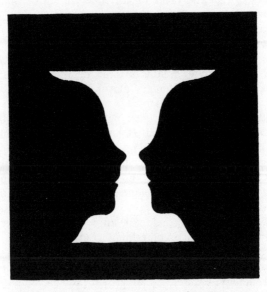

Figure 14. Figure-ground reversal (Rubin's vase).

gerontology: the study of all phenomena pertaining to senescence.

Gestalt (pl. Gestalten): organized wholes or configurations.

Gestalttheorie: a point of view in contemporary psychology which began as a protest against reductive analysis and which emphasized total configurations (Wertheimer, 1912); a system developed from von Ehrenfels' observations of spatial and temporal totalities in perception (Gestaltqualität, 1890).

gestation: the interval between conception and birth.

gifted child: one with an IQ of 140 or above; one with some high degree of specialized ability.

giantism (gigantism): genetically determined huge stature or the result of hyperactivity of the pituitary, anterior lobe (acromegaly, hyperpituitarism. Marie's disorder).

gland: a specialized organ of secretion (e.g., cytogenic, secreting cells; endocrine, secreting hormones; and duct, secreting on an external or internal surface).

glaucoma: hardening of the eyeball, with impairment or loss of vision.

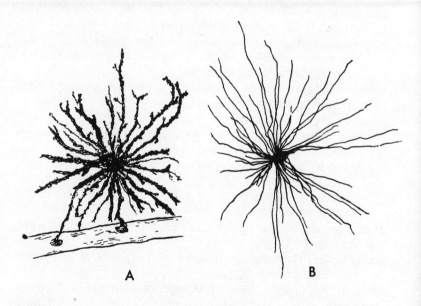

Figure 15. Neuroglia. A has branched, and B unbranched, processes.

glia cells: the supporting cells of nervous tissues; the neuroglia.

glioma: a tumor developing from the glia cells.

globus hystericus: a choking sensation or a swelling of the thyroids in hysterical emotional outbursts or prolonged tensions.

glossal: pertaining to the tongue.

glossolalia: incoherent speech or use of an artificial language by a person in a state of religious excitement; "speaking in unknown tongues."

glove anesthesia: a form of hysterical paresthesia in which insensitivity to pain seems to have occurred on hand and wrist (Janet).

glutamic acid: a chemical which may induce hyperactivity, and hence facilitate the maze learning of a rat.

goal: the objective for which purposeful activity was initiated and sustained.

goal-directed behavior: in Adler's theory, those fictional or realistic objectives which, though attainment may lie in the remote future, are the strivings and urges operative in the immediate present.

goal gradient: the influence of nearness to the goal as it causes increments or decrements of energy output.

goiter: enlargement of the thyroid (simple goiter often found in cretins; exophthalmic goiter marked by great irritability, protruberant eyeballs, tremors).

golden rectangle: one in which width is to length as length is to the sum of both width and length.

gonads: ovaries or testes.

goodness of fit: a measure of a given array of scores from a theoretical or a problematic array of scores.

Goodenough test: the measurement of intelligence from children's drawing of a man, the drawing scored for parts included, thus yielding a point score which is converted into a mental age equivalent.

grade equivalent: the school grade for which a given test score is the mean score.

grade norm: the mean score obtained by pupils of any given placement in school grade.

gradient: an orderly change in strength or weakness of response.

grand mal: a major convulsive seizure, which, classically, follows the pattern of aura, cry, fall, tonus-clonus spasms, fugue state, amnesia, and furore.

grandiose delusions: expansive, unrealistic beliefs of having great importance or power.

graph: a diagram picturing the array of scores and of score values by means of bars, straight lines, or curved lines.

graphic rating scale: a line, usually with guiding phrases below, on which an individual's status on a given trait may be indicated by a check.

graphology: the pseudoscience which diagnoses personality traits from handwriting.

graphomania: psychotic compulsion to write, usually to write meaningless gibberish.

grasping reflex: the tendency of the neonate's fingers to curl over an object, in some instances strong enough to be briefly supported by the grasp.

Graves' disease: mental and physical symptoms associated with exophthalmic goiter.

gray matter: popularly, the outer layer of the cortex of the cerebrum.

group: two or more persons in psychological relationship to one another.

group dynamics: the study of interactions among members of a group and the changing patterns of interpersonal relationships.

group mind: in Le Bon's theory, the distinctively different psychological processes which take over the consciousness of any individual in a crowd, thereby causing irrational and irresponsible behavior.

group therapy: the technique of directed interviews with small groups of disturbed persons whereby, through shared experiences, each patient may gain new perspectives and insights.

growth curve: a graphic representation of changes which occur during the processes of achieving maturity.

guidance: helpful and systematic aid in self-discovery given in an educational or vocational agency by some one who is professionally qualified.

guilt: a pervasive and disruptive feeling of having failed to meet some high expectation or standard; in psychoanalysis, a dysphoric condition of prolonged anxieties resulting from superego promptings (moral anxiety).

gustation: the sense of taste.

gustatory sensations: the qualities of sweet, sour, bitter, and salty.

gutturophonia: a throaty voice.

gynandromorphy: in Sheldon's somatotypes, a body which resembles that of the opposite sex.

gynephobia: morbid fear of women.

gyrus (gyre): a convolution on the surface of the cerebrum or the cerebellum.

habenula: a band-like structure; any of the zones of the basilar membrane.

habit: a learned response which is relatively permanent and which requires a minimum of voluntary direction.

habit hierarchy: the organization of simple habits into a complex pattern (e.g., in telegraphy).

habitat: the region where a group normally dwells.

habituation: the condition of being thoroughly accustomed to a given situation or response pattern.

habitus: the physique.

habromania: cheerful delusions.

Haeckel's law: ontogeny recapitulates phylogeny.

hair bulb or follicle: a tubular sheath in the epidermis from which a hair emerges and which is sensitive to pressure stimuli.

hair cell: a cell with hairlike projections located within the cochlea and said by Helmholtz to be the receptor for audition (hair cells are located in the organ of Corti).

hair esthesiometer: apparatus devised by v. Frey to locate pressure spots on the skin, the instrument consisting of a hair affixed to a handle.

hallucination: a pseudoperceptual experience; the perception of what has no apparent basis in sensory stimulation.

hallucinogenic: drugs which induce pseudoperceptual experiences.

hallucinosis: a mental disorder characterized by pseudoperceptions.

halo effect: the tendency in using a rating scale to be influenced by subjective impressions or by ratings on one trait.

handedness: preference for using the right (dextrality), the left (sinistrality), or either (ambidextrality) hand in motor activities.

handwriting scale: a guide for rating obtained specimens of penmanship with a scale based upon expert judgments of differences in quality.

haphalgesia: intense pain caused by objects resting on the skin.

haploid: having half the number of chromosomes of the somatic cells.

haptic: pertaining to sensitivity for pressure or, loosely, touch.

haptics: the study of cutaneous sensitivities.

harmonic: an overtone or upper partial, the vibration frequency of which is a multiple of the fundamental tone.

harmonic mean: the reciprocal of the arithmetic mean of the reciprocals of the scores.

Hartshorne-May Tests: situational tests designed to measure the ethical character development of children, designed for the Character Education Inquiry (CEI) of 1928-1930.

headache: cephalgia.

healer: popularly, one who effects cures by suggestion.

healthy-minded: in James' account of religious experience, one whose personality is well-organized and free from dramatic conversion experiences.

Healy Picture Completion Tests: formboards used (1911 *et seq.*) in appraisals of the nonverbal intelligence of children, especially in the pioneer investigations of juvenile delinquency.

hearing: audition; sensitivity to double vibrations, normally, ranging from about 16 to 20,000 per second.

heat: the sensation resulting from simultaneous stimulation of contiguous warmth and cold spots.

hebephrenia: that form of schizophrenia (dementia praecox) characterized by dilapidation and childish emotionality.

hebetude: dullness.

hedonic: pertaining to feelings of pleasantness.

hedonic tone: the pleasantness-unpleasantness quality of an affective experience.

hedonics: the study of the pleasantness-unpleasantness aspects of behavior.

hedonism: in ethics, that point of view which equates the highest good (*summum bonum*) with pleasure.

helix: the curved rim of the outer ear.

Helmholtz theory of audition: the theory that segments of the basilar membrane of the cochlea are involved in the analysis of sound, the projecting hair-like cells being arranged, metaphorically, like a harp.

Helmholtz theory of vision: the Young-Helmholtz explanation of color vision by reference to three independent processes in the retina for, respectively, red, blue, and green, all other color experiences being analyzable into these.

hemetal:　pertaining to the blood or to the blood vessels.

hematophobia:　morbid fear of blood.

hemi-:　Greek prefix, *half;* one side of the body.

hemiablepsia:　blindness in half the visual field.

hemianalgesia (hemialgia):　insensitivity to pain on one side of the body or in one leg or one arm or both.

hemianesthesia:　absence of sensation in one half of the body or in one arm or one leg or both.

hemianopia (hemianopsia, hemiopia):　blindness in half the visual field.

hemidystrophy:　inequalities in the development of one side of the body as compared to the other side.

hemiplegia:　paralysis of one half of the body or of one leg or one arm or both.

hemisphere:　either half of the cerebrum or of the cerebellum.

hemiteria:　the condition of malformation of the physique due to congenital factors.

hemo-, haemo-:　a combining form denoting *blood.*

hemophilia:　susceptibility to profuse bleeding.

hemophobia:　morbid fear of the sight of blood.

hemorrhage:　rupture of a blood vessel.

hepatic:　pertaining to the liver.

Herbartian method:　an educational procedure which emphasizes the integration of new material with that already known (*apperceptive mass*) of the learner.

herd instinct:　(Trotter) the gregarious impulse.

hereditarian:　one who upholds the doctrine of hereditary (genetic) determinants in development of physical and psychological characteristics.

hereditary:　transmissable through the genes.

heredity:　the transmission from parents to offspring of genetic determinants of growth and development.

hereralopia:　day blindness.

Hering theory of color vision:　the statement that visual sensations are mediated by three antagonistic pairs of retinal processes; namely, black-white, red-green, and blue-yellow, one of which is catabolic and the other anabolic.

hermaphodite:　one possessing both female and male sex organs.

hetero-:　Greek prefix meaning *unlike.*

heterogeneous grouping: the system of disregarding differences in IQ's when assigning pupils to classes.

heterophonia: the voice change at puberty.

heterophoria: imbalance in the eye muscles.

heterosexual: one who is normal sexually (as opposed to homosexual).

heterosuggestibility: uncritical acceptance of suggestions given by others.

heterotropia: syn., *strabismus;* cross-eyedness.

heuristic question: one which motivates the learner to find the answer through reflection.

higher-order conditioning: (Pavlov) conditioning on the basis of conditioned reflexes already established.

hind-brain: the medulla oblongata, the pons Varolii, and the cerebellum.

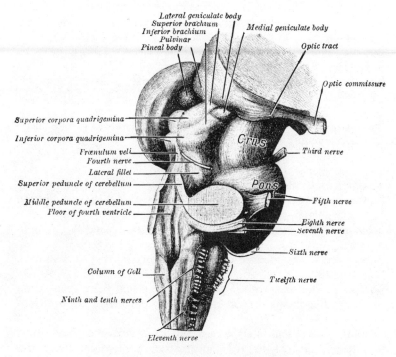

Figure 16. The hindbrain and the midbrain.

hippocampal convolution: nerve tracts (hippocampus major and hippocampus minor) along the floor of each descending horn of the lateral ventricles of the brain.

hircine: resembling the odor of cheese.

histogram: a graphic representation of a frequency distribution, the score values on the abscissa and the frequencies being vertical lines or rectangles above them.

histology: microscopic study of tissues.

hodology: (Lewin) study of forces, directions, and distances of movements in psychological space.

Holmgren worsteds: a test of color blindness as shown by matching various hues to red, green, and purple.

holophrase: a word connoting many concepts and much affectivity.

homeopathy: in ancient Greek medicine, the cure of like by like (e.g., melancholia by seeing a tragedy).

homeostasis: the tendency of the organism to maintain constant states; the self-regulatory physiological mechanisms (Cannon).

homo-:   Greek prefix meaning *like, similar*.

homo-eroticism: homosexuality.

homogeneous grouping: in assigning pupils to classes, grouping on the basis of IQ's.

homolateral: on the same side.

homonymous association: a word of the same sound but different meaning (e.g., bare/bear).

homosexuality: limitation of erotic interests to members of the same sex.

hormic: ·purposive; teleological.

Hormic Psychology: McDougall's theory that behavior, human and animal, is purposive in character.

hormone: the specific product of an endocrine gland (e.g., adrenalin).

horn: any of the columns of gray matter in the spinal cord (dorsal, lateral, and anterior horns).

horopter: the locus of all points in the visual field upon corresponding points in each eye, whereby the images are perceived as single.

hostility: persistent anger as a result of frustrations, the hostility being directed toward the frustrating situation, being displaced upon some other situation, or being generalized.

House-Tree-Person Test (HTP): (Buck) an appraisal of psycho-dynamics through drawings and interrogations about them.

hue: color; the correlate of the wavelength of a visual stimulus.

human engineering: psychology applied to increase of efficiency.

humerus: the large bone from shoulder to elbow.

Humism: the doctrine in philosophical psychology that all knowl-edge is relative and arises from experience (Hume).

humor (humour): in ancient medicine, one of the four fluids within the body (blood, phlegm, yellow bile, and black bile); a liquid (e.g., vitreous humor in the eyeball); response to a comic situation.

hybrid: progeney of parents of different species; having incon-gruous parts.

hydrocephaly: excessive pressure from cerebrospinal fluid in the cranial cavity if internal (usually causing a large skull and a thin cortex) or if external an accumulation of fluid between the skull and the brain.

hydrophobia: morbid fear of water; rabies.

hydrotherapy: treatment by baths.

hygiene: the science of preservation of health, physical or mental.

hypacusia: slight deafness.

hypalgia: diminished sensitivity to pain.

hyper-: Greek prefix meaning *an excess of*.

hyperacusia: high degree of auditory acuity.

hyperalgesia: abnormal sensitivity to pain.

hypercritical: captiously fault-finding.

hyperemotility: given to abnormal outbursts of emotions.

hyperesthesia: abnormal responsiveness to sensory stimulation.

hyperfunction: the functioning of an organ at an abnormally high level.

hyperkinesia: restless motility.

hyperopia: farsightedness (due to shortness of the eyeball or to defect of the refractive media).

hyperosmia: abnormal keenness of smell.

hyperorexia: abnormal craving for food.

hyperpituitarism: a morbid activity of the pituitary gland result-ing gigantism or acromegaly.

hyperprosexia: unusual fixity of attention.

hypersthenia: abnormal muscular strength.

hyperthyroidism: syn., *exophthalmic goiter;* restlessness, loss of weight, protruberant eyeballs, and irritability due to hyper-functioning of the thyroid.

hypertonia: muscular rigidity or abnormally great tension.

hyperventilation: exhaustion of carbon dioxide by forceful exhalations, thus inducing muscular rigidity in a temper tantrum or in an attack of hysteria.

hypnagogic period: the time before the onset of deep sleep.

hypno-: Greek prefix meaning *sleep, drowsiness.*

hypnopompic period: the time before awakening from sleep.

hypnosis: a condition of apparent drowsiness in which the subject accepts the suggestions given by the operator; a state of extreme suggestibility.

hypo-: Greek prefix meaning *an insufficiency of.*

hypobulia: inability to make decisions.

hypochondria: affliction by imaginary illnesses.

hypochondriac: one who is obsessed by imaginary afflictions.

hypogastrium: lower region of the abdomen.

hypoglossal nerves: the 12th pair of cranial nerves.

hypomania: a slight degree of excitement; in a manic-depressive disorder, manic type, great emotional tensions but less than those occurring in acute and in hyperacute mania.

hypometropia: near-sightedness.

hypophonia: inability to speak above a whisper.

hypophrenia: mental deficiency.

hypophysis: the pituitary gland.

hypopituitarism: a condition of obesity and diminished sexual vigor due to underfunctioning of the pituitary.

hypoprosexia: inability to maintain attention.

hypothetico-deductive method: system building that begins with established facts, and then goes on to testable hypotheses and corollaries which may be empirically investigated (Hull).

hyposynergia: poor coordinations in motor responses.

hypothalamus: a part of the forebrain which lies below the thalamus and forms the floor of the third ventricle and which includes the mallary bodies, the tuber cinereum, the infundibulus, the pituitary (hypophysis), and the optic chiasm.

hypothesis: a proposition which is empirically tested to ascertain whether or not it is valid.

hypothyroidism: underfunctioning of the thyroid gland, which, if occurring from the earliest months of life, may cause cretinism, and if at a later time in the lifespan, myxedema.

hysteria: a neurosis (psychoneurosis) which assumes protean forms, such as anesthesias, dissociations, paralyses, and other functional disorders; in psychoanalysis (early Freud) the representation of unconscious, repressed fantasies or (later Freud) the result of a breakdown of defenses against unconscious anxieties.

hystero-epilepsy: a neurotic convulsive seizure resembling to some extent a grand mal attack but actually being a psychogenic motor outburst.

I concept: the developing child's self-awareness as indicated by increasing use of first person pronouns.

ictus: a sudden stroke of convulsive seizure.

id: in psychoanalysis, the unconscious, unorganized source of all instinctual drives, the reservoir of all phylogenetic acquisitions, and the directive force towards amoral, immediate gratifications; that part of the psyche which, more or less effectively is controlled by the ego and the superego.

idea: a composite of mental images; any concept or thought of a situation not immediately present to sense.

ideal: a standard of desirability or of excellence.

idealism: in philosophy, the doctrine that the spiritual, or the mental, is of ultimate primacy, and that, conversely, states that the physical is basically nonexistent or of little importance.

idealization: in psychoanalysis, the overestimation of a person or an object, the faults of which are held to be nonexistent; sexual overevaluation of a person or an object.

identical elements: the perceived similarities between the new situation and a situation which was previously learned, and hence the explanation for transfer of training.

identical twins: same-sex twins developed from one fertilized ovum; twins with identical genetic constitutions.

identification: in psychoanalysis, the process of unconsciously gaining ego strength by taking another person as a model to imitate.

ideographic writing: that which is communicated by pictures or symbols of pictures rather than by phonograms.

ideology: the subjective views about the power relationships which should be enforced, or should prevail, in a group.

ideomotor activity: that which ensues immediately upon ideas about it.

idio-: Greek prefix meaning *personal*.

idioglossia: speech so unintelligible that it seems as if an unknown language were being spoken.

idiographic method: an extension of Windelband's suggestion about an intensive, thorough study of a single case; the procedure of a complete investigation of one person without making comparisons to other persons or without isolating traits for psychological measurement.

idiopathic epilepsy: convulsive seizure, the cause being unknown.

idiot: a mental defective whose mental age is 2 or less and whose intelligence quotient is not more than 20, according to Terman.

idiot savant: a person who seems to be a mental defective but who, according to anecdotes, possesses a single remarkable ability, such as in arithmetic calculations, visual imagery, or rote memory.

illumination: the third stage in creative thinking, in which the new idea or the inspiration seems to appear all of a sudden; an "ah-ha" experience.

illusion: a misperception of sensory data; a perceptual distortion.

image: a more or less clear representation of an object or situation not present to sense; a reproduction of a former sensory-perceptual experience in the absence of overt stimulation.

imageless-thought controversy: the discussions about the possibility of thoughts which entirely lack any sensory reference or revival in mental images.

imagination: the radical recombination of elements of former experiences into a present experience.

imago: in analytical psychology, the idealized, unconscious representation of a parent or some one else closely associated with the individual in early childhood.

imbecile: a mental defective whose intelligence quotient is not more than about 50 nor less than 20 or 25 and whose mental age lies between 2 or 3 and 6 or 7, according to Terman.

imitation: any response which more or less closely resembles the stimulus; a behavior sequence elicited by observing a similar behavior sequence in another person.

imitation theory of language: the opinion that language developed out of the attempts of primitive people to duplicate the sounds of animals and of natural events.

impairment: an injury; loss of a function; destruction of an organ.

imperception: faulty interpretation of sensory-perceptual data.

implicit behavior: subdued responses; minimal, often unobservable, muscular activities, as of speech organs in subdued mental activities.

impotence: weakness, feebleness; loss of or absence of capacity for sexual intercourse.

impulse: an irresistible urge to action but with a minimum of anticipation of consequences or of planning.

impulsion: an urge to some type of overt behavior.

inadequacy: feeling of impotence, severe lack of self-confidence, or general incompetence.

inappropriate stimulus: one which elicits a response even though the particular form of energy is not normally the stimulus for a given receptor (e.g., sensation of light when the eyeballs are pressed).

inbred: innate.

inbreeding: producing offspring from closely related parents; to give rewards to none but the members of a close in-group.

incentive: that which initiates and sustains a behavior sequence leading to some reward or to avoidance of punishment.

incest: sexual intercourse between persons forbidden to have such relationships by the law or by the mores of the group.

incidental learning: the acquisition of certain skills or understandings which accrue as a by-product of some other activity.

incoherence: the condition of being illogically put together.

incoordination: a lack of harmonious adjustment among the parts especially that between pairs of antagonistic muscles in motor acts.

incorporation: in psychoanalysis, the acquisitiveness or greediness ensuing from inadequate libidinal gratifications from intake of food in early life.

incorrigible: a child or an adolescent who is defiant, hostile, and unmanageable in relationships with others, especially with teachers, parents, and law-enforcement officers.

incus: syn. *anvil;* one of the three small bones or ossicles in the middle ear.

independent variable: that factor in a psychological experiment which is varied by the scientist; the cause of the phenomenon which is observed in the experiment, the measured changes, occurring as one factor is varied at a time, being known as dependent variables or effects.

Individual Psychology: the point of view, based upon clinical observations, developed by Alfred Adler (1870-1937).

individual test: a psychological examination that is administered to but one person at a time.

induced movement: a visual illusion in which a stationary object seems to be in motion because other objects in the visual field are actually moving.

induction: the reasoning process which proceeds from particular instances or cases to a general conclusion.

industrial psychology: the application of psychological facts and principles to the selection, training, and management of personnel in industry, their morale and efficiency.

infant psychology: that division of genetic psychology which is concerned with growth and development during the first two years of life.

infantilism: the persistence of childish modes of behavior into adult life.

inference: the end result of an act of inductive reasoning which reaches a conclusion.

inferiority feeling: a sense of personal incompetence and lack of self-confidence, particularly in competitive social relations; in psychoanalysis, the result of a failure to resolve the oedipal situation, giving rise thereby to a sense of failure and disappointment.

information test: items presented verbally or in pictures designed to measure factual knowledge about a specific field (e.g., mechanical devices) or general information.

infundibulum: a stalk-like organ connecting the pituitary gland to the tuber cinerium.

ingenerate trait: any congenital characteristic.

ingest: to take into the stomach.

inhibit: to restrain.

inhibited personality: one lacking in spontaneity and personal freedom in making choices; in psychoanalysis, the result of an overdemanding superego.

inhibition: the arrest of one muscular contraction by activity in an antagonistic group of muscles; a conflict between incompatible motives; in psychoanalysis, the condition in which there are unconscious renunciations of wishes in order to obviate the need to find new defenses against the id.

inkblot test: blobs of ink used to elicit imaginative responses (as in Whipple's inkblots); a series of blots used as a projective technique to appraise the global aspects of personality (e.g., the Rorschach Ink Blots).

innate: unlearned; congenital.

innervation: nerve fibers activating a muscle group or a gland; the amount of nervous impulse to elicit a response in a muscle or a gland.

inorganic: nonliving matter.

insanity: a popular and legal term for psychosis.

insight: the sudden discernment of a solution to a problem or of a new concept; the redintegration of a Gestalt to closure; an "ah-ha" or "Eureka" experience.

inspiration: intake of breath; loosely, the sudden awareness of a novel concept.

inspiration-expiration ration (I/E ratio): the quotient obtained by dividing average time for inspiration by that for expiration, an an index of emotion.

instigator: a stimulus.

instinct: a complex, unlearned response that is now, or was phylogenetically, adaptative, and that is normally present in all members of a species; in Hormic Psychology, the inner spring of purposive behavior; in psychoanalysis, the psychic energy lying within the id.

instinctive: popularly, unintended or involuntary.

instinctivist: one who defends the view that all psychosocial behavior is directed by inherited forces which may wax and wane and which, though controlled by habit, remain as the primary springs of action.

institution: a relatively enduring organization of folkways, customs, and mores perpetuated by the elders of the group through the education of children and having a rather well-defined system of habits and beliefs.

instrumental conditioning: that form of learning in which an intermediate response must be learned as a means for obtaining the reward.

instrumentalism: in philosophy, the doctrine that thinking is a means for efficient action, not an end in itself.

insula: the island of Reil, one of the cerebral lobes.

integrated personality: a loose, normative concept relating to an individual who behaves in a purposeful, altruistic manner and who is free from symptoms of maladjustment.

integration: organization into a coherent, unified pattern; the condition of harmonious, meaningful relationships among parts.

intellect: the totality of cognitive functions; the totality of understandings acquired during one's lifetime.

intelligence: a broad concept variously defined; e.g., ability to adjust to a novel situation making best use of past experience; ability to think abstractly; ability to organize parts of a situatio ninto a coherent whole (from the Latin *intelligere,* to relate or organize); the speed and the accuracy with which an individual performs in a graded series of test items; and so on.

intelligence quotient (IQ): the ratio between mental age and chronological age; *MA/CA times* 100.

intelligence scale: a graded series of items, verbal or nonverbal, used in individual or group measurement to predict an individual's likelihood for success, usually in school or in work allied to academic studies; predictive measures of efficiency in adjustment to academic studies, to mechanical studies, or to social relationships.

intensity: the magnitude or the quantity of a sensation.

intensity discrimination: ability to detect small differences between stimuli presented simultaneously or sequentially.

inter-: Latin prefix meaning *between.*

interactionism: in philosophy, the doctrine that mind influences body and that body influences mind; Descartes' doctrine that mind and body have directive influences upon each other.

interest: an effectively toned choice or preference.

interest test: a list of items which, previously marked by persons in different occupational fields, gives the individual a basis for comparing his interest pattern with theirs.

internal consistency: the degree to which test items, subtests, or other parts of a psychological examination yield scores comparable to scores on the entire examination.

intero-: Latin prefix meaning *within, from the inside.*

interoceptor: a receptor located within muscles, tendons, joints, or internal organs.

interpersonal theory: H. S. Sullivan's belief that personality as a concept has no meaning apart from the social group of the individual and that psychiatry and social psychology have a basic unity.

interpolation: any statistical or reasoning process whereby intermediate values may be determined between two known values.

interval: spatial or temporal separation between experiences or data; the distance from one statistic to another.

intervening variable: a logically postulated construct to account for the intermediate processes between observable stimuli and observable responses.

interview: a planned or self-motivating sequence of questions designed to elicit information or attitudes or to appraise a person.

intra-: Latin prefix meaning *within.*

intracranial: within the skull.

intrapsychic conflict: a rivalry between two or more incompatible motives; in psychoanalysis, a conflict between unconscious instinctual tendencies.

intrinsic motive: a drive, need, motive, or wish that requires no external incentive.

intro-: Latin prefix meaning *turned inward.*

introception (internalization): the uncritical acceptance of beliefs and values of another person (usually the parents or parent surrogates).

introjection: in psychoanalysis, the process of enhancing the ego by assuming the qualities of another person, such as some one towards whom a strong emotional tie exists and from whom ethical standards and values are learned.

introspection: popularly, self-study or analysis; in the Titchenerian system, the analysis of the elements of consciousness by a trained experimentalist; the process which results in a verbal report of psychological contents or events.

introversion: a personality trait marked by reflectiveness, preference for quiet activities, some withdrawal from others, and (often) a bit of shyness.

introversion-extraversion inventory: a list of statements or questions designed to distribute persons along a continuum from those who live psychologically in an inner world to those who are concerned primarily with objective reality.

intuition: the sudden apprehension of a concept or generalization without prior investigation or prolonged reflection.

intuitionism: a philosophical doctrine that truths do not necessitate empirical investigations but may be reached through insights.

invalidism: unconscious assumption of incapacitating ailments; the persistence into postconvalescence of behavior patterns learned during an illness.

invert: a homosexual.

invertebrate: an organism without a spinal column.

inverted Oedipus complex: in psychoanalysis, a fixation upon the parent of the same sex.

investigation: a research undertaking.

investment: in psychoanalysis, the expenditure of instinctual energy upon some object or outlet.

involuntary response: a reflex response or an habitual action without intent or conscious direction, respondent (as opposed to operant) activity; a reflex.

involution: the period of life when physiological and psychological functions undergo marked alterations, usually at age 45-50.

involutional melancholia: emotional disorganization and depression associated with the menopause or the male climacterium, usually attributed to psychosomatic factors and to endocrine changes.

involutional psychotic reaction: a severe disorder occurring in old age and including such symptoms as pettiness, suspiciousness, periods of disorientation, wandering, hypochondria, and the like.

iris: diaphragm suspended in the aqueous humor before the lens of the eyeball and perforated by the pupil.

iris reflex: expansion and contraction of muscle fibers in the iris to regulate the amount of light admitted into the eye.

irradiation: the stage at which any stimulus may elicit the response which, at a later stage in the conditioning process, will be elicited only by the conditioned stimulus alone.

Ishihara Test: a widely used appraisal of the type of color blindness, consisting of plates in which numbers and pathways are embedded in variegated fields of hues.

iso-: Greek combining form meaning *equal*.

isolate: a person who is rejected in sociometric choices by the rest of the group.

isolation: in psychoanalysis, the unconscious process whereby an unpleasant repression is divested of its affective component.

isomorphism: in Gestalt theory, the correspondence between the fields of excitation in the brain and the conditions of awareness which are experienced.

item: a fact or datum for investigation; a single question or exercise on a psychological test or measure.

item analysis: the process of evaluating the relative difficulty of separate test questions or exercises with reference to the difficulty of the test as a whole.

-itis: Greek suffix meaning *an inflammation of*.

J-curve hypothesis: the view that when institutional pressures are strong, most persons conform, a few deviate slightly, and some do not conform at all (F. H. Allport).

jabber: in psychopathology, rapid unintelligible gibberish.

Jacksonian epilepsy: tonic-clonic spasms in a small group of muscles or a limb; localized muscle spasms resulting from excitants in the motor area of the cerebrum (Hughlings Jackson).

Jackson's law of mental deterioration: in progressive dilapidation, most recently acquired habits are lost first, next those acquired earlier in the patient's life history, and finally those dating from childhood (Hughlings Jackson).

James-Lange theory of emotions: the view that "the bodily changes follow directly the perception of the exciting fact, and that our feeling of the same changes as they occur is the emotion."

Jendrassik effect: the increased vigor of the knee-jerk reflex when the hands are locked tightly together or when the table edge is firmly grasped.

job analysis: an objective study of abilities, habits, skills, and personality qualifications necessary to insure success on a given industrial job; all the separate functions required for any industrial job in order to predict success or failure on the part of applicants.

job satisfaction: the zest of a worker as measured by output, absenteeism, scales and questionnaires pertaining to morale, and interviews.

joint sense: a loose term for awareness of interoceptive stimulation from joints and immediately contiguous areas.

Jost's law: the principle which states that, if two associations are of the same strength, further reviews strengthen the older one more than the most recently formed one.

judg(e)ment: the statement of a decision or an opinion; a formal expression or proposition which asserts something; the ability to relate the particular data to a general conclusion.

Jukes family: the pseudonym for a family of misfits living in the Finger Lakes region of New York and investigated by Dugdale in 1877 and Estabrooks in 1915, the family including about 2,800 mental defectives.

Jurgensen Classification Test: a personality inventory, in the form of forced choices, for use in business and industry (1944 *et seq.*).

juvenile: a person below the age of 16 or 18, as the law of the state decrees.

just noticeable difference (j.n.d.): the minimal discrimination an individual can make when, simultaneously or successively, a sense organ or receptor is stimulated; the minimal change in stimuli if differences are to observed.

juxtaposition: side by side.

kainophobia: morbid fear of the new.

Kallikak family: a family line, reported by Goddard (1912), descended from Martin Kallikak (Good-Bad), from one mother there being 496 good citizens and from another mother 480 trouble-makers and mental defectives.

katabolism: the tearing down of tissues; in the metabolic process, the opposite of anabolism (building up).

Kent-Rosanoff Free Association Test: one hundred stimulus words with the response frequencies obtained from a thousand normal adults (1910), scored in terms of commonality and idiosyncrasy of associations.

kinesthesia (kinaesthesia): the complexity of sensations arising from interoceptive stimulation; sensations from tendons, muscles, and joints.

kinesthetic method: the teaching of reading by having the child trace the letters and, simultaneously, pronouncing the sound.

kinetic: pertaining to motion.

klang association: in a free association test, the response being a sound like that of the stimulus word, but often a meaningless response (a neologism).

kleptolagnia: stealing accompanied by sexual excitement.

kleptomania: compulsive stealing, often of objects of no real intrinsic worth; in psychoanalysis, pathological stealing motivated (if done by females) by unconscious penis-envy.

knowledge: the totality of what one knows; measured achievement in information.

Knox Cube Test: a measure of immediate memory for a series of taps on four cubes, used with non-English speaking arrivals at Ellis Island (1914 *et seq.*).

Kohs Block Design: a graded series of designs to be made with one-inch cubes, each side being painted in a different color, used as a measure of performance intelligence (1923).

Korsakow (Korsakoff) syndrome: loss of immediate memory and presense of other deteriorative symptoms in chronic alcoholism.

Krause bulbs: round-end bulbs of sensory nerves located in the cornea, the conjunctiva, some blood vessels, and the mucous membranes (said by von Frey to be the receptors for cold).

Kuhlmann-Binet. a revision of the Binet-Simon Scale down to 3 months of age (one of the first infant tests, 1912).

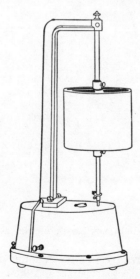

Figure 17. A simple, spring-wound kymograph.

kurtosis: the state of curvature of a frequency-distribution curve as compared to the Gaussian curve. (If the curve is broad and flat, it is platykurtic; if broad at the top, mesokurtic; and if small at the base, leptokurtic.)

Kwakiutl: Indians living in British Columbia whose culture emphasizes boasting and outdoing one another in destruction of their possessions (potlatch).

Kwalwasser-Dykema Music Tests: ten tests administered by use of phonograph records used to measure aptitude for benefiting by education in music.

kymograph: a moving drum on which lines may be traced to record physiological responses.

labile affects: changeable emotionality, often with suddenness.

laboratory: a place for experimentation; the outgrowth of Wundt's psychological laboratory at Leipzig (founded in 1879).

labyrinth: the inner ear.

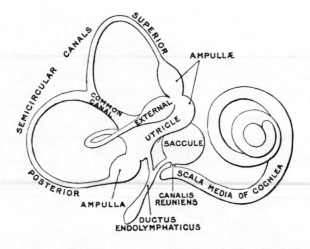

Figure 18. The membranous labyrinth, with associated structures.

labyrinthine sensitivity: the static and the dynamic sense mediated by the semicircular canals and the utricle and the saccule of the inner ear.

lachrymals: the tear glands.

lachrymose: tearful.

lacuna: a gap or hiatus, as in free associations or in memory.

lag: the persistence of physiological activity in the sense organ or the sensory nerve after the stimulus has ceased to act.

-lalia: Greek combining form meaning *speech.*

lallation: infantile babbling; the repetition of sounds in very low-grade mental deficiency.

lalophobia: morbid fear of speaking.

laloplegia: paralysis of speech muscles other than those of the tongue.

Lamarchism (Lamarckianism): the doctrine that acquired traits are transmitted to offspring and that alterations in environment induce changes in inheritable structure.

lambdacism: difficulty in articulating *l* "ell".

lambert: the physical unit of brightness reflected by a surface.

lamella: an instrument to measure the lower limit of the auditory threshold, usually consisting of a thin sheet of metal affixed to a holder (Appunn's lamella).

lancination: a stabbing pain.

language: any one of the thousand or more systems of communication by speech, writing, or gestures used over the world, with innumerable dialects.

laryngograph: apparatus for recording the movements of the larynx in speech.

larynx: the vocal cords and accessory organs.

latency period: the interval between the stimulus and the start of physiological activity in a sense organ or in the nerve fiber; the reaction time; in psychoanalysis, the years between 5 and 12.

latent content of dreams: in psychoanalysis, the unconscious wishes which motivate a dream.

law: a proposition which relates to verifiable uniformities and which generally holds true, within the limits of probability, for the phenomena in question.

law of effect: (Thorndike) a satisfying outcome strengthens, and an annoying outcome weakens, a modifiable connection between a stimulus and a response; the strength of a response depends upon the number of past occurrences when the need-state was satisfied or left unsatisfied.

law of exercise: (Thorndike) use increases, and disuse weakens, the strength of a modifiable connection between a stimulus and a response; in trial-and-error learning, the frequencies and the recencies of any given response increase the probability of a repetition of that response when the same or a like stimulus recurs.

law of parsimony (Occam's Razor): (Morgan) of two or more theories to account for all observable data, the simplest (most parsimonious) should be chosen. (Also known as *C. Lloyd Morgan's canon.*)

law of readiness: (Thorndike) "for a conduction unit ready to conduct to do so is satisfying; for it not to do so is annoying."

laws of thought: (Aristotle) (1) law of identity: A is A; (2) law of contradition: A is not not-A; No A is not-A; (3) law of excluded middle: Everything is either A or not-A; A either is or is not B; (4) law of sufficient reason: No event without a cause. (*Principle* is often preferred to *law* in these four instances.)

learning: a very broad term designating the acquisition of skills and understandings; (Gestalt) the processes of perceptual reorganizations; the relatively permanent effects of practice or understandings.

learning curve: (Bryan and Harter) a graphic representation of progress in mastering skills, which rises rapidly during the initial periods of practice, reaches a plateau or apparent halt in progress, and then slowly advances towards the limit for the learner.

legend: in social psychology, unverifiable tales, popularly accepted as historical facts, regarding eminent personages and events of bygone times.

Leiter International Performance Scale: a nonverbal measure of intelligence requiring a minimum of instructions to the testee (1936 *et seq.*).

lenitive: that which eases pain or grief.

lens: a transparent, biconvex organ located between the iris and the vitreous humor of the eyeball; often called the crystalline lens.

lenticular nucleus: the large, external nucleus of the corpus striatum, the outer part being reddish (the putamen) and the two inner parts being yellowish (both these comprising the globus pallidus).

leptophonia: an unusually weak, thin voice.

leptosome: a weak, thin physique, with schizothymic personality (Kretschmer).

Lesbian: a female homosexual.

lesion: a diseased or injured organ or part of an organ.

levator palpebrae: a muscle which raises the eyelid.

leveling: the tendency of rumors to shrink in details as they are passed from person to person.

libido: in psychoanalysis, the unconscious energy through which the life instincts (or the sexual instinct) perform their work; in Jungian theory, life energy or psychic energy; in pre-Freudian writings, sexual cravings, particularly those relating to perversions or to excessive and deficient outlets.

lie detector: a popular name for instruments which measure the physiological changes accompanying strong emotion.

life cycle: the span from conception to death.

life instinct: syn. *eros instinct;* in psychoanalysis, the totality of sexual and self-preservative impulses.

life space: in Lewinianism, the sum total of all the determinants of a person's behavior at any given moment.

ligament: any band of tissue which connects bones or holds organs in place.

light waves: luminous radiant energy that gives rise to visual sensations.

limbus: the edge or border of an organ.

limen: threshold.

liminal: the lowest value of any given form of energy that will arouse a receptor and cause a sensation.

linear: in a straight line.

lingualis: all the muscles of the tongue.

linked character: a trait which is transmitted through heredity along with another trait (e.g., congenital blindness and mental deficiency in amaurotic family idiocy).

liparous: obese physique.

literate: able to read and write.

Lloyd Morgan's canon: syn. *the law of parsimony;* of rival theories to account for observable phenomena, the simplest should be chosen.

lobe: an area marked off by surface fissures or divisions, as the lobes of the cerebrum (frontal, parietal, occipital, temporal, and island of Reil).

lobectomy: surgical removal of a lobe.

lobotomy: surgical severance of some of the nerve fibers leading from one lobe to another, particularly of some fibers from the frontal lobe to the hyopthalamus.

local sign: (Lotze) the nativistic doctrine that each receptor and each afferent nervous impulse differs in character from every other sensation and that the mind organizes them into meaningful perceptions.

Locke's adaptation demonstration: the reversal effects experienced when one hand is adapted for cold and the other for warmth, and then both hands immersed in water of intermediate temperature. (See cut below.)

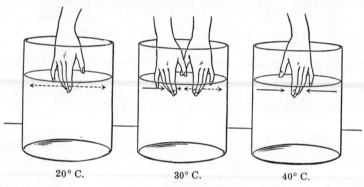

20° C.   30° C.   40° C.

Figure 19.

localization of function: the doctrine that each separate part of the brain is concerned with one single psychological function (e.g., "centers" for written language, motor speech).

localization of sound: determination of the precise source of auditory stimulation in all aspects of the horizontal and the mesial planes, monaurally (one ear) and binaurally (both ears).

locomotor ataxia: syn: *tabes dorsalis;* a disturbance of gait resulting from lesions in the posterior column of the spinal cord due to syphilitic infection.

logic: the normative science dealing with the procedures in valid thought and with the ways of demonstrating the accuracy of thought processes.

logical: thought which, the premises being accepted, proceeds according to the principles of some system of logic.

log(o)-: Greek combining form meaning *speech*.

logorrhea: excessive verbosity, usually with rapid, jumbled phrases.

Lombrosion theory: the doctrine, now discarded, that criminals have physical stigmata and are atavistic (throwbacks in heredity) and degenerated beings.

longitudinal method: studies by tests, measures, and observations of the same individual over a long period of time.

looking-glass self: the concept of the self which is developed through observations of the responses of other persons to the individual.

loudness: the intensity of the auditory stimulus, usually recorded in terms of decibels.

lunacy: in legal documents, unsoundness of mind.

luster: the sheen or gloss of an object.

lymph: a colorless fluid which drains the tissues and fills the lymphatics.

lypemania (lypothymia): melancholia.

lyssophobia: morbid fear of contracting hydroprobia.

Machover Draw-a Person Test: a projective technique for personality diagnosis from drawings of a human figure (1949).

macro-: Greek prefix meaning *large*.

macrocephaly: mental deficiency together with an abnormally large skull.

macrocosm: the universe; society at large.

macro-esthesia: overestimation of the size of perceived objects or of the intensity of stimuli.

macrogenesia: gigantism.

macromania: delusions of great wealth, importance, or power.

macropsia: overestimation of the size of visual sensations.

macrosplanchic: having an abnormally large trunk and relatively short arms and legs.

macula acustica: minute spots in the utricle and the saccule, the receptor cells of which may be involved in equilibrium.

macula lutea: syn. *yellow spot;* a small area on the retina, within which lies the fovea centralis, or point of clearest vision.

mad: a popular term for psychosis; enraged.

magic: in anthropology, the use of supernatural powers which, allegedly, influence physical events and objects.

magical use of language: syn. *open-sesame incantations;* the use of language in the hope that natural events and objects may thereby be influenced.

magnetism: mesmerism; purportedly, a mysterious force by which an occultist works miracles.

maidism: malnutrition, with concomitant dullness and weakness.

maieusiomania: psychosis associated with childbirth.

maieutics: the method of instruction used by Socrates, who believed that learning is actually the revival of memories.

maintenance reactions: physiological and learned reactions which foster healthful living.

Make-a-Picture Story: a projective technique (Shneidman, 1952) in which a story is related as it is developed around a miniature stage scene created by the child; popularly known as the MAPS test.

mal-: Latin combining form meaning *defective, disordered.*

mala: cheek bone.

maladjustment: inability to meet the common problems of everyday life, particularly as a result of emotional immaturity.

maladroit: clumsy.

malaise: a general feeling of vague illness or discomfort.

malaria therapy: treatment of paresis by induction of fever through injections of malaria germs.

malevolent transformation: the child's belief that he is surrounded by enemies; hence, he withdraws from others (Sullivan).

malingerer: one who feigns a disability or a disorder in order to gain personal advantage.

malleus: syn. *hammer;* one of the small bones in the middle ear.

malnutrition: improper diet, which may result in dullness and physical weakness.

Malpighian layer: the deeper portion of the epidermis.

Malthusian law: the doctrine that population increases in geometric ratio and food supply in arithmetic ratio; hence, population increase should be checked if poverty is to be avoided.

mammalia: all vertebrates that suckle their young.

mandala: in Jung's theory, a symbol in the collective unconscious which represents the striving for wholeness of self.

mania: a condition of uncontrolled excitement.

manic-depressive psychosis: extreme alterations in mood, from dilapidated elation to profound depression,

manifest content: in psychoanalysis, the conscious, remembered part of a dream.

manikin test: a performance measure of intelligence, the testee to assemble parts of a small human figure (Pintner, 1917).

mannerism: an idiosyncrasy of a person (e.g., individualistic gestures or postures).

manoptoscope: apparatus for determining eye dominance (as in sighting a rifle).

marasmus: progressive emaciation due to malnutrition.

marginal person: one who has no clear group memberships but who seems to be relegated to a peripheral status.

marijuana (canabis indica): weed leaves which, smoked, create a sense of elation and remove inhibitory controls.

Mariotte's blind spot: the area where the optic nerve joins the retina and where there are no receptors for vision.

MAS: the Manifest Anxiety Scale.

masculine protest: in Adler's early theory, a compensatory re-action for a feeling of inferiority, femininity, or weakness.

masculinity complex: in psychoanalysis, the castration anxiety which causes hostility for the father in the boy and the penis envy which causes hostility towards the mother in the girl.

mask: syn. *persona;* in Jung's theory, the role necessitated by the culture; the facade which more or less conceals the private personality.

masochism: sexual stimulation through passively enduring pain.

mass action: (Coghill) the diffuse, general, primitive behavior out of which, by the processes of individuation, specific re-sponses gradually emerge as the organism matures; in social psychology, the vigorous protest of the group against whatever is perceived as frustrating their needs.

mass media: ways in which large numbers of people are reached as through radio, newspapers, TV, popular books, or motion pictures.

mastery motive: the need to surmount obstacles and to achieve self-actualization; the need to dominate.

masturbation: achievement of sexual excitement through friction of the genitals.

matched-groups procedure: syn. *equivalent-groups method;* the equating of two separate groups, one of which may serve as the experimental group and the other as the control group, to measure the effect of some variable.

materialism: the theory that psychological data should be interpreted in terms of physical data, without any recourse to mentalistic concepts.

maternal drive: the need of the mother to take care of her offspring.

maturation: development which occurs through the biological processes of growth as distinguished from development resulting from learning or exercise.

maturity: realization of the fullest potentiality for development; adulthood.

maze: a series of pathways only one of which leads from the starting point to the reward and which must be learned principally by trial and error.

McNaughton (Daniel) case: the acquittal in 1834 of a defendant in a murder trial, the grounds being inability to distinguish right from wrong with respect to the act upon which he stood trial.

mean: the arithmetic average; $M = \dfrac{\Sigma\,(X)}{N}$.

mean deviation: the average of the deviations of individual scores from the arithmetic mean of the distribution, with plus and minus signs ignored; $MD = \dfrac{\Sigma/x/}{N}$.

mechanism: in philosophical psychology, the view that all psychological data should be accounted for in terms of necessary cause-effect, mechanical concepts; in psychoanalysis, the unconsciously adopted modes in which the urges of the id find some outlet in consciousness and behavior.

medial (mesial):   in or towards the midline.

median: the score or score value which divides the distribution into two equal parts; the second quartile; $Md = \dfrac{N}{2}$ or $\dfrac{N+1}{2}$.

mediate: interposed.

medical psychology: psychiatry.

medium: in occultism, a person allegedly endowed with power to communicate with departed spirits.

medulla: the innermost portion of an organ.

medulla oblongata: the lower posterior part of the brain which tapers off into the spinal cord and which includes centers for such functions as respiration, swallowing, circulation.

medullary sheath: syn. *substance of Schwann, myelin sheath;* the whitish membrane covering medullated nerve fibers.

mega-, megalo-: a Greek combining form meaning *large.*

megacephalia: an abnormally large skull.

megalocephalia: megacephalia.

megalomania: exaggerated pride in one's own achievements, real or imaginery.

Meissner corpuscles: sensory nerve endings in the skin, thought by von Frey to be responsive to touch and pressure.

mel: a subjective unit in judgment of pitch differences.

melancholia: extreme depression.

meliorism: (James) the view that day-by-day efforts to improve one's personality organization and the social order are more effective than an all-or-none perfectionistic method.

memoranda: the materials which are to be learned.

memoriter: that which is learned by rote, not by understanding.

memory: a broad term which includes learning, retaining, recognizing, recalling, and relearning—a term which is verbal in its connotation (Woodworth), not substantival.

memory drum: apparatus for serial learning of items briefly exposed, and then for testing, by the anticipation method, the retention of the material.

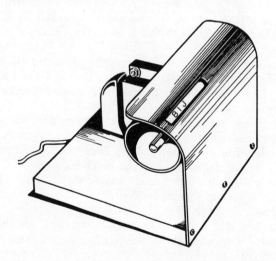

Figure 19a. A typical memory drum or tachistoscope.

memory span: the amount of unrelated or meaningful material which, after a single presentation, can be correctly reproduced.

menacme: the interval between the menarche and the menopause.

menarche: first onset of the menses in the female.

Mendelian law: the biological principles which determine the inheritance of many characters of organisms; the principles which determine the operation of dominant and recessive characters in inheritance.

meninges: the membranes covering the brain and the spinal cord, namely, dura mater, arachnoid, and pia mater.

meningitis: inflammation of the membranes covering the brain and/or the spinal cord.

meningo-:   Greek combining form which means a *membrane.*

menopause: cessation of the menstrual cycle in the female.

menses: monthly flow of blood in the female, typically lasting three to five days.

mental: pertaining to psychological activities or functions.

mental age: the test level reached by a person as compared to the test level reached by the average person of any given chronological age.

mental alienation: a legal term for a psychotic condition.

mental chemistry: (J. S. Mill) the fusion of associations into new compounds, which are different from the elements of which they were composed.

mental conflict: rivalry between incompatible urges or wishes. Mental conflicts are said, by Lewin, to be of the following major types; approach-approach, avoidance-avoidance, and approach-avoidance.

mental defective: an idiot, imbecile, or moron; one who cannot adjust to the community by reason of low intelligence.

mental deterioration: loss of efficiency in psychological functions, as in senile dementia or alcoholic psychosis.

mental discipline: the discarded belief that certain studies strengthen various mental faculties.

mental disease: a psychosis.

mental faculties: the doctrine, long since discarded, that the mind is divided into separate powers (e.g., reason, imagination, perception).

mental hygiene: a broad field which comprises preventive and melioristic procedures in promoting personality development in the widest sense.

mental image: ideational reproduction of sensory-perceptual experience.

mental test: (Cattell, 1890) a brief exercise or series of exercises, administered in a standardized manner, whereby one person may be compared with other persons who have taken the same test.

mentalism: the doctrine that mind is the ultimate reality.

Merrill-Palmer Scale: a verbal and nonverbal intelligence test for preschool children (1931).

mesencephalon: midbrain.

meso-: Greek combining form meaning the *middle*.

mesomorphy: typical athletic build.

meta-: Greek combining form meaning *beyond, along with, after*.

metabolism: the sum of building up and tearing down of tissues; anabolism and catabolism considered together.

metamorphosis: loosely, a sudden alteration in personality, usually as a result of disease or psychosis.

metaphysics: (Schopenhauer) "the branch of philosophy concerned with the analysis of experience."

metapsychology: speculative principles to account for behavior; any systematic point of view which supplements empirical data by hypotheses and conjectures.

meter: 39.37 inches (in USA).

metromania: neurotic or psychotic obsession to write poetry of questionable merit.

metronoscope: an exposure apparatus used to speed up reading habits.

micro-: Greek combining form meaning *small*.

microcephalia: an adult skull 1350 or less in cubic centimeters of capacity.

microcosm: a miniature universe.

micromania: psychotic self-depreciation.

micromillimeter: one millionth of a millimeter; m μ; millimicron.

microsplanchic build: relatively long arms and legs and small trunk.

midbrain: the middle part of the brain; mesencephalon.

midparent: (Galton) the mean of physical measurements of both parents (e.g., their average height at maturity).

mid-point: the halfway point between the lower and the upper limit of any given score or class interval.

migraine headaches: intense and recurrent pains, sometimes involving but half the head, often accompanied by nausea.

milieu: the environment.

military psychology: an application of psychological methods and principles to selection, placement, training, and morale of members of the military forces.

Miller Analogies Test: syn. *MAT;* a reasoning and vocabulary test to predict success or failure in advanced studies (1947).

millimeter: 0.03937 inch.

millisecond: 1/1,000 of a second; sigma or σ.

mimesis: imitation.

mind: the psyche; the sum total of all psychological contents or functions.

mind-body problem: the philosophical, speculative debate about the relationships between mind and body.

mind-healer: a nonmedical person who professes to cure mental disorders through such techniques as hypnotism, persuasion, exhortation, and the like.

mind-twist hypothesis: the view that mental disorders may be caused by mental conflicts, repressions, or other psychological factors.

miniature situation test: for purposes of mental measurement, the reduction of a total activity to its bare essentials.

miniature system: a theory which subsumes the facts and the principles of such a psychological process as perceptual functions or theory of learning.

minimal cue: the smallest stimulus that can arouse a response.

Minnesota Multiphastic Personality Inventory (MMPI): 550 statements for self-report, as True, False, Cannot Say, indicating presence of or freedom from maladjustment (1940).

minor: (generally) a person under 21 years of age.

mirror-drawing experiment: tracing a design with the hand concealed from direct view and the figure seen in a mirror.

mirror writing: syn. *strephographia;* writing backwards, so that only by holding the material up to a mirror can it be read.

misanthropy: intense dislike of fellow men.

miscegenation: the production of offspring by parents of diverse ethnic backgrounds; in U.S.A. the production of offspring by whites and Negroes.

misdemeanor: a crime legally regarded as less serious than a felony and graver than misconduct.

miso-: Greek combining form meaning *hatred.*

misogamy: intense aversion to marriage.

misogyny: pathological dislike of women by a man.

misopedia, misopaedia: morbid dislike of children, even one's own.

misophobia, mysophobia: morbid aversion to dirt.

misperception: an error in organizing sensory data into a meaningful Gestalt; an illusion.

missing-parts test: (Binet) pictures with a part omitted, the testee to name what has been left out.

mitosis: cell division by the halving of chromosomes (prophase, metaphase, anaphase, and telophase).

mnemonic device: an artificial scheme for introducing meaning into unrelated series of items to be learned (e.g., Thirty days hath September . . . .)

-mnesia: a Greek combining form meaning *memory.*

mob: a collection of persons temporarily directed by primitive impulses and emotions and bent upon irrational or antisocial activities.

mobility: in social psychology, the upward or the downward movement of a person from one social class to another.

modality: any given area of sensory-perceptual experience (e.g., taste modality).

mode: in a distribution of scores, the score which occurs most frequently.

mogigraphia (mogographia): writer's cramp.

molar behavior: integrated segments of large patterns of activity.

molar concepts: those which, opposed to molecular concepts, pertain to the whole personality or large segments of it.

molecular concepts: those based upon detailed analysis.

monads: (Leibnitz) physical units which, within themselves, somewhat reflect the total universe and which combine into systems of varying complexity (e.g., into mind).

monaural, uniaural: pertaining to one ear.

mongolian: a mental defective with an oblique epicanthus, fissured tongue, flat head, and stubby toes and fingers; Langdon-Downs' imbecility or idiocy.

monism: in philosophical psychology, the view that ultimate reality is either mind (idealism) or body (materialism).

mono-: Greek combining word meaning *one, single.*

monochorionic twins: identical twins; one-sac twins.

monoideic somnambulism: (Janet) sleepwalking in which one dominant, obsessive idea seems to be carried out.

monocular: pertaining to one eye.

monomania: psychotic obsession with a single idea.

monoplegia: paralysis of one limb.

monozygotic twins: twins with the same heredity; identical twins.

mood: a long-lasting affective state, usually mild in intensity.

moral imbecile: (Pritchard, 1835) an outmoded term to denote a person who is wholly lacking in scruples, loyalty, or adherence to the moral code of the group.

moral realism: (Piaget) the older child's belief that standards of good and bad conduct are unquestionably objective and obvious.

moral relativism: in cultural anthropology, the doctrine that ethical standards vary from group to group and age to age, they being social products.

morale: the degree of zest for purposeful endeavor, whether in personality development or in group participation.

morbid: pathological.

mores: (Sumner) social customs evaluated from the standpoint of ethics.

Morgan's canon: in choosing among various theories which seem to account for all observable and inferred data, the simplest is likely to be the most nearly valid; a restatement (1894) of Occam's razor.

moron: (Goddard) a mental defective with an IQ between 50 and 70 and with a mental age of from 7 to 12, roughly; the highest grade of mental deficiency.

Moro reflex: upward movements of limbs in a newborn infant when the mattress of the crib is vigorously patted

morphinism: pathological changes, physiological and psychological, due to addiction to morphine.

morphology: that branch of biology which deals with the form and the structure of organisms (anatomy, histology or microscopic anatomy, organography, cytology, and embryology).

mosaic test: Lowenfeld's projective test, consisting of 465 small blocks of various sizes and colors, the subject told to make anything he pleases.

mother's complex: in Jung's theory, the resultant of both racial and personal experiences with mothers, which comprise the nucleus of an intense attachment.

mother fixation: in Freud's theory, the after-effects of a failure to resolve the oedipal attachment; loosely, an intense attachment to the mother which carried over into the male's adulthood.

mother surrogate: an older woman who serves as a substitute mother for a younger (and neurotic) man.

motile: one who learns best through motor activities (e.g., writing out the assignment).

motivation: the incentives, both intrinsic and extrinsic, which initiate and sustain any given activity; a complex and ambiguous concept to denote (usually) sustained, goal-directed behavior.

motive: (Woodworth) an activity-in-progress; the inferred cause for an action; a need.

motor: glandular and muscular activities; a response.

motor aphasia: inability to speak or write, though ability to understand speech and writing may be unaffected (Head).

motor area: that part of the cortex of the cerebrum directly in front of the fissure of Rolando and extending to the upper part of the medial surface of the hemisphere.

motor fiber: syn. *motor nerve, efferent nerve;* a nerve fiber which transmits nervous impulses to muscles and glands.

motor function: muscular activity.

motor theory of consciousness: (Washburne) the doctrine that consciousness, or awareness, is a concomitant of muscular activities or bodily responses.

motor neuron(e): a nerve cell which is in contact with an effector.

motor sensitivity: responsiveness to proprioceptive stimulation; response to sensations from receptors in muscles, tendons, joints, and (by some) the utricle and the saccule.

motorium: all the parts of the brain which are involved in muscular and glandular responses, particularly the area which mediates the skeletal musculature.

ms: 1/1,000 of a second; one sigma.

mμ: 1/1,000 of a micron; the unit for measuring length of light waves.

mucous membranes: soft tissues lining cavities of the body; the corium, or deep layer, and the soft layer moistened by cell secretions and by secretions from embedded glands.

Müller-Lyer illusion: a well-known visual-space misperception in which direct and reversed arrowheads make lines of identical length appear to be unequal.

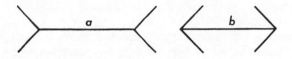

Figure 19b. The Müller-Lyer illusion. (Note: a and b are equal in length.)

multimodal: a frequency distribution with two or more intervals containing the same number of scores.

multimodal theory of intelligence: Thorndike's teaching that intelligence is not a single entity but a large number of specific abilities or capacities.

multiple causation: the view that a symptom or a response may be determined by more than a single factor or cause.

multiple-choice test item: one in which the testee must decide between two or more possibilities for the correct answer.

multiple factor analysis: in statistics, a procedure for determining the basic factors which underlie a series of psychological tests or measures.

multiple personality: two or more distinct personalities, which coexist or alternate, in the same individual, each more or less dissociated from the other.

multiple sclerosis: deterioration of brain and/or cord, with concomitant ataxia, disorientation, weakness, and other symptoms of deterioration.

Mundugumor: in cultural anthropology and social psychology, a New Guinea tribe characterized by aggressive behavior (Mead).

Munsell system: a procedure in identifying the hue, saturation, and brilliance of a surface color by referring it to a standard atlas of colors (1926).

muscae volitantes: small particles in the vitreous humor of the eyeball which are sometimes observed.

muscle: a bundle of contractile fibers, which may be striated or striped, unstriated or smooth, and intermediate (e.g., heart muscle).

muscle tonus: the amount of contraction in a muscle fiber.

"muscle-twitch psychology": a term of opprobrium for systems which dispense with all mentalistic concepts and emphasize muscular and glandular responses.

musculature: all the muscles together, usually the skeletal system.

musicotherapy, music therapy: the use of appropriate music, chosen by professionally qualified experts, as adjuvant therapy in mental disorders.

mutation: (De Vries) a sudden variation which is transmissible, as a dominant or a recessive, through heredity.

mutism: refusal to speak (e.g., in catatonia); inability to speak because of congenital or early deafness.

mutualism: in biology, both the host and the parasite benefiting from the relationship; symbiosis.

myasthenia: great lassitude or weakness of muscles.

myelin tissue: syn. *substance of Schwann;* the fatty, whitish covering of medullated nerve fibers.

myelon: spinal cord.

myesthesia: syn. *kinesthesia, muscle sense;* the pattern of proprioceptive stimulation; myoesthesia.

myiodesopsia: a pathology of vision in which the patient complains of particles floating in the eyeballs.

myograph: apparatus for objectively measuring strength of muscles.

myo-: Greek combining form meaning *muscle*.

myopia: near-sightedness.

myotonia: muscle spasm.

mysophobia, misophobia: morbid fear of dirt or infection.

mysticism: in philosophy, the doctrine that truth is reached through intuitions or nonsensory experiences.

myth: in social psychology, a tale generally accepted as historically true but which has no factual basis and meets the subjective needs of its adherents.

mythomania: pathological lying or exaggeration of the facts.

myxedema: syn. *hypothyroidism;* reduction in thyroid activity, with concomitant thinness of hair, dryness of skin, and physical weakness.

N, n: number of cases.

Nancy School: a systematic presentation of psychiatric theory by Bernheim; particularly, Bernheim's teaching that hypnosis is hypersuggestibility (1882).

nanism: dwarfism.

narcissism, narcism: in psychoanalysis, direction of libidinal energy towards the self as the object-choice; the arrest of psychosexual development at the level of childish ego gratification.

narco-: Greek combining form meaning *stupor*.

narcolepsy: abnormal spells of sleepiness.

narcosis: the state of being under the influence of drugs.

narcosynthesis: in psychiatry, the use of mild, quick-acting drugs (e.g., sodium pentothol) to induce the patient to ventilate the tensions and to assimilate their interpretation by the analyst.

narcotism: addiction to sleep-producing drugs.

nares: nostrils.

nasopharyngeal: pertaining to the cavities above the soft palate.

nation: a group of persons united under a common system of government or ideology, almost always with a shared belief system, and usually with strong in-group loyalties.

national character: an integrated pattern of habits and values which are said to differentiate one national group from another and which the older generation teaches children.

native: unlearned; inherited.

nativism: (Kant) the mind possesses innate categories not acquired through the senses or learned in any other way.

natural philosophy: an outmoded term for such sciences as chemistry and physics.

natural selection: (Darwin) the theory that favorable variations in heredity facilitate, and unfavorable variations impede, survival of a species; survival of the fittest.

nature-nurture controversy: the arguments about whether heredity or environment plays a larger role in growth and development; eugenics vs. euthenics.

nausea: intestinal distress, with a tendency to vomit.

Neanderthal man: an extinct race with a cranial capacity similar to that of contemporary man (named from the Neanderthal Valley in the Rhine Province).

nearsightedness: syn. *myopia; a focus* of light waves in front of, not on, the retina.

Necker cube: one cube superimposed on another, with the edges connected, which appears to fluctuate.

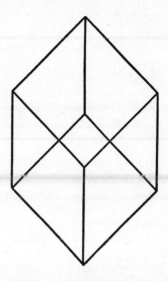

Figure 20. The Necker cube.

necro-: Greek combining form meaning *dead*.

necromancy: in occultism, foretelling the future by communication with the dead.

necrophilia: abnormal excitement in presence of corpses.

necropsy: autopsy.

need: a tissue lack; a motive.

neëncephalon: the cortex of the cerebrum.

negative acceleration: said of a frequency curve which rises rapidly, and then flattens into a plateau (e.g., a familiar type of learning curve).

negative adaptation: (Guthrie) learned indifference to a stimulus.

negative afterimage: sensation of the complement of a color after removal of the stimulus following exposure to it or during prolonged exposure. (Newton, 1704).

negative practice: syn. *the beta hypothesis;* continued practice of an error, with knowledge of what is wrong and how the act ought to be performed (Dunlap, 1932).

negative transfer: a reduction of efficiency because learnings from one performance are carried over to another activity.

negative transference: in psychoanalysis, the dislike or hatred of the analyst by the analysand at one period during the therapeutic relationship.

negativism: uncooperativeness; doing the opposite of what is requested.

neo-: a Greek combining form meaning *new*.

neo-Freudian: one who has extended the theories of classical psychoanalysis, usually from teachings and references made by Freud during the latter part of his life.

neologism: meaningless jargon coined by the patient or by a young child.

neonate: the infant during the first three or four weeks of life.

neopallium: the cortex of the cerebrum, which is the most recent portion to appear in evolution.

neoplasm: a tumor or cancerous growth.

nerve fiber: a bundle of neurons.

nerve cell: syn. *neuron* (*e*); the structural-functional unit of the nervous system, consisting of a dendrite (receiving end), the cell body (including the nucleus), collateral branchings, and the axon(e) (which transmits the impulse).

nerve (neural) impulse: the electrochemical discharge from dendrite along axon, which travels at about 120 meters a second in the human nervous system.

nerve trunk: nerve fibers surrounded by neurilemma (sheathing).

nervous arc: the afferent, the connectors, and the efferent neurons involved between the receptor and the effector.

nervous breakdown: popularly, a condition of being physically debilitated and emotionally keyed up.

nervous system: in man, the cerebrospinal and the peripheral nerve fibers together with the autonomic nervous system.

nervus: in anatomy, a nerve fiber.

neurasthenia: syn. *Beard's disease;* vague complaints and great fatigability; an outmoded term to denote a common type of neurosis.

neurilemma: the whitish, delicate covering of medullated (sheathed) nerve fibers.

neuritis: painful inflammation of a nerve or of nerves.

neuro-: Greek combining form meaning *nerve*.

neurobiotaxis: (Kappers) the tendency of dendrites to develop towards the axons of nerve cells in which nervous impulses are frequently discharged.

neuroblast: embryonic nerve cell.

neuroglia: cells which form the supportive tissues of the nervous system, especially the brain, the spinal cord, and the ganglia.

neuroglioma: syn. *glioma;* a neoplasm in the nervous system; a tumor.

neurology: the study of the structure and the functions of the nervous system.

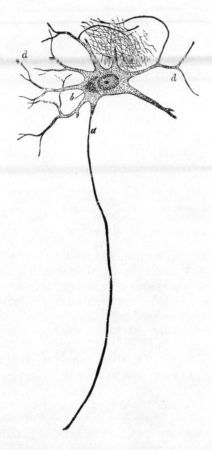

Figure 21.   Schematic representation of a neuron from the human spinal cord.   (a is the axon; b, the cell body, with nucleus and pigment; and d, dendrites.)

neuron(e):   a nerve cell; (Waldeyer, 1891) the structural-functional unit of the nervous system.

neuropathological: caused by an organic disorder of the nervous system.

neurophysiology: the science which investigates the functions of the nervous system in health and illness.

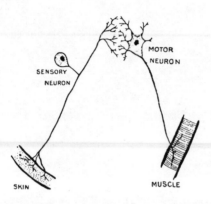

Figure 22.   Hypothetical representation of the simplest functional unit in reflexive activity.

neuropsychiatrist: a medical specialist who combines both neurology and psychiatry in diagnosis and treatment of disorders.

neurosis (psychoneurosis):   a functional disorder which is more grave than a simple personality maladjustment but more benign than a functional psychosis.

neurosyphilis: infection of the nervous system by terponema pallidum.

neurotic inventory: a list of questions or problems usually for self-report to indicate whether any given pattern of neurosis is present.

neurypnology: (Braid, 1843) hypnosis.

nightmare: syn. *nocturna parvor;* a terror dream.

nihilistic delusion: the psychotic belief that nothing is real.

nil est in intellectu quod prius in sensu: loosely, all ideas are derived from sensations, a statement which, in philosophical psychology, protests against the doctrine of nativism.

nirvana principle: in psychoanalysis, the tendency for mental functions to proceed on a minimum of psychic tension; the principle which leads "our throbbing existence towards the stability of an inorganic state."

Nissl bodies: minute structures in the cytoplasm of nerve cells.

nociceptor: a sense organ, or receptor, for pain.

noctambulism: syn. *somnambulism;* sleepwalking.

nodal points: points on the axis of a lens system which make rays transversing one point emerge from the other point in a parallel direction.

noegenetic principles: (Hamilton, posthumously 1859) those arising from pure reason, independently of sensory bases.

noise: unpleasant, nonperiodic sound waves.

nomadism: tendency to wander.

nominalism: in philosophy, the doctrine that universals are actually nonexistent, only the term is general (e.g., a term like group mind).

nomothetic method: a procedure which leads to general laws or principles on the basis of detailed observations of the behaviors of many individuals.

non-: Latin prefix meaning *not.*

non compos mentis: in law, incapable of managing one's personal affairs; psychotic.

nonadjustive behavior: that which does not meet the demands of the situation but which serves to ease pent-up tensions.

nondirective counseling: syn. *Rogerian psychotherapy;* client-centered procedure, the counselor serving merely to help by permissive acceptance and clarification, not by assuming responsibility for solving the problem.

nonliterate society: in cultural anthropology, a people who have no written form of communication.

nonparametric statistics: procedures which do not assume that the true arrays of all data (the universe) are distributed according to the frequency curve of theoretical probability but that other types of distributions may occur.

nonsense syllable: (Ebbinghaus) a vowel separating two consonants, and hence equal in difficulty to others and equally devoid of associations (in the German); a meaningless word used in experiments on rote learning.

non sequitur: a conclusion which does not logically follow from the premises adduced to support it.

nonverbal test: one which uses pictures, manipulative materials, or imitative situations in order to measure intelligence (e.g., formboards, Goodenough Draw-a-Man, Army Beta).

nor-adrenalin: a hormone secreted by the medulla of the adrenal gland, said to be involved in rage reactions.

Nordic race: North Germans and Scandinavians who are long-headed (*dolichocephalic*); blond, and large.

norm: standard type or value (e.g., social norms); the value representing the average for any given chronological age, school grade, etc., whereby a raw score may be interpreted.

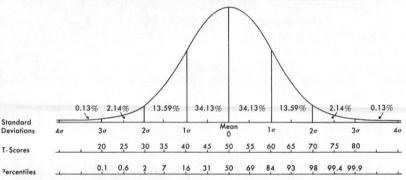

Figure 23.   The normal frequency (or Gaussian) curve, with t-score and percentile (%-ile) equivalents.

normal curve: the bell-shaped curve or curve of theoretical probability.

normal personality: a broad concept defined statistically as the most common type in a group; evaluatively, as the ideal type; and, often, as an individual free from defects or disorders, especially from psychiatric involvements.

normative subject: a field of study in which standards are derived a priori (e.g., as in ethics or logic); a study, or (loosely) a science, which establishes standards for evaluating data or behavior.

noso-:   Greek combining form meaning *disease* or *disorder*.

nosology: the branch of medicine which classifies disorders according to their patterns of symptoms (e.g., as by Kraepelin, in psychiatry the great nosologist).

nosomania: obsession with imaginary ailments.

nosophobia: morbid fear of contracting a disease.

nostalgia: homesickness.

notalgia: pain in the back.

notochord: in the embryo, the tissues from which brain and cord are developed.

nous: in the history of psychology, the faculty of reason or the intellect (Anaxagoras).

nuclear complex: in psychoanalysis, the Oedipus complex, which is regarded as the forerunner of later maladjustments if not properly resolved.

nucleus: a mass of gray matter in the nervous system; the ovoid mass of protoplasm which is enclosed in the nuclear membrane and which is surrounded by the cytoplasm of the cell.

nucleus ambiguus: an elongated group of cells in the medulla oblongata.

nucleus caudatus: syn. *caudate nucleus;* a mass of gray matter in the corpus striatum.

nucleus cuneatus: a mass of gray matter in the medulla oblongata.

nucleus dendatus: syn., *corpus dentatum;* wavelike sheet of gray matter in the cerebellum and in the olivary bodies of the medulla oblongata.

nucleus lenticularis: syn. *lenticulate nucleus;* a large and external mass of gray matter in the corpus striatum.

nucleus of Bechterev: syn. *vestibular nucleus;* the gray matter in which the fibers of the vestibular nerve end (a branch of the VIIIth cranial nerve mediating the nonauditory senses of the inner ear).

null hypothesis: the assumption of the opposite of the hypothesis being investigated.

number factor (N): (Thurstone) one of the primary mental abilities; facility in dealing with numbers and number concepts.

nurture: the totality of all the environmental factors which influence growth and development, as opposed to heredity (nature).

nyctophobia: morbid fear of darkness.

nymphomania: insatiable sex drive in women.

nystagmus: rapid oscillation of the eyeballs.

O: in structural psychology, the observer or trained introspectionist.

obcecation: partial blindness.

object: in psychoanalysis, that which is required for libidinal gratification.

object blindness: a form of aphasia in which familiar objects cannot be identified.

object-cathexis: in psychoanalysis, the direction of the libido toward that which is not obviously, or consciously, sexual in connotation; the investment of unconscious energy in whatever will gratify an instinct.

object-choice: syn. *object-cathexis;* direction of the libido toward the idea of some object in the outer world.

objective psychology: systematization of empirically derived facts and principles, as opposed to mentalism and subjectivism.

objective test: one yielding the same, or about the same, score, no matter who grades it; a standardized, impersonal measure, often taking the form of true-false, completion, multiple-choice, or matching items.

objectivism: in philosophical psychology, the point of view emphasizing empirical, verifiable inquiries of an impersonal nature.

oblique muscles: those which move the eyeball upward and outward (superior oblique) or downward and inward (inferior oblique).

oblivescence: material in a state of partial or complete loss through forgetting.

obmutescence: mutism.

obnebulation: confusion.

obnubilation: confusion and stupor.

obsession: a persisting, intrusive ideational component, usually disquieting and anxiety-producing.

obsessional-compulsive reaction: a neurosis characterized by persistent, troublesome fixed ideas together with purposeless motor expressions (e.g., hand-washing by Lady Macbeth).

obsessional neurosis: the presence of vague anxieties and forebodings as disruptive, persistent ideational components; a maladjustment marked by troublesome fixed ideas.

obstruction method: the use of apparatus to measure the strength of various animal drives, usually by determining the amount of electric shock the animal will endure to reach the goal.

obtained score: syn. *raw score;* the value before statistical treatment is given.

obtundent: that which eases pain.

Occam's razor: in logic, the view that the simplest theory to account for all observed facts should be preferred to complex theories.

occasionalism: in philosophical psychology, the theory (Geulincx and Malebranche) that God occasionally intervenes to produce bodily activity corresponding to mental activity; one of the classical theories of body-mind relationships.

occipital lobe: that part of the cerebral hemisphere which lies behind the parietal lobe and above the temporal lobe.

occiput: posterior area of the skull or the brain.

occultism: belief in, or practice of, mysterious, supernatural ways of controlling or understanding the forces or events of nature.

occupational therapy; purposeful activities which facilitate the rehabilitation of the convalescent patient.

ochlophobia: morbid fear of crowds or crowded places.

oculist: syn. *opthalmologist;* a medical specialist trained in diagnosis and treatment of disorders of the eye.

oculo-: Greek combining form meaning the *eye.*

oculomotor: pertaining to movements of the eyeball.

oculomotor nerve: the 3rd cranial nerve.

od: in occultism, the mysterious force (odylic force) producing hypnosis.

odor prism: Henning's representation of six fundamental odors and their interrelationships.

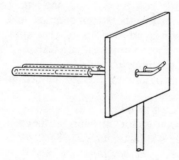

Figure 24. A Zwaardemaker olfactometer, used for studies of sensitivities to odors.

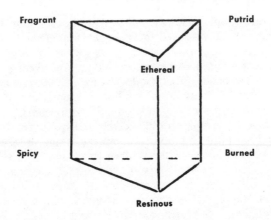

Figure 25. The smell, or odor, prism of Henning (1915).

odorimetry: measurement of the strength of olfactory sensations and stimuli.

Oedipus (Edipus) complex: in psychoanalysis, libidinal cathexis upon the parent of the opposite sex.

oesophagus (esophagus): passage from the mouth to the stomach.

oestrus (estrus) cycle: periodic sexual receptivity in female animals.

ogive: a curve representing a cumulative frequency distribution of scores.

ohm: the resistance of an electric circuit in which a potential difference of one volt produces a one-ampere current.

Ohm's law: in acoustics, the statement that auditory perceptions of complex sounds are fusions of sensations aroused by the components of the complex sound wave.

-oid: Greek suffix meaning *like.*

olfactie: the unit in describing the strength of an olfactory sensation.

olfaction: the sense of smell.

olfactometer: apparatus for measuring the sensitivity to odors (Zwaardemaker's olfactometer, 1888).

olfactory bulb: syn. *olfactory lobe;* an extension of the cerebrum lying above the nasal passages and consisting of an ovoid mass of gray matter; the rhinencephalon.

oligo-: Greek combining form meaning *few* or *a minimum of.*

oligolalia: impoverished vocabulary.

oligophrenia: mental deficiency.

-ology: Greek combining form meaning *the study,* or *the science of.*

omnibus test of intelligence: one in which the items are not grouped into patterns, or subtests, according to similarity of function to be measured (e.g., Binet's tests as contrasted to the Wechsler-Bellevue tests).

omnicompetent: having legal authorization to act for the patient in all matters.

omnipotence: in psychoanalysis, the belief of the young child that all wishes may be granted; in abnormal psychology, the delusion of having unlimited power and wisdom.

onanism: coitus interruptus; (masturbation).

oneiro-: Greek combining form meaning *a dream.*

oneirocritics: the interpretation of dreams, usually by non-empirical methods.

oneirology: the study of dreams.

one-trial theory of conditioning: (Guthrie) the view that the conditioned response is established, or not, on the initial presentation of the conditioned stimulus along with the unconditioned stimulus.

oniomania: psychotic or neurotic "buying spree."

onomatopoetic theory: the view that language originated in the attempts of primitive man to imitate the sounds of nature (also known as the "bow-wow" theory of the origin of speech).

onomy: in biology, the appropriate choices of nomenclatures.

ontogeny: growth and development of the individual, as opposed to phylogeny (evolution of the species).

ontology: in philosophy, the study of the ultimate nature of being, as such; a branch of metaphysics which investigates ultimate relationships, essential properties, and basic nature of being.

onychophagia: neurotic nail-biting.

opeidoscope: apparatus for displaying sound waves on a screen.

open-end question: one which gives the informant an opportunity to state opinions, rather than to answer by yes-no-don't know.

operant conditioning: a form of learning in which a response made by the organism becomes potent, through repetition or insight, to obtain a reward or to escape from a noxious situation.

operant response: one defined by the stimulus which it leads to rather than by the stimulus which elicited it.

operational definition: (Bridgman) a definition which does not pertain to the absolute properties of any given concept but which derives meaning from the operations to which they are directed in an investigation or experiment.

operationalism: in logic, the view that concepts derive meaning from the use to which they are put or from the methods of research by which they are derived.

ophthalmology: the branch of medical science which deals with diseases and imperfections of the eye.

ophthalmoplegia: paralysis of the muscles of the eyeball.

ophthalmoscope: apparatus devised by Helmholtz (1851) for looking into the eye chamber.

ophthalmometer: apparatus for measuring the saccadic movements of the eyeballs, as in reading.

opinion: the verbal expression of a belief; a judgment.

opinion poll: an investigation, by methods of sampling, of beliefs relative to a current issue of importance.

opistognathous: having a retreating lower jaw (e.g., as in microcephaly).

opisthotonos: a muscular spasm in which the head is bent backward.

oppilative: obstructive or frustrating.

opportunity class: in educational psychology, a class for pupils who do not satisfactorily adjust to the normal program of the school.

opposites test: a form for test items in which the examinee must choose the antonym or, in nonverbal material, the obverse of the stimulus given (e.g., up ——; 2, 4, 6, 8 - - - - - -).

optic chiasm: the decussation of the optic nerves (in front of the tuber cinereum).

optic lobe: the anterior portions of the corpora quadrigemina.

optic nerve: the 2nd cranial nerve.

optic thalamus: syn. *thalamus;* gray matter at the base of the cerebrum; an oval-shaped mass in the diencephalon.

optic tract: the optic nerve.

optician: an expert, or dealer, in eyeglasses and optical instruments.

optimism: the belief that life is essentially and basically good.

optimum: in biology, the situation most conducive for the reproduction and the survival of a species.

opto-: Greek combining form meaning *vision* or *the eye*.

optometer: apparatus for measuring visual distance and accommodation of the eyeballs.

optometrist: a nonmedical expert in testing visual acuity.

optophone: apparatus for converting light waves into sound waves, thereby aiding the blind.

oral: pertaining to the mouth.

oral aggressive: in psychoanalysis, sarcasm, zeal to exploit, meanness toward others, as a result of residual fixations at the oral level in psychosexual development.

oral anxiety: in psychoanalysis, the persistence of fears associated with early failure to satisfy food needs and need for affection.

oral character: in Abraham's extension of psychoanalysis, the residual effects of failure to gratify sucking needs, resulting in a pessimistic, fearful, melancholic personality.

oral dependence: in psychoanalysis, the unconscious wish to regress to the warmth and security of the mother's breast.

oral eroticism: in psychoanalysis, an excessive and unconscious preoccupation with the oral region, which may (Abraham) lead to excessive biting or lip play.

oral-incorporative behavior: in psychoanalysis, the residual effects of infantile efforts to take into the body the mother's person, resulting in behavior that is possessive, greedy, and selfish.

oral sadism: in psychoanalysis, the unconscious urge to bite, devour, or destroy.

oral stage: in psychoanalysis, the earliest period in pregenital psychosexual development, in the early phase of which sucking, swallowing, incorporating are the chief activities and in the later stage of which biting is a principal activity.

order-of-merit ranking: a procedure for recording impressions of the relative merits of persons, traits, or stimuli along a single continuum.

ordinate: the *y*-axis of a graph.

Orestes complex: (Wertham) a son's unconscious impulse to kill his mother.

-orexia: Greek combining form meaning *hunger* or *appetite*.

orexis: appetite and affective impulses as distinguished from intellectual functions or aspects of experience.

organ: in anatomy, a structure which performs some particular function.

organ of Corti: a spiral membrane in the inner ear.

organ inferiority: (Adler) awareness of a physical deficiency which leads to efforts to overcompensate for the handicap.

organic disorder: a pathological condition arising from a physiological or anatomical deficiency or defect.

organic memory: a persisting alteration in structure as a result of experience in the life history of the organism.

organism: any living being.

organismic point of view: one which takes cognizance of the whole organism, not of the separate parts of which it is made up.

organology: syn. *splanchnology;* the science dealing with the organs of the body and their relationships to one another in structure and function.

orgasm: the climax in sexual excitement.

orientation test: in a mental examination an assay of the person's ability to answer questions relating to temporal and spatial topics.

origin: the zero point on a graph where the y-axis and the x-axis intersect.

original nature: the totality of traits and characteristics due wholly to heredity.

ortho-: Greek combining form meaning *rectification, correct, proper, normal.*

orthobiosis: life in accordance with best knowledge of hygienic principles.

orthodox: sound; approved; the accepted norm.

orthopsychiatry: preventive psychiatry; therapy for incipient disorders.

orthoscope: apparatus for examining the iris.

Oseretsky Tests: measures of motor development between ages 4 and 16 (1923).

osseo-: Latin combining form meaning *bony.*

osseous labrynth: part of the internal ear; the semicircular canals and the cochlea.

ossicle: a small bone (e.g., malleus, incus, stapes).

ossification index: syn. *anatomical index;* the result of x-ray examination of the rate at which cartilaginous tissues are changing into bones in the wrist.

OSS: Office of Strategic Services, the work of which was reported in 1948.

osteo-: Greek combining form meaning *bone.*

osteology: the science which deals with the bones of vertebrates.

Ostwald System: a method for identifying chromatic and achromatic hues by a number-letter system.

ot-; oto-:   Greek combining form meaning *ear*.

otocleisis: middle ear obstruction.

otolith, otolite: small particle of calcareous matter in the endolymph of the inner ear which stimulates nerve endings in the utricle and the saccule.

otology: the science dealing with the ear and its functions in health and disease.

-ous: Latin suffix meaning *full of, possessing the qualities of*.

outbreeding: producing offspring from parents who are relatively unrelated.

out-group: a social group with which the person has no affiliations, as opposed to the in-group.

outlet: in Kinsey's sexology, any manner of inducing an orgasm, whether by intercourse or by any other means.

outpatient: a patient who receives treatment from, but is not a resident in, a hospital, clinic, or mental institution.

oval window: syn. *fenestra ovalis, fenestra vestibuli;* an oval-shaped aperture into which the footplate of the stapes is inserted in the middle ear.

ovary: the essential female organ of reproduction.

overachievement: a performance which exceeds the level predicted by tests or other measuring techniques.

overage: an excess in chronological age over educational or mental age; a schoolgrade status with pupils younger in chronological age.

overcompensation: (Adler) persistent effort to strengthen a defective organ by intensive training; a direct attack upon the situation held responsible for producing inferiority feelings.

overdetermination: in psychoanalysis, the union of two or more unconscious wishes to bring about the latent content of a dream or a neurotic symptom.

overlearning: practice beyond the point of a single correct recall.

overprotection: excessive zeal in sheltering the child from all dangers, real or imagined.

overt response: one which is directly observable.

overtone: one of the upper partials which, with the fundamental tone, make up the complex musical note.

ovum: the egg cell produced in the ovary.

oxy-: Greek combining form meaning *acute*.

oxyaphia: keen sense of touch.

oxyblepsia: hyperacute vision.

oxycephaly: an unusually high skull.

oxyesthesia: abnormally acute sensitivity to any stimulation of a receptor.

oxyopia: extremely acute vision.

oxyphonia: shrillness of voice.

pacificism: an attitude of complete rejection of war as a means for settling disputes between nations; opposition to force.

pacing: the adjusting of school subjects and other tasks to the present level of the child's development.

Pacinian corpuscle (or body): an ovoid ending of certain sensory nerves, especially those in the skin of feet or hands.

paedarchy: rule by children; extreme form of child-centered school.

paedicatio: syn. *pederasty;* coitus per anum by two males.

paideutics: pedagogy.

paido-: syn. *pedo-;* Greek combining meaning *child*.

paidology: syn. *paedology;* child study.

paidophilia: syn. *pedophilia;* erotic attachment to small children.

pain: a sensation, usually but not always unpleasant, varying from a slight prick to an intense and overwhelming reaction.

pain principle: in psychoanalysis, the antithesis of the pleasure principle; the unconscious wish for destruction of self.

pain spots: cutaneous areas especially sensitive when touched by a sharp-pointed instrument, usually called an algesimeter.

painless region: syn. *Kiesow's area;* a small region in the cheek where there are no pain receptors.

paired associates: words or other symbols presented together until the learner is able to recall or to recognize the second when only the first member of the pair is presented.

paired comparison: the method, often used in measures of esthetic preference, whereby each member of the series (words, pictures, tonal sequences, etc.) is compared with every other member of the series.

palaeo-: syn. *paleo-;* Greek prefix meaning *ancient*.

paleaopsychology: in Jung's theory, the investigation of racial memories or archetypes in the racial unconscious

palaeosophy: ancient knowledge.

palaestra (palestra): gymnasium.

palatability: that quality of food which makes it acceptable to the person who eats it.

palilalia: repetition of syllables or words in speech.

palingenesis: the metaphysical doctrine of successive rebirths; the doctrine that individual development (ontogeny) recapitulates the development of the species (phylogeny).

palingraphia: mirror writing.

palinlexia: the condition in which words are perceived in reversed form.

pallesthesia: the sense of vibration.

pallium: the cortex of the cerebrum.

palmar reflex: the grasping response in the newborn.

palmesthesia: the sense of vibration.

palmistry: in folklore, the superstition that lines on the hand indicate occult characteristics about the individual.

palpebra: eyelid.

palpebral: pertaining to the eyelids.

palpebral fissure: the space between the eyelids.

palpitate: to beat rapidly.

palpitation: an extremely rapid pulsation.

palsy: a form of paralysis marked by tremors and "shakes."

pan-: Greek combining form meaning *all*.

panacea: in folklore, a cure-all.

pancreas: a gland partly duct and partly endocrine situated behind the stomach.

panel: a group chosen to discuss a topic from various points of view.

panic: a sudden, intense, overwhelming fear.

panmnesia: complete recall of all former experiences.

panpsychism: in philosophy, the doctrine that all reality is basically mind, not matter.

pansexualism: the doctrine that the universal and basic interests are derived from the sex drive.

pansophy: (Comenius) universal, encyclopedic knowledge.

pansphygmanometer: apparatus for recording simultaneously respiration, pulse rate, and heart beat.

pantheism: the doctrine that everything, both mind and so-called matter, is God.

pantophobia: syn. *panphobia;* irrational fear of everything and anything.

papilla: a small protuberance.

papilla spiralis: the organ of Corti.

para- (par-): Greek prefix meaning *distorted* or *near.*

para-analgesthesia: loss of all sensation in the lower portion of the body.

parabiosis: temporary loss of excitability in a nerve fiber.

parablepsia: abnormal visual sensation.

parabulia: gross abnormality in drives or motives.

paracentral gyrus (lobule): a convolution on the inner side of the cerebral hemisphere.

paraconscious activity: consciousness that is parallel to, but differentiated from, the main stream of thought.

paracusia: gross distortion in the field of auditory sensitivity.

paradigm: a model or schematic representation.

paradoxical temperature sensation: the reversal of cold and warmth sensitivity when the receptors are intensely stimulated; paradoxical cold and paradoxical heat.

parageusia: distorted taste sensitivity.

paragnosia: a misperception or misunderstanding due to neurological disorder.

parakinesia: motor disorder.

paralalia: disorder in pronouncing words.

paralambdacism: a speech disorder in which *l* is sounded as if it were *w.*

paralexia: a form of aphasia in which words are misread.

paralgesia: anomalous pain sensitivity.

parallax: the apparent change in the visual field of an object that is viewed from different positions or angles.

parallelism: the doctrine that mind and body are totally different entities which function simultaneously but which have no causal relationship.

paralogia: incoherence in speech.

paralogism: fallacious reasoning.

paralysis: loss of function.

paralysis agitans: a neurological disorder marked by progressive impairment, tremors, and difficulty in walking (festination); palsy.

paralytic dementia: mental and motor impairment, often associated with aftereffects of syphilitic infection.

parameter: the property or quality of an infinite number of data, from which the sampling has been drawn; hence, popularly, the graphic representation of the data in the form of a curve, with corrections for true probability.

paraminia: inability to gesticulate meaningfully in speech.

paramnesia: any defect of memory; involuntary retrospective falsification.

paramorphy: any physical anomaly not due to hereditary factors.

paranoia: the condition in which systematized delusions, often internally consistent, occur.

paranoid: resembling true paranoia but having unsystematized, bizarre delusions.

paranomia: a form of aphasia in which objects are incorrectly named.

paranosia: the primary gains a person achieves through becoming ill.

paraphasia: a form of aphasia in which words are incorrectly used; jumbled speech.

paraphia: anomalies in the sense of touch.

paraphilia: a general term for any form of sex perversion.

paraphrasia: gross incoherence in speech.

paraphrenia: psychosis, especially dementia praecox (schizophrenia).

paraplegia: paralysis of both sides of the lower part of the body.

parapraxia: gross incoordinations in habitual motor activities.

parapsychology: the application of methods of psychological research to investigations of occult phenomena.

parasympathetic portion of the autonomic nervous system: those nerve fibers which originate in the cranial or the sacral portions and which are thought to exert a calming effect upon smooth muscles and endocrine glands.

parathyroid: four small endocrine glands lying adjacent to the thyroid and secreting a hormone which regulates the calcium-phosphorus balance.

parathyroid tetany: intense muscular spasms caused by absence or reduction of the parathyroid hormone, usually resulting in death.

parencephalon: the cerebellum.

parent figure or surrogate: a person who meets the psychological needs usually satisfied by the real parent.

paresis: a severe and progressive disorder resulting from syphilitic infection within the brain.

paresthesia (paraesthesia): unusual cutaneous sensations which arise from no objective stimulation.

paretic: a person who is a victim of paresis and who often has delusions of grandeur, talks in a slurred manner, rapidly deteriorates, and behaves imprudently.

parietal lobe: one of the major divisions of the cerebrum, situated in back of the central gyrus, above the fissure of Sylvius, and before the parieto-occipital fissure.

Parkinson's disease: paralysis agitans.

Parkinson syndrome (or facies): the masklike, expressionless appearance of a victim of encephalitis lethargica (sleeping sickness).

parorexia: craving for unusual food substances.

parosmia: illusions or hallucinations in the sense of smell.

paroxysm: a convulsion.

part method: the piecemeal procedure of breaking up the whole, and then memorizing it section by section.

partial (partial tone): any part of a compound tone, the lowest being the fundamental and the others the upper partials.

partial correlation: in statistics, the correlation between two arrays of scores when one or more other variables are held constant or eliminated. The general formula for partial correlation is

$$r_{12.34\,\ldots\,n} = \frac{r_{12.34\,\ldots\,(n-1)} - r_{1n.34\,\ldots\,(n-1)}r_{2n.34\,\ldots\,(n-1)}}{\sqrt{1 - r^2_{1n.34\,\ldots\,(n-1)}}\sqrt{1 - r^2_{2n.34\,\ldots\,(n-1)}}}.$$

parturate: the newborn before the umbilical cord is severed.

parturition: childbirth.

passive: lacking in assertiveness; inactive.

passive decay: loss of ability to recognize or recall materials once known but not used or reviewed subsequently.

passivism: a form of male sex perversion marked by total submission.

patella: kneecap.

patellar reflex: the knee jerk when the patellar tendon is tapped.

patheticus: the trochlear, or 4th, cranial nerve.

pathetism: hypnotism.

patho-: Greek combining form meaning *disease* or *suffering*.

pathogenic: that which causes a disorder.

pathognomic: that which is definitely known to be a characteristic of a disorder.

pathognomy: scientific diagnosis of disorders.

pathology: the science of diagnosing and treating disorders.

pathomania: psychopathic behavior.

pathomimesis: malingering.

patrilineal society: one in which lines of descent are traced from the male.

Pavlovianism: that system of psychology (or reflexology) which emphasizes classical conditioning as the major explanatory principle for learned behavior.

parvor nocturnus: nightmare.

pausimenia: the menopause.

peccatophobia: neurotic fear of sinning, even by small acts.

pecking order: the dominance-submission relationships among inmates of the henyard; hence, popular, the lines of authority controlling members of a group.

pectoral: relating to chest or lungs.

peculation: embezzlement.

pedagogy: the science of teaching.

pedal: pertaining to the foot.

pederasty: intercourse per annum.

pediatrics: the medical specialty dealing with infants and small children.

pedology (paedology): child study.

pedophilia: erotic attachment to small children.

peduncle: a band of white matter joining parts of the brain.

peer: an equal.

pegboard: a device, usually a measure of speed, requiring the testee to insert small pegs into holes.

penilingus: syn. *fellatio;* insertion of the penis into the mouth.

penis: the external sex organ of the male.

penis envy: in psychoanalysis, the sense of deprivation suffered by the girl after she has discovered what she regards as an anatomical lack.

penmanship: syn. *chirography;* the style (sometimes expressive) of handwriting.

penology: the social science dealing with the treatment of the offender.

pentathol interview: a psychiatric procedure in which the patient receives a small amount of pentathol sodium in order to overcome resistance and to facilitate "talking it out" with the therapist.

peptic: relating to the digestive functions.

peptic ulcer: a lesion in the stomach walls or the duodenum, said to be occasionally due to psychosomatic difficulties.

percentile curve: an ogive in which the scores within each interval are distributed in terms of their percentages of the total distribution.

percentile rank: the relative position of each score in the distribution as arranged on a scale of one hundred. (Thus a %-ile rank of 80 indicates that 79% of the scores lie below the given raw, or obtained, score.)

percept: that which is perceived.

perception: awareness; the organization of sensory data into patterns of experience.

perceptionism: the doctrine that all knowledge is based upon sense perception.

perceptive: capable of making sharp and accurate discriminations among sensory or ideational contents.

perceptual defense: the hypothesis that the individual tends not to perceive that which might threaten the ego (sense of self-esteem).

perceptual speed: (Thurstone) a primary mental ability which is measured by tests of quick, accurate grasping of visually presented items or of similarities and differences among them.

percipient: in parapsychology, the receiver of a message sent in a manner which cannot be explained by any known natural law or principle.

perfectionism;   neurotic obsession with achieving unattainably lofty goals, even when working at tasks of minor importance.

performance test: a measure, often making use of manipulative materials, which involves no, or a minimum of, verbal instructions (e.g., the Kohs Block Design or the Army Beta).

periencephalitis: inflammation of the pia mater, often with concomitant mental symptoms.

perimetry: the use of special apparatus for mapping the color zones of the retina.

peripheral nerves: those which connect brain and cord with receptors and effectors.

peripheral vision: visual sensitivity mediated by other portions of the retina than the fovea.

peripheralism: the systematic presentation of psychological facts and principles which emphasize the role of receptors and effectors rather than the cerebral cortex.

permissive attitude: that which, adopted by the counselor, encourages full expression by the client and which allows neither condemnation nor condoning but full acceptance of the problem as it is verbalized or otherwise expressed.

persecutory delusions: paranoidal suspiciousness; the unfounded belief of being a victim of maleficent influences.

perseveration: obsessive-compulsive persistence of an activity long after the circumstances originating it have disappeared.

persona: in Jung's theory, the public aspects of the personality or the mask which conceals the deep components of the psyche.

Personal Data Sheet: a famous self report inventory or questionnaire consisting of 116 items used to locate neurotic soldiers in World War I (Woodworth); the first successful psychoneurotic screening device.

personal document: any record, whether a diary or correspondence and the like, which serves to give insights into the subjective life of an ndividual.

personal equation: differences in scientific research as the result of variability among the observers (e.g., different reaction times).

personalism: the systematic position that the Self is the basic and the central concept in psychology and that it must be regarded as the highest value.

personality: a term with a wide variety of meanings, but with a few basic connotations (Allport and others), namely, the role one plays, one's social-stimulus value, an assemblage of traits, and a unique and priceless value.

personality inventory: standardized, printed, scorable items such as are used in psychiatric interviews, the purpose being to obtain a self-report about the quality of adjustment.

personality problem: any difficulty which lowers personal efficiency and rapport with other persons, but which is not severe enough to be a grave disorder.

personnel: the employees of a business or an industrial organization.

Personnel Classification Test: a rapid screening device appraising verbal reasoning and number facility (Wesman, 1951).

persuasive therapy: a counselor-centered approach in which appeals are made to alter feelings and understandings about the issue in question.

perversion: any type of sex behavior condemned by the mores of the group.

petit mal: loss of consciousness, dizziness, staggering, but no fall or violent convulsion as in a grand mal convulsive seizure.

PGR: the psychogalvanic, or electrodermal, reaction.

-phagia (phagy):   Greek combining form meaning *eating*.

phagomania: syn. *bulimia;* pathologically insatiable craving for food.

phallic: pertaining to the male sex organ.

phallic stage: in psychoanalysis, the period in psychosexual development from about age three to seven, when the penis or a substitute thereof is the center of interest.

phallicism: a primitive form of worship in which the male sex organ is the principal symbol.

phallus: the male sex organ; in psychoanalysis, any object which symbolizes the penis (e.g., a tower, cane, etc.).

phantasy: a daydream.

phantom limb: the anomalous sensations reported by amputees, as if the body were still intact.

pharmacological: pertaining to drugs.

pharmacopoeia: a list of approved drugs and other medications.

pharynx: the region from the mouth to the esophagus, including the Eustachian tubes.

phase: a transitory stage in growth and development; an aspect of sound waves.

-phasia: Greek combining form signifying a *speech disorder* based upon a neuropathology.

-phemia: Greek combining form usually signifying a *speech disorder* arising from neurotic or functionally psychotic causes.

phenakistoscope: apparatus for demonstrating the illusion of visual movement.

phenobarbital: a drug used to induce relaxation or sleep and often prescribed for treatment of nervous disorders.

phenomenal data: those which are directly observed through the senses.

phenomenology: the doctrine that knowledge is built up through observation of actual data, not by subjective procedures.

phenomenon (pl. phenomena):   observable, not inferred, datum (pl. data).

phenotype: (Lewin) similarities in the behavior of many persons, as distinguished from hereditary determinants (the genotype).

phenylpyruvic (phenylketonuric) mental deficiency: a form of amentia, said to be hereditary, associated with a gross imbalance of acid.

phi coefficient: an index of the degree of association between two arrays of discrete scores.

phi phenomenon: a visual illusion of movement.

-phily (-philia): Greek combining form meaning *love*.

philosophical psychology: the systematic exposition of a priori (rational) theories, with a neglect of a posteriori (empirical) validation.

philosophy: the body of knowledge derived from speculation or rational thought.

phlegm: one of the four classical humors, causing a lethargic (phlegmatic) temperament.

phobia: an irrational fear.

-phobia: Greek combining form denoting a *morbid fear* (e.g., claustrophobia).

phobophobia: fear of becoming afraid.

phon: a unit in measurement of intensity of an auditory stimulus.

phonautograph: syn. *phoneidoscope, phoneloscope, phonodeik, phonscope;* apparatus used in making visible records of sound waves.

phoneme: a unit of sound in speech, there being about 45 in spoken English.

phonetics: the representations of speech sounds by an arbitrary list of symbols.

-phonia: Greek combining form meaning *speech* (e.g., aphonia—speechlessness).

phono-: Greek combining form meaning *voice, sound*.

phonography: the science which investigates speech; also denoted phonology.

phonopathy: any disorder of the voice.

phoria: the axes maintained by the eyeballs.

-phoria: Greek combining form meaning *feelings* (e.g., euphoria).

phot: a unit of measurement of the degree of illumination.

photoma: the sensation of experiencing a flash of bright light, but without an objective stimulus; a photism (visual hallucination).

photon: a unit in measurement of brightness of a visual sensation.

photopia: vision in bright daylight.

photoreceptors: rods and cones.

-phrasia: Greek combining form meaning *a disorder in speech*.

phratry: a group of related families.

phrenasthenia: syn. *oligophrenia;* mental deficiency.

phrenetic: delirious.

phrenology: a psuedo-science which relates protrusions and re-cessions in the skull to psychological characteristics; also known as craniognomy.

phrenopathy: an organic brain disease.

phrictopathic: an unpleasant cutaneous sensation without objec-tive cause (e.g., a limb "going to sleep").

phthisis: a wasting away of the body or an organ.

phylogeny: the evolution of a species or race, as distinguished from ontogeny, which is the development of the individual.

phylum: the most inclusive category in the Linnean classification of fauna and flora.

physical: pertaining to natural things and processes as opposed to mentalistic concepts.

physical examination: an appraisal of bodily functions as the procedures are directed by a physician and members of spe-cialties related to medicine.

physical therapy: treatment of disorders by such methods as continuous baths, heat and fever, diet, rest, and the like, as differentiated from psychotherapy; physiotherapy.

physiogenic causation: a disorder arising from organic pathology.

physiognomy: the procedure of inferring psychological and char-acter traits from the shape and the characteristics of the face, generally regarded as a fallacious method.

physiological age: the level of glandular, muscular, and skeletal development an individual has attained as compared to the normal level at any given chronological age.

physiological limit: the highest level to which, by continued prac-tice, a learned performance can be brought.

physiological psychology: that branch of general psychology which investigates the relationship between body functions and structures and the behavior which accompanies these events and reactions.

physiological zero: the temperature at which an object must be if no sensation of warmth or cold is experienced.

physiology: the science dealing with the functions of a living organism or with the functions of any organ.

physique: the general shape (morphology) of the body.

pia mater: the innermost of the membranes covering the brain and the cord.

piano (or harp) theory of hearing: the Helmholtz theory that rods in the organ of Corti vibrate like strings and thus mediate pitch sensitivities.

pica: perverted food cravings.

Pick's disease: brain deterioration resulting in a premature psychosis resembling senility.

Picture Frustration Test: (Rosenzweig, 1947) sets of cartoon-like drawings (one set for children; another for adults) presenting various frustrating situations, the testee indicating what he or she would likely say.

picture tests: subtests in measures of intelligence which may require the logical arrangement of a series of pictures or which require the testee to tell what would be necessary to complete the picture (picture arrangement tests and picture completion tests, respectively). Still another form requires the testee to interpret the meaning of a picture.

Piderit's drawings: simplified line drawings of various facial expressions in emotions (1859), on the basis of which interchangeable parts may be constructed to build up patterns of facial expressions in emotions.

pilomotor reaction: gooseflesh; a movement of the hairs in the skin.

pilot study: a brief and relatively simple trial before an extensive experiment or investigation is undertaken.

pineal gland: syn. *conarium, epiphysis;* a small gland, function unknown, attached to the roof of the third ventricle of the brain (thought by Descartes to be the point at which mind and body interact).

pinna: the outer part of the ear; the auricle.

Pintner-Cunningham Primary Test: long one of the most widely used measures employed in group testing of kindergarten and first-grade children.

Pintner-Paterson Performance Scale: the first important and successful test involving the use of fifteen formboards to obtain a mental age (1917).

pitch: that quality of auditory sensitivity experienced as high, low, etc.; sensitivity to differences in vibration frequencies of sound waves.

pitch discrimination: ability to judge whether the second member of paired tones is higher or lower than the first; a measure of just noticeable differences between successive paired tones, the frequency interval being more and more reduced throughout the test.

pituitary gland: syn. *hypophysis,* the "master endocrine"; a ductless gland lying at the base of the brain.

pituitary type: popularly, a physique characterized by obesity, large bones, and masculine distribution of hair (thought to be the result of hyperpituitarism).

placebo: a harmless medication which the patient believes to be a cure for his or her ailment.

placement test: a measure used to determine the grade in which a pupil should be enrolled or the type of job an employee should fill.

placenta: the membranous, vascular covering of the fetus in the uterus.

planchette: a freely moving table on which the arm or the hand rests while automatic writing is being produced.

plantar response (or reflex): the flexion of the toes when the sole of the foot is lightly scratched or stroked.

plasticity: (James) the ready modifiability of the nervous system in early life.

plateau: the stage of no apparent progress on a typical learning curve, occurring between the rapid progress at first and the slow ascent to the end.

Platonism: the doctrine of innate ideas: complete subjectivism and rejection of empiricism in psychology.

platoon-volley theory: in audition, the theory that the discharge of the nervous impulse occurs in rapid sequences over different fibers in the auditory nerve.

platycephaly: having a flattened crown to the skull.

platykurtosis: the condition in a frequency curve with a flattened appearance in the region of the central tendency.

platyrhinism: having a broad, flat, short nose.

play therapy: the use of spontaneous, enjoyable activities whereby the child works off tensions and achieves a better adjustment through the help of the psychotherapist.

pleasure-pain principle: in psychoanalysis, the ambivalence between the Eros and the Thanatos (life and death) instincts.

pleasure principle: in psychoanalysis, that characteristic of the id which demands immediate gratification; hence, the principle of tension reduction upon which the id operates.

plethysmograph: apparatus for determining the amount of blood volume in any part of the body.

plexus: a network of nerve fibers lying outside the central nervous system.

plot: to arrange scores in a tabular or graphic pattern.

pluralism: (James) the doctrine that ultimate reality consists of many, not one (monism) or two (dualism), aspects.

plurality of causes: the doctrine that disorders seldom arise from a single factor; the multiple causation of disorders.

PMA: (Thurstone) the primary mental abilities.

pneumo-: Greek combining form meaning *breath*.

pneumogastric nerve: syn. *vagus nerve;* the 10th cranial nerve.

pneumograph: apparatus for recording inspiration-expiration ratios.

poetry appreciation test: typically, a measure of aptitude for distinguishing between a mutilated version and a version written by an eminent poet (e.g., the Abbot-Trabue Exercises in Judging Poetry, 1921).

Poetzl effect: subliminal stimulation.

point scale: a measure with norms expressed in terms of the amount of credit earned (or points achieved), these to be converted into a mental age equivalent (e.g., the Yerkes-Bridges-Hardwick 1915 revision of the Binet-Simon Scale).

polarities: in psychoanalysis, the doctrine that instinctual tendencies polarize about opposite extremes (e.g., life-death, love-hate, etc.).

polarity of the nerve cell: the principle that the nervous impulse travels in but one direction, from dentrite to axon.

poll: a sampling of public opinion on some issue, as about a forthcoming election.

poly-: Greek combining form meaning *many*.

polyandry: marriage to more than one husband (e.g., Tibet).

polyarchy: rule by many.

polydactylism: having supernumerary fingers.

polydipsia: intense thirst.

polyesthesia: an anomaly of touch, in which a single stimulus is sensed as two or more touches on the skin.

polygamy: plural marriages, as opposed to monogamy.

polygenesis: the view that the human species has evolved from different types of lower animals; hence, that there are inherent racial differences.

polygraph: apparatus for making simultaneously records of various items of behavior or responses.

polylogia: syn. *logorrhea;* a rapid, incoherent flow of speech.

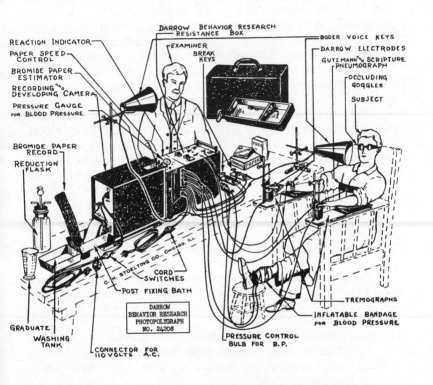

Figure 25a.   A polygraph.

polymorphous-perverse: in psychoanalysis, the nonspecific and diffuse attachments of the libido in early infancy.

polyopia: having more than one retinal image; multiple vision.

polyphagous: having a ravenous, undiscriminating appetite.

polyphrasia: rapid, incoherent speech.

polypnoea: unusually rapid breathing.

polyspermia: the entrance of more than one spermatozöon into an ovum.

polytechnical institute: a school devoted to instruction in several applied sciences and arts.

pons: syn. *pons Varolii;* a band of transverse nerve fibers lying in front of the medulla, beneath the cerebellum, and below the cerebrum.

poriomania: wanderlust.

pornography: obscenity.

Porteus Maze Tests: a nonlinguistic point scale used as a performance test of intelligence, consisting of a series of mazes to be traced with a stylus (1924).

posit: to make an assumption, as in stating an hypothesis which is to be empirically investigated.

position: in social psychology, the status which determines the role of the individual.

position habit: the continued use of a response pattern even though it is not adjustive in the situation; an inflexible use of a learned reaction.

positive afterimage: the persistence of a retinal image after the stimulus has ceased to be operative.

positivism: (Comte) the rigorous exclusion of all mentalistic or philosophical concepts, and the application of controlled observations to natural phenomena, to the end that the procedure may be repeated and verified.

possession theory: the folk belief that a mentally disordered person is a victim of possession by evil spirits.

posterior: situated behind.

posthypnotic behavior: the carrying out of a suggestion given during hypnosis, usually with amnesia for the command, after the subject has been awakened.

postmortem examination: an autopsy.

postnatal: occurring after birth.

post partum: after the birth of a child.

postpuberal stage: the year or so after the onset of puberty, during which the bony structures usually achieve their fullest development.

postulate: an assumption or inference which is to be tested empirically.

postural reflexes: the intricate pattern of nervous impulses which maintains muscular tonus and holds the body in position.

posture: an attitude or set.

potlatch: (Boas) among the Kwakiutl Indians, the display of wealth by destruction of one's possessions or by conspicuous, foolish give-away.

power figure: a person who represents, consciously or unconsciously, the possession of an enviably high status and authority.

power test: syn. *unspeeded or work-limit test;* a series of items of increasing difficulty, the testee to complete as many as possible within a reasonable limit of time.

PR: the percentile rank of a raw score.

practical curve: a graphic representation of improvement with repeated opportunities to practice or to review; a representation of the practice (or review) effect, as in mastering a motor skill or learning by rote.

practical experiment: (Aschaffenburg) the measurement of improvements as new motives and incentives are introduced into the task to be learned.

practice limit: the ultimate limit of improvability, beyond which further practice is of no value in effecting gains.

pragmatism: the doctrine that meanings are to be sought in the practical applications of propositions or thought.

pragnanz: syn. *pregnance;* (Wertheimer) the tendency of Gestalten (configurations) to become as well-defined as the circumstances permit; also called the eidotropic principle or the law of precision.

praxiology: the scientific study of behavior and experience.

pre-, prae-: Latin prefix meaning *before.*

pre-adolescent stage of development: the two or three years immediately preceding the onset of puberty.

preciosity: affection.

precocious: unusually rapid development.

precognition: in parapsychology, a foreknowledge of what eventually occurs in reality, the awareness achieved without natural causation.

preconsciousness: in psychoanalysis, all the material not immediately in consciousness but readily brought there.

pre-established harmony: (Leibniz) the doctrine that mind and body are separate but that changes in one accompany changes in the other by reason of divine will.

preference test: a measure of vocational or avocational interests or esthetic judgments by requiring the testee to make forced choices between members of paired or grouped items.

prefrontal lobotomy: syn. *prefrontal leucotomy;* the excision of connections from the thalamus to the frontal lobes. (Note that prefrontal lobectomy literally denotes complete removal of the frontal lobes.)

pregnancy: the stage (in the human female lasting about 40 weeks) from conception to childbirth.

prehuman: referring to primates thought to be ancestors of *homo sapiens*.

prejudice: a preconceived, stereotyped judgment; bias for or against.

preliterate culture: one that has not developed a system of writing.

prelogical thinking: (Piaget) the reasoning procedures of small children, who do not follow orthodox rules of logic but who, nevertheless, have their own private logic.

premise: in logic, either of the two propositions from which a conclusion is drawn in the syllogism; hence, either the major premise or the minor premise in syllogistic reasoning.

prenatal: before birth.

prenubile years: those which antedate the onset of puberty.

pre-Oedipal stage of development: in psychoanalysis, the years antedating the first appearance of the Oedipal complex.

preparation: (Wallas) the first stage in a complete act of creative thinking, during which skills and understandings are acquired and which enriches the stage of incubation.

preperception: (McDougall) a preparatory set, or conative tendency, to respond to certain aspects of a situation; an anticipatory reaction or condition of readiness.

prepotent reflexes: (Sherrington) the reflex patterns which serve to protect the organism or to favor perpetuation of the species.

prepuberal stage: the year or two antedating the onset of puberty.

presby-: Greek combining form meaning *old*.

presbyophrenia: a form of senile psychosis occurring in women.

presbyopia: farsightedness resulting from inelasticity of the lens.

preschool: a nursery school or kindergarten.

presenile psychosis: premature onset of mental deterioration usually associated with andvanced age (e.g., Alzheimer's psychosis or Pick's disease).

press: (Murray) the power that a situation appears to have in affecting, for better or worse, the total welfare of the person.

pressure of thoughts: a descriptive term denoting a manic flight of ideas which seem to outspeed the patient's ability to express them.

pressure sensitivity: responsiveness to stimulation of spots in the skin; the kinesthetic sense as a whole.

pressure spots: minute areas on the skin which are stimulated by touches or by deforming the surface of the body.

prestige: having an enviable role and status in the group; having the power to make prestige suggestions, whereby attitudes are uncritically changed.

pretest: a practice exercise intended to familiarize the testee with a procedure; a test administered before a unit of instruction is introduced to determine how much the learner already knows about it.

priapism: prolonged erection of the penis.

primary mental abilities: (Thurstone) those various abilities sampled by measures of the level of intelligence (e.g., verbal meaning, spatial relations, perceptual speed, and so on).

Primary Mental Abilities Test: (Thurstone) a measure of the following abilities (determined by factor analysis): Spatial (S), Perceptual (P), Number (N), Verbal (V), Word Fluency (W), Memory (M), and Reasoning (R)—(1938).

primary attention: (Titchener) spontaneous, unforced, unlearned attention.

primary hues: (Young-Helmholtz) red, green, and bluish violet; (Hering) black-white, red-green, and blue yellow.

primary quality: (Locke) that which inheres in the object or stimulus itself as distinguished from the manner in which it is sensed or perceived (secondary quality).

primate: in the Linnean classification, the Lemuroidea and the Anthropoidea (apes, monkeys, marmosets and lemurs, and man, respectively).

primipara: a woman who has borne only one child.

primitivization of behavior: (Lewin) a retrogression to less constructive activities as the result of tensions arising from frustrations.

principal: (*principal teacher*) the administrative director of a school.

principle: a general inference or truth that is derived from empirical studies, but that cannot be stated unequivocally as a law.

private data: those which are not directly observable by another person but which may be revealed through a verbal report, a projective technique, or expressive behavior; traditionally, those data reportable through introspection

proactive inhibition: (Ebbinghaus) the loss of efficiency in learning a new task as a result of prior learning immediately before.

probabilism: the doctrine that certainty can never be achieved, but that knowledge is valid only within statistical limits of probability.

probability curve: syn. *Gaussian curve, curve of normal probability,* (popularly) the bell-shaped curve; in statistics, the graphic representation of the distribution of all data within any given field that is sampled; hence, the basis for making corrections in inferences based upon the sample.

probable error: syn. *P.E.;* on a curve of probability, the middle 50% of the scores, or plus and minus 25% from the measure of central tendency, a measure of the reliability of a score or an array of scores. The probable error of a mean is derived by the following formula, where sigma σ is the standard deviation and N is the number of cases:

$$P.E.M_N = .6745 \frac{\sigma}{\sqrt{N}}$$

problem box: (Thorndike) a box fastened by a concealed method, the animal or the human subject to discover the method by trial and error behavior.

problem-solving behavior: that which involves a delayed response in overt action while "as-if" or alternative procedures are explored more or less by implicit behavior.

process: in anatomy, any structure or part thereof.

procreation: sexual reproduction of a species.

prodigy: an unusually precocious child.

prodromal symptom: that which warns of the onset of a grave
• disorder.

product-moment correlation: syn. *product-moment coefficient of correlation, r;* a convenient statistical device for expressing the possible degree of relationship between two arrays of scores, the statistic ranging from -1.0 to + 1.0 and a basic formula

$$r = \frac{\Sigma xy}{\sqrt{\Sigma x^2} \cdot \sqrt{\Sigma y^2}},$$

in which the x and y deviations are from the averages and $\sqrt{\Sigma x^2}$ and $\sqrt{\Sigma y^2}$ are the sums of the squared deviations from the two averages.

profile: a graphic representation of an individual's test scores on a number of psychological tests and measures; a profile chart or psychograph.

profile: syn. *psychograph;* a graphic portrayal of an individual's scores (expressed in statistically comparable units) on a number of tests and measures.

progeny: offspring.

progeria: early senility.

prognathous: having a facial angle of 70 to 80 degrees; protruding jaw.

prognosis: prediction of the outcome of a disorder.

prognostic test: a measure which predicts how well a person is likely to do in a certain school subject or task (e.g., the Iowa Placement Examinations).

Progressive Education Association: once a lively organization promulgating the philosophy underlying the pupil-centered school, the project method, and the learner's own desires as the guide to education.

Progressive Matrices Test: a series of abstract designs, the testee to find the missing part and thus indicating a measure of the Spearman *g* factor (1941).

project: a self-initiated, self-planned, self-sustained, and self-evaluated activity, as opposed to a task imposed upon the learner.

projection: in psychoanalysis, the unconscious mechanism where one's own faults are seen in other persons' rather than in one's own personality; in other systems of psychology, the act of objectifying what is actually a subjective or internal experience.

projection fiber: a nerve fiber connecting an area in the cerebral cortex with a motor or sensory area in the brain.

projective technique: the use of unstructured, or relatively unstructured, materials which the person organizes, interprets, or uses, thereby revealing the psychodynamic aspects of the personality which would not be directly accessible otherwise (e.g., fingerpaints, inkblots, toys, etc.).

promiscuous: having indiscriminate sexual intercourse.

promnesia: syn. *paramnesia;* retrospective falsification or distortion.

pronation: the act resulting in the palm being turned downwards.

propaganda: methods carefully planned to influence the attitudes and actions of other persons (now usually employed in a bad sense).

propensity: (McDougall) syn. *instinct;* an inborn tendency or driving force to some type of action (e.g., migratory propensity)

prophylaxis: preventive methods against disorders.

proprio-:   Latin combining form meaning *one's own.*

proprioceptor: a receptor lying in muscles, tendons, and joints and in the vestibule and the semicircular canals of the ear.

proprium: the ego or the self.

prosencephalon: the forebrain; the telencephalon and the diencephalon.

prosopography: a complete description of the face or of the total appearance of an individual, as for purposes of identification.

prosthesis: an artificial replacement for a part of the body (e.g., dentures, glass eye, etc.).

prostitution: sexual intercourse for hire.

protagonist: one who takes a leading role in popularizing a theory or doctrine.

protanopia: red-blindness.

protensity: (Titchener) the duration of a sensation, an image, or a feeling.

proto-:   Greek combining form meaning *first in time, chief.*

protocol: the notes or records made by a clinical psychologist or psychiatrist during, or immediately after, the interview or diagnostic session.

protoplasm: the simplest of all living substances; also, the contents of the living cell, the nucleus being excepted (the supportive network being called spongioplasm and the fluid called hyaloplasm).

prototaxic: (H. S. Sullivan) pertaining to the uncoördinated, undifferentiated behavior of the newborn.

prototype: the earliest form.

proverbs test: (Binet) a list of proverbs, graded in difficulty, for the testee to interpret.

proximal: referring to that portion of a limb or an organ which lies closest to the point of attachment.

proximodistal axis: the axis extending from the center of the body to the fingertips (arms extended), or from the midline to the most distant point.

prurient: syn. *libidinous, lascivious;* being preoccupied with sex longings.

psellism: speech disorder.

pseudesthesia: hypochondrical pains; the sense of pain or discomfort in an amputated limb.

pseudo-:   Greek combining form meaning *false.*

pseudochromia: misperception of colors.

pseudofeeblemindedness: syn. *pseudo-amentia;* the appearance of mental retardation because of sensory defects or emotionality.

pseudomania: pathological lying.

pseudoscience: theories and doctrines that appear to be plasuible but that have no empirical support.

pseudoscope: a system of lenses which transpose the retinal images. (A pseudophone transposes auditory stimuli from the normal ear to the other.)

psych(o)-: Greek combining form meaning *mind, mental functions.*

psychasthenia: (Janet) a neurotic disorder characterized by phobias, loss of psychic energy, obsessions and compulsions, tics, and anxieties.

psyche: the mind.

psychesthesia: illusion; sensory hallucination.

psychiatric social work: special aids for the patient and the family given by a professionally qualified person.

psychiatry: the medical specialty that investigates, diagnoses, and treats mental disorders (in England known as medical psychology).

psychic: (as a noun) in occultism, a person who has supernormal powers; also, pertaining to mental, or subjective, data.

psychic monism: the doctrine that mind or spirit is the one basic reality.

psychical research: syn. *parapsychology;* the serious investigation of phenomena that apparently are not to be understood in terms of any known natural laws.

psychoanalysis: the method, the point of view in psychiatry, and the general facts and principles developed by Sigmund Freud.

psychoasthenics: study of mental defectives.

psychobiology: a study of the relationships between the organism and its unlearned and learned ways to adjusting to the environment.

psychodiagnostics: the study of behavioral traits (manner of speech, walking, etc.) and responses (e.g., to Rorschach inkblots) as data for making inferences regarding the presence or absence of personality disorders.

psychodometer: apparatus for measuring reaction times.

psychodrama: (Moreno) the spontaneous acting out (under a qualified therapist) of conflictual situations more or less typical of those which disturb the patient, thereby achieving insights into the nature of the problem.

psychogalvanic response (PGR): syn. *electrodermal response;* the lowering of skin resistance to electrical conduction, as when an unexpected stimulus is presented to the individual.

psychogenetic disorder: one which, presumably, arises solely from mental conflicts and/or psychic tensions, the causes having their basis in the life history of the individual or in some traumatic experience.

psychogram: a graphic representation of standings, expressed in comparable units, on various psychological tests and measures.

psychography: (G. Bradford) a literary characterization of a personality, often based upon the method of critical incidents or revealing episodes in the person's life history.

psychography: in occultism, the communication by automatic writing with the spirits; conventionally, the literary, or clinical, description of a person's traits, qualities, and subjective life.

psychokinesia: a violent motor reaction, as in mania.

psychokinesis: in parapsychology, the production of movements or actions in an inanimate object through the mediation of subjective influences; often abbreviated as PK effect.

psycholagnia: intense imaginative preoccupation with erotic themes.

psycholepsy: (Janet) loss of drive and a sense of hopelessness, as in psychasthenia.

psycholinguistics: the study of the art and the science of communication, both from the standpoint of the communicator and from that of the reader or auditor; the psychological factors involved in communications.

psychological atomism: the doctrine that mental contents or functions are reducible to units of sensations (or images and feelings as well).

psychological clinic: an organized institution where psychological tests and measures are expertly administered and interpreted, and where remedial programs and psychotherapy may be carried out; traditionally, a clinical psychologist, a psychiatrist, and a social worker pooling their skills in bringing help to individuals in difficulties, (e.g., in connection with schools, a psychoeducational clinic).

psychological determinism: the doctrine that no behavior occurs by chance but that there is always a cause, whether conscious or unconscious, for each action.

psychological environment: syn. *life space;* (Lewin) the sum total of all the perceptual and the conceptual data which at any given moment are operative in directing the behavior of an individual or of a group.

psychological test (or measure):   a standardized procedure for comparing the performances of two or more persons on abilities, aptitudes, achievements, and the like, the test itself being classified according to its purposes, the method of administration (e.g., individual or group, speed or power, etc.), and the manner in which it was standardized (e.g., age scale or point scale, etc.).

psychology: (James) the science of mental life, both of its phenomena and of their condition; a term with so many variant definitions as to defy an attempt to be dogmatic about it, no two psychologists being in total agreement, though scientists do agree that a psychologist is one who has met the rigorous requirements for status in the American Psychological Association.

psychometrics: the administration and interpretation of psychological tests and measures by a specialist (a psychometrician or psychometrist); at one time, the study of sensory thresholds, reaction times, and the like.

psychomotor attack: a seizure which supposedly results from intense mental conflicts or tensions.

psychomotor test: a measure or test of motor skills (e.g., rapid insertion of a stylus into holes of varying sizes).

psychoneurosis: syn. *neurosis;* a functional disorder of the personality which is more grave than a minor personality problem but not so severe as a psychosis; a psychogenic disorder.

psychoneurotic inventory or questionnaire: a list of questions or items designed to elicit self-report answers about the quality of adjustment or the presence-absence of major neurotic symptoms.

psychopath: a loose term denoting an antisocial or hostile individual.

psychopathic hospital: syn. *receiving hospital;* an institution where patients suffering from serious mental disorders are temporarily kept for early diagnosis and treatment (psychopathic ward in a general hospital also filling a similar expedient purpose).

psychopathic personality: a loose term denoting a person who is free from gross symptoms of a psychosis but who does not accept the mores of the larger society and acts, therefore, as a trouble maker or is so defined.

psychopathology: the science dealing with all forms of behavioral deviations.

psychopathy: a loose term meaning literally "a sick mind"; any form of mental disorder.

psychophysical parallelism: the doctrine that mind and body are separate entities but that their activities are simultaneous, though not causally related (accepted in modified form by Wundt).

psychophysics: (Fechner) the science which investigates quantitative relationships between the stimuli and the resultant sensations.

psychosis: a grave mental disorder.

psychosomatics: syn. *psychosomatic medicine;* that medical specialty which combines the standard methods of a general practitioner with the art of psychiatrists in treating the patient or in fostering mental-physical health.

psychosurgery: a popular term for prefrontal leucotomy and other brain operations in certain types of grave mental disorders.

psychotechnology: the application of psychological facts, methods, and principles in business, industry, or any other form of institutional endeavor.

psychotherapist: one who is professionally accredited to deal with individuals in difficulties, through the use of such techniques as lie within the field of social work, clinical psychology, or psychiatry; one who is qualified to make use of all such resources (psychotherapy) in aiding an individual.

psychotic disorder: a grave mental affliction which usually indicates an imperative need to commit the patient to a hospital for treatment.

psychotomimetic drugs: those which induce mental conditions resembling grave psychoses (e.g., LSD-25).

psychrophiliac: organisms that thrive in intense cold.

psychrophobia: morbid fear of anything cold.

pubertas praecox: syn. *precocious puberty;* the premature development of primary and secondary sex characteristics; abnormally early achievement of adolescence.

puberty: the achievement of full generative powers, together with the secondary sex characteristics associated therewith.

puberty age: roughly, about age 14 in boys and 13 in girls, though with wide variations.

puberty rites: in cultural anthropology, the ceremonies of initiation whereby the elders of a tribe recognize the new status of those who have reached the puberal growth stage.

pubes: the hair which appears on the lower abdomen and the crotch (hypogastric region) with the onset of puberty.

pubescence: the growth stage during which puberty is being reached, a pubescent being a boy or a girl who has just reached this stage.

public: that which is repeatable, observable, and verifiable, as contrasted with that which is subjective; also, the general community.

public opinion: the views or attitudes which, through a random sampling or opinion poll, appear to be shared by a majority of individuals.

public relations work: the art of applying all sorts of procedures, including psychotechnology, to the creation and the maintenance of favorable attitudes toward an individual or an institution.

pudendum (plural **pudenda**): the external sex organ or any part thereof.

puerile behavior: childishness on the part of one who has chronologically passed that phase of growth and development, usually as a symptom of a personality disorder.

puerperal period: childbirth.

pulmonary: relating to the lungs.

pulse rate: the throbbing caused by the rhythmic contractions of the ventricles of the heart, which (though varying with age, etc.) is normally detectable in the arteries at the rate of 70-75 a minute.

pulsimeter: any apparatus for measuring the force and the rate of pulsations in the arteries.

punctiform stimulation: exploration of cutaneous sensitivities by means of a pointed stylus.

pungent: that quality of a sensory experience which is described as sharp, stinging, or painful.

punishment: treatment by a penalty; historically, the successive methods of retaliation, retribution, restoration, and rehabilitation; in Thorndike's system, anything which results in annoyance, and which thus favors the disuse of the stimulus-response bond involved.

pupil: the contractile opening in the iris of the eye; also, one who attends an elementary or secondary school.

pure perception: a response that, theoretically, pertains to nothing but the sensory elements or the stimuli eliciting it.

pure stimulus: a form of physical energy (light waves, chemical substances, sound waves, etc.) which affects a receptor without having any concomitant or complicating forms of energy, thus, in theory, defining any given elementary sensitivity.

Purkinje afterimage: the appearance of the complementary of the hue which was briefly the stimulus for a visual sensation.

Purkinje effect: the apparent darkening of hues, like red, orange, and yellow under conditions of twilight vision, as contrasted with the relative stability of hues like green and blue.

Purkinje's figures or images: the shadow-like appearance of the retinal network of blood vessels, to be observed if a light is directed through a tiny aperture before the eyeball.

Purkinje images: syn. *Purkinje Sanson images;* the three reflections observed, respectively, on the cornea and on the front and the back of the lens.

purposive accident: in psychoanalysis, a slip of tongue or pen or other apparently chance form of behavior which, actually, is unconsciously determined.

purposive psychology: syn. *teleological psychology;* (McDougall's hormic psychology) a systematic exposition of psychological facts and principles which emphasizes the ends to which all actions are directed and the needs or purposes which instincts (or propensities) serve for the organism.

pursuitmeter: apparatus for recording motor efficiency in keeping a stylus on a moving or rotating pathway, as a measure of hand-eye coordinations.

puzzle box: syn. *problem box;* (Thorndike) a device in which the reward is confined by a system of locks or levers, the animal to learn how to get it by trial and error.

pyknic build: (Kretschmer) a rounded, fat body, which is associated with a cyclothymic personality and which is especially characteristic of patients with a manic-depressive psychosis.

pylorus: the opening from the stomach into the large intestine.

pyramidal tract: either of the two columns of motor fibers in the spinal cord.

pyretology: the division of medicine which treats fevers or uses fever therapy (as in treatment of paresis by malaria).

pyrolagnia: sexual excitement by watching or setting fires.

pyromania: obsessive-compulsive incendiarism.

pyrophobia: obsessive anticipatory fear of fires.

Pyrrhic victory: a success, or an attempt at psychotherapy, gained at too great a cost to justify the effort.

Q: the quartile deviation.

Q sort: a technique for making an inventory of personality by sorting statements into piles, each representing the degree to which a given characteristic is applicable to the individual being studied.

quadrant: one of four areas on a graph; an area bounded by the *y*-axis and the *x*-axis at the point of their intersection on a graph.

quadrate lobe: syn. *quadrate lobule;* a convolution, roughly square in outline, on the middle (or mesial) surface of the parietal lobe of the cerebrum.

quadrigeminal: fourfold.

quadriplegia: paralysis of both arms and both legs.

quadrivium: in the early university, the four "higher studies" of the curriculum: arithmetic, astronomy, geometry, and music.

quale: (Titchener) an item of sensory experience considered separately from all associations, context, and other complexities.

quality: (Titchener) that aspect of a mental content whereby it may be differentiated from all other elements (e.g., each individual taste, odor, and so on).

quantify: to convert data into numerical equivalents for statistical analysis or classification.

quartile: one of three points along the horizontal axis of a typical graph which separate the distribution into four equal groups.

quartile deviation: one-half the range between the 25th percentile and the 75th percentile; half the interquartile range.

quasi: in a sense or to a certain degree; seemingly but not actually.

querulant: given to unfounded suspicions, accusations, and complaints.

questionnaire, questionary: planned statements or queries on any given topic, usually designed for submission to a large number of persons for the purpose of eliciting information about their opinions, attitudes, or behavior.

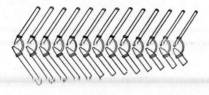

Figure 26. Quincke's tubes for study of auditory sensations.

Quincke's tubes: a series of small tubes made of glass, used for study of high pitches, difference tones, and interference effects.

quintile: a point which divides an array of scores into fifths.

quotient: the number obtained by dividing one number by another number (e.g., intelligence quotient = mental age divided by chronological age).

R: symbol for the unconditioned response or, simply, response.

r: symbol for product-moment correlation coefficient.

ʳbis: biserial correlation coefficient.

ʳ12.3: partial correlation; the correlation of variables 1 and 2 when 3 is held constant.

ʳtet: tetrachoric correlation coefficient.

rabdomancy: dowsing; the employment of divining rods to locate water or lost objects.

race: a main division of the human family Hominidae; commonly, a naturally homogeneous ethnic division (e.g., Australoid, Negroid, Mongoloid, etc.) .

racial memory: those ideas, impulses, emotions supposedly resulting from experiences in the remote past of the human race and hence a part of every individual's mental equipment.

racial unconscious: (Jung) archaic memories presumed by Jung to reside in the unconscious and to be derived from the race's accumulated experiences, knowledge and traditions; the collective unconscious.

radiant energy: light considered in terms of electromagnetic waves emanating from a source.

radix: a nerve root or bundle of nerve fibers at the point of their emergence from, or entrance into, the central nervous system.

rami communicants: those bundles of nerve fibers connecting the spinal nerves and the sympathetic ganglions.

ramus: the nerves connecting the central and sympathetic nervous systems; generally, a branch of a nerve or vein.

random error: chance or unsystematic error.

random movement: in effect, movement for which the observer cannot determine a definite cause.

random numbers: tables of numbers arranged at random within rows and columns for use in random assignment of subjects to groups or for assigning groups at random to one of a number of experimental conditions.

random sample: a number of persons or objects drawn by chance from a larger population, frequently on the assumption they will be representative of the larger group.

randomize: to select on a chance basis; treatment or arrangement in such a fashion as to eliminate selective factors.

range: difference between the largest and smallest values in a distribution.

range effect: in situations requiring the observer to track or pursue a moving target, the tendency to make too large a movement when the movement of the target is slow and two small a movement for fast moving targets.

range of sensation: the continuum of sensations accompanying and corresponding to the range of stimulation.

rank-difference correlation: a measure of correlation based upon the relative ranks assigned to individual scores on two variables; $p(\text{rho}) = 1 - \dfrac{6\Sigma D^2}{N(N^2 - 1)}$, where D is the difference between ranks and N is the number of cases.

Rankian psychology: a dissident offshoot of Freudian psychoanalytic theory established by Otto Rank.

rapport: the empathic relationship between two individuals, especially between counselor and counselee or therapist and patient, characterized by mutual confidence and freedom from constraint.

rate of change: the ratio between the amount of change in a variable and the value of the variable before the change.

rational psychology: a systematic organization of psychological facts, concepts, and principles based upon value judgments or theological views.

rating: estimating, on some systematic basis, the presence or absence or the magnitude of some trait, characteristic, or quality of a person, thing, or process.

rating scale: a device or procedure for establishing an individual's position on a continuum, usually with respect to some personality variable or characteristic.

ratio: relation of a number, amount or degree, e.g., height to weight; proportion, as in the ratio of men to women in a population.

rational: based on reason or having the power or capacity to reason.

rationale: underlying reason or theory upon which a particular action or belief is based.

rationalization: giving socially acceptable or plausible reasons for one's actions or beliefs to avoid acknowledgment of the real, possibly improper or unworthy reasons.

reaction: the integrated pattern of responses to a situation; the behavior of an organism when stimulated.

reaction formation: in psychoanalysis, the development of behavior directly opposed to unconscious, forbidden behavior tendencies.

reaction levels: a conceptualization of the operation of the nervous system in which functions are carried out, depending upon their complexity, by different levels of the nervous system, the simplest ones by the spinal, the most complex by the forebrain.

reaction potential: (C. Hull) the possibility, measured in units of the *wat,* of a particular response occurring. (Estimated, according to Hull, by multiplying habit strength by relevant drive.)

reaction psychology: an orientation emphasizing behavior as reaction-to-stimulus and especially concerned with motor activity.

reaction time: interval between stimulation and response. (Simple reaction time is the time interval between a prearranged stimulus and a previously determined response. Choice reaction time involves a variety of stimuli, for each of which a different stimulus has been specified. Cognitive reaction time is the interval between stimulus recognition and response. Discrimination reaction time measures reaction time when the subject is required to respond to only one of several stimuli.)

reaction type: categorization of reactions on the basis of the subject's focus of attention, e.g., sensory reactions in which the subject's set is to apprehend the stimulus, or motor type reactions in which the set is to make the required motor response as quickly as possible; a specific psychiatric syndrome such as paranoid reaction type.

reactional biography: life history stressing the individual's behavior rather than environmental or situational factors.

reactive depression: a state of despondency arising from the attempted reduction of acute anxiety by prolonged depression and self-depreciation; neurotic depressive reaction.

reactive psychosis: psychosis precipitated by, or resulting from, primarily environmental factors such as traumatic war experiences or imprisonment.

reactive reinforcement: the arousal of unconscious, and opposite, tendencies by conscious processes, e.g., the lover unconsciously hating the loved one.

readiness: the sum of the individual's intellectual, sensory and motor development, needs, and acquired abilities and ideas, as a result of which he is more likely to respond in one fashion than another.

realism: the acceptance of what is experienced as being real.

reality feeling: the unreflective experiencing of the world as being real and immediately apprehended.

reality principle: that part of the ego structure which operates to achieve satisfaction of instinctual drives while regulating behavior in accordance with demands of one's environment.

reality testing: in therapy, the verifying by the patient of his ways of thinking and perceiving in a situation devoid of anxiety.

reasoning: thinking in accordance with principles of logic or the solving of problems by application of these principles, the reasoner being aware that his conclusions must take certain premises into consideration.

reassurance: a directive counseling technique in which direct and indirect suggestion is used to restore the patient's self-confidence and encourage optimism.

recall: the experiencing or evoking of a representation of that which had been previously experienced.

recall method: a method of measuring retention by requiring the subject to reproduce previously learned material.

recapitulation theory: the view that the stages of development of the individual are representative of evolutionary stages of the species; summarized in the statement: "ontogeny recapitulates phylogeny."

recept: the change taking place in the neuron during a neutral discharge from receptor to effector.

receptor: specialized bodily structures which operate to receive and translate stimuli into neural activity. Receptors are classified according to the type of energy (light, heat, sound, and so on) by which they are stimulated.

recessive: receding or failing to be manifested; genetically, a gene which produces no determinable effect unless paired with another recessive gene.

reciprocal inhibition: failure to recall either of two closely associated items due to the interference of one with the other.

reciprocal innervation: relaxation of one of a pair of antagonistic muscles when the other contracts.

reciprocity principle: Bronsen-Roscoe Law: the principle, applicable only within narrow limits, that response to a stimulus is a product of both its duration and intensity; e.g., a brief extremely loud stimulus is equivalent to a prolonged stimulus of low amplitude.

recognition: the awareness of objects as being those to which one previously responded or which were previously experienced.

recognition method: a measure of retention in which the subject is required to select those items which have been previously presented.

recognition span: the number of words or digits which an individual can perceive in a single fixation.

reconditioning: reintroduction of the unconditioned stimulus to prevent experimental extinction or to strengthen the conditioned response.

reconstruction: the process of evolving past experiences and their associated emotional states whereby therapist and patient may consider present inappropriate emotions in the light of past conditions which gave rise to them.

reconstruction method: measurement of retention by requiring the subject to re-establish a series in the order in which it was learned.

recovery time: the interval following a response during which the response cannot be repeated; refractory period.

recruitment: the involvement of an increasing number of effectors under prolonged stimulation.

rectilinear coordinates: two straight lines or axes intersecting one another at right angles; units on both axes are used to locate points representing values of individual cases with respect to both axes.

red-green blindness: dichromatism or partial color blindness in which red and green are perceived as gray (blue or yellow being confused).

reduced cues: the theory that, with repetition, a response previously attached to a total situation can be elicited by progressively smaller portions of that situation.

redintegration: the completion or renewal of a complex mental state upon the recall or renewal of a single part of it.

reduction-division: the final stage of cell division in the process of formation of male or female elements, whereby the number of chromosomes is reduced by one-half.

reductionism: the position that the more elementary components of complex phenomena are real and that the whole is completely explicable in terms of only these parts.

reduction screen: a vertical, opaque screen with two small holes so positioned that binocular vision through them does not result in their fusing.

re-education: in therapy, the process of aiding the individual to relearn appropriate and efficient behavior patterns which have been lost.

refer: 1. assigning a sensory impression to its actual or supposed source; 2. to send a person to some other professional agency or individual for assistance.

referent: that thing which is denoted by a word or by some other symbol.

referred sensation: the localization of sensation in some other area other than that actually stimulated.

reflected color: color which is preceived to be reflected from the surface of an object as opposed to color coming directly from a light.

reflecting back: restating by the counselor of a counselee's remarks to afford him the opportunity for new perceptions or to direct his attention to significant material.

reflex: an unlearned, immediate, and unreflective response to stimulation.

reflex arc: theoretically, the basic unit of function of the nervous system which includes an afferent neuron, a synaptic connection and a motor neuron.

reflex circle: the tendency of proprioceptors to be stimulated by muscular contractions, resulting in re-stimulation of the muscles.

reflex inhibition: the inhibition of one reflex by the reaction of another reflex.

reflexogenous zone: an area of the body's surface in which several points of stimulation give rise to the same reflex.

reflexology: (Bekterev) a form of behaviorism in which all behavior is reduced to reflex arcs, with total exclusion of all mentalistic concepts.

reformism: obsessive zeal in promulgating one's own plans for the welfare of the group.

refraction: the deflection of energy (e.g., light waves) as it passes from one medium to another (e.g., from the cornea through the lens).

refractory phase: the brief interval after a muscle contraction or a nervous discharge in which no physiological activity of a similar type can occur.

regard: the visual fixation point; the point at which vision is clearest.

regimen: the total style of living that promotes health.

region: any relatively large area or of an organ; in Lewin's theory, any major subdivision of life space.

regnant process: (Murray) the physiological concomitant of a dominant psychological activity (Not all regnant processes, however, are accompanied by consciousness.)

regression: in psychoanalysis, the resumption of childish modes of behavior; in Jung's theory, the return of the libido to the unconscious, introverted outlets, both personal and collective, wherein new modes of progression may be discovered; in Lewin's theory, a loss of ability to make effective discriminations (hence, dedifferentation); in Galton's eugenics, the tendency of successive generations to revert towards the average (law of filial regression); also, (Ribot) the decline of memories for recent events.

regression equation: in statistics, the technique for determining, within the limits of probability, the most likely value of Y from the known value of X; also, the formula for drawing straight lines (or curves) adjusted to the means of one array of scores in a two-way (or double-entry) table. One standard formula is: $Y = a + bX$.

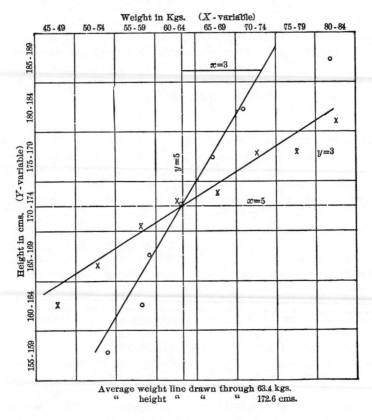

Average weight line drawn through 63.4 kgs.
     "   height   "   "   "   172.6 cms.

Figure 27. Two regression lines, one "best fitting" heights, and the other, "best fitting" weights.

regurgitate: syn. *retch;* to vomit.

rehabilitation: techniques of re-education whereby the patient is able to resume life as a self-supportnig, effective member of the community.

reification: syn. *hpyostization;* the fallacy of using an abstract concept to denote a specific entity.

reincarnation: the belief that souls return to earth and inhabit the bodies of successive generations of mankind or lower animals.

reinforce: in physiology, the strengthening of a response to one stimulus by the response elicited by another stimulus.

reinforcement: in learning theory, the strengthening of a response by the reward or the satisfying condition which ensues; the modern extension of E. L. Thorndike's law of effect.

reinstatement test: any measure of retention which requires the learner to recall, recognize, relearn, or repeat what was previously learned (with special reference to retention for rote material).

rejection: exclusion from affectionate relationships or from acceptance (e.g., parental rejection) as the cause for severe frustration.

relapse: the recurrence of a disorder from which a recovery had been made.

relatedness: in Lewin's theory, the principle that behavior is always the result of interaction between two or more facts (e.g., the person and the environment, inner personal and perceptual regions, etc., etc.).

relational thinking: that in which chance associations, not logical coherence, determine the sequence of ideas.

relativism: in social psychology, the doctrine that folkways and mores are established within the group at any given time or in any given area, and that, consequently, there are no absolute standards.

relaxation: the return of muscles and ligaments to their normal level of tonus after a period of contraction.

relaxation therapy: instructions in how to reduce tension levels in group of skeletal muscles, one by one (Jacobson).

relearning: the reinstatement by reviews of what was previously acquired (Ebbinghaus).

releaser: a stimulus which elicits a response characteristic of the species to which the organism belongs; broadly, any situation which has social-stimulus value.

release therapy: that form of counseling in which the individual expresses, verbally or through manipulation of objects, all hostile impulses and anxieties in a permissive situation.

reliability: the extent to which a test or a series of observations is dependable, self-consistent, and stable.

reliability coefficient: a coefficient of correlation between such variables as scores on test repetition, one half vs. the other, chance halves, comparable forms, and the like.

religious psychology: syn. *psychology of religion;* systematic investigations of conversion experiences, beliefs, motives, and the like, as they relate to religion and its practices.

remedial program: in education, instruction to suit the needs of a pupil in difficulties.

reminiscence effect: the supposed gain in the efficiency of a learning as a lapse of time supervenes, no reviews having consciously taken place during the interim.

remission: the temporary abatement of a disorder.

renal: relating to the kidneys.

renifleur: one who derives erotic responses in connection with strong odors.

renunciation: in psychoanalysis, the denial of gratification to the basic instinctual drives of the id because they would conflict with the ego (reality principle) or with the demands of the superego.

reorganization: in Gestalt theory, the achievement of new Gestalten (or configurations) by complete alterations in the patterns of past experience and the current perceptual functions.

repertoire: the totality of all the responses, unlearned and learned, that an individual is capable of making.

repetition-compulsion: in psychoanalysis, the unconscious tendency to repeat nonadjustive or maladjustive, infantile responses, even when the behavior brings no pleasure.

replacement: the substitution of socially acceptable, or ethically approved, modes of behavior for former modes of behavior that were unacceptable or that interfered with personality growth.

replantation: the rearrangement of tissues in the embryo (usually of the chick) by techniques of microsurgery; transplantation.

replicate: to repeat an experiment or field study precisely as it was first carried out.

representation: a mental content or idea, as a copy of what is actually in the world.

repression: in psychoanalysis, the unconscious mechanism whereby unwelcome knowledge is kept from the conscious.

reproduction: in education, a proof of learning and of retention in which the original materials are reinstated (as in an examination); in biology, the production of an offspring.

reproof: a form of negative reinforcement (as in a censure or blame for an action).

reputation: the value judgments pertaining to a person.

required actions: syn. *folkways;* the social techniques demanded by the group.

research: a serious inquiry into a definite problem (as by experiment, historical analysis, field studies, or observations).

resignation: (Horney) neurotic withdrawal from life; defeatism.

resilience: the elasticity of an organ (e.g., of the ciliary muscles).

resistance: in psychoanalysis, the analysand's unconscious wish to keep from achieving full self-knowledge, and hence a failure in rapport with the analyst.

resolution: in mental conflicts and interpersonal conflicts, making compromises which ease or palliate the tensions, but which do not solve the problem.

resonance theory: in audition, the view that the nerve endings on the basilar membrane of the organ of Corti vibrate (like a piano or a harp) in tune with the frequency of the sound waves initiating them (Helmholtz); in memory, the tendency of memoranda to be reproduced (by recall or recognition) more readily when the original mental set established at the time of learning is dominant.

respiration ratio: the index of inspiration vs. expiration.

respirometer: apparatus for measuring inspiration-expiration rates and vigor of breathing, the record being called a *respirograph.*

respondent behavior: that which is directly identified by the stimulus which elicits it.

response: the reaction elicited by a stimulus, often being symbolized as *R.*

restraining influences: in Gestalt psychology, all those forces which keep a Gestalt from following the law of closure (completeness) or pragnanz ("goodness").

restraint: a drastic form of confinement designed to keep the patient from self-injury.

restructure: in Lewin's theory, the shifting of parts of the psychological field without diminishing their size or relative importance.

results: the outcomes of an empirical investigation upon which the conclusions are based.

retained-members method: a measure of retention in which a record is kept of ability to reproduce the original section by section (e.g., in poetry, keeping a score on reproduction of verses or stanzas).

retardate: a pupil who, because of dullness, cannot keep up with age mates in school.

retardation: in educational practice, all those influences which keep a pupil from proceeding in the regular grade-by-grade mastery of the curriculum, and, hence, that necessitate repetition of grades or special education.

retention: the process of retaining what has been learned as evidenced by some proof (e.g., recall or reproduction).

reticulum: a network of fibers or tissues.

retifism: erotic stimulation from feet or shoes.

retina: the innermost membrane of the eye, wherein are located the rods and the cones (visual receptors).

retinal rivalry: the result of stimulating the retinas by colors or designs which cannot be fused, and hence, which fluctuate.

retinitis: inflamation of the retina, resulting in diminished vision and/or insensitivities in color discrimination and in adaptation to darkness.

retinoscope: a device for use in looking at the retina (or optic ground).

retro-: Latin prefix meaning *backward*.

retroactive inhibition: the interference effects upon efficiency in reproducing a learned task when it was immediately followed by a task closely resembling it.

retrograde amnesia: forgetfulness at first of recent events, and then of events of episodes long past, as in senility; in traumata, the inability to recall events just prior to the injury or shock.

retrogression: a psychological reversion to infantile or childish forms of behavior.

retrospection: a verbal report about a past experience; reminiscence.

retrospective falsification: syn. *paramnesia;* the involuntary distortions of memory.

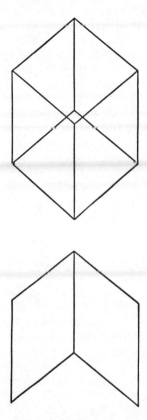

Figure 28. Familiar reversible figures, often used to demonstrate fluctuations in attention.

reversible figure: an illusion of perspective in which a figure (e.g., the Necker cube or the Schröder staircase) seem to fluctuate back and forth.

reversion: a characteristic arising from a recessive character in the ancestral line.

reward: a reinforcement; an attained incentive; a satisfier (Thorndike).

-rhagia: Greek combining form meaning *a bleeding* (e.g., as in hemorrhage).

rhathymia: a merry disposition.

rhesus: a species of Catarrhine monkey of the genus Macaca.

rhigosis: the sense of cold.

rhigotic spots: cold spots distributed on the surface of the body.

rhinencephalon: the olfactory lobe of the cerebrum.

rhino-: Greek combining form meaning *nose.*

rhinolalia: syn. *rhinophemia, rhinophonia;* a nasal quality in the speech.

rhinorhagia: syn. *epistaxis;* a severe nosebleed.

rho: the rank difference coefficient of correlation:

$$p = 1 - \frac{6\Sigma D^2}{N(N^2 - 1)},$$

rhodopsin: visual purple, found in the rods.

rickets: a nutritional disease in children.

rigidity: in physiology, an intense and prolonged contraction of the muscles; in psychology; inflexibility and resistance to new (and appropriate) methods.

riot: a violent disorder or disturbance of the peace by excited, unruly persons.

raparious group: people who live along river banks; riparians.

risible: provoking laughter.

rite: a prescribed method of conducting a religious ceremony.

ritualistic behavior: stereotyped actions directed toward meticulous, unimportant details (as a defense against unconscious anxieties).

rivalry: competition for status in the dominance-submission struggle.

RL: stimulus threshold (*Reiz-limen*).

robot: an automaton; one who, dominated by authoritarians, obeys orders in a machine-like fashion and never exercises initiative.

rods: those receptors (in the retina) which have a rodlike appearance and which are said to mediate achromatic and twilight vision.

Rolandic fissure: syn. *fissure of Rolando, central sulcus;* the deep sulcus which separates the frontal and the parietal lobes on the lateral surface of the cerebrum.

role: that characteristic pattern of behavior imposed upon an individual because of his or her status in the group.

role-playing: the acting out of conflicts, both personal (role rivalries) and social, under the direction of a therapist, who helps the individual to achieve insights or to gain an ability as a leader.

Romberg sign: inability to maintain erect posture when the feet are close together and the eyes are closed, usually indicating pathologies in the posterior column of the spinal cord.

root: the point at which a nerve fiber or a muscle originates.

Rorschach Inkblot Test: ten cards, each with a symmetrical inkblot, to which the subject is asked to attach meanings, which are said to reveal characteristics of the personality (one of the most discussed projective techniques).

Rosenzweig Picture-Frustration Study: cartoon-like drawings of two persons, one of whom is saying something and for the other person the testee is to write in the reply; (sometimes called the Rosenzweig P-F Study).

rotary-pursuit task: a measure of ability to hold a stylus on a rotating pattern of irregular form.

rotation chair: syn. *Barany chair;* an apparatus for testing the aftereffects of rotation of liquid within the semicircular canals upon the individual's ability to orient spatially.

rote learning: that which involves little or no understanding but much parrot-like repetition.

round window: syn. *fenestra rotunda;* an opening (covered by a membrane) between the middle ear and the inner ear, against which the strapes (stirrup) rests.

RT: the reaction time.

Ruffini corpuscle: a nerve ending in the deep layer of the skin, which may be the receptor for warmth sensitivity.

rumor: an unverified story passed about, principally by word of mouth, sometimes, not always, of a disquieting nature.

run: a single trial of an experiment; a procedure that can be repeated later.

rut: male counterpart of estrus; readiness for copulation (male animal).

rypophagy: the eating of filthy substances.

S (plural Ss): the subject in an experiment or psychological study.

saccadic movements: the jerking of the eyeballs from one point of fixation to another while S is reading.

saccule: syn. *sacculus;* a small sac lying within the labyrinth of the inner ear.

sacral: pertaining to the portion of the spinal column directly connected with the pelvis.

sacral nerves: those which are attached to the lower portion of the spinal cord.

sadism: a form of sex perversion in which the loved one must be tortured; erotic thrill derived from cruelty.

sadomasochism: erotic thrill derived from both receiving and inflicting pain.

saggital axis: an imaginary line in the median plane of the body or any other line which is parallel to it.

saltation: growth by spurts, as in the puberal years.

samples: data which are considered to be representative of the universe from which they have been chosen.

sampling: the procedure used in choosing a representative array of data from the universe to which the data relate, the data, usually selected at random, then being evaluated statistically by reference to the probability curve.

sane: a legal concept meaning freedom from symptoms of grave mental disorder, and hence responsible for behavior.

sanguine temperament: (Galen) one characterized by optimism, cheerfulness, and hope (said to be due to a relative excess of blood).

sapphism: syn. *lesbianism, tribadism;* homosexuality among women.

satiation effect: the deleterious results of boredom or fatigue in a long test or experiment, which lowers the final score or the quality of the work.

satisfier: (Thorndike) a gratifying outcome of a response, thus favoring its repetition.

saturation: the amount to which a psychological test or measure is loaded with any given factor.

saturation of color: (Titchener) the amount by which any given hue differs from a hue on the white-black dimension of the color pyramid of the same brilliance; a hue composed of a single wavelength.

satyriasis: insatiable sex desire in the male.

savings method: (Ebbinghaus) the need for less frequent reviews of material that is to be relearned.

scala media: that part of the cochlea which contains the organ of Corti.

scala tympani: one of the spiral tubes into which the cochlea is divided.

scale: in music, a graduated, conventional series of pitches; in mental testing, a series of items experimentally arranged from easy to difficult (e.g., the Binet-Simon Scale for measurement of intelligence).

scapegoat: a recipient of displaced hostilities and frustrations.

scapula: shoulder blade.

scatologic speech: obscenities.

scatter: the variability of scores around the measure of central tendency in a frequency distribution.

scattergram: a graphic portrayal of an individual's scores on subtests or on a series of psychological tests.

scedasticity: the tendency of scores to be distributed regularly or irregularly on a two-way table, as measured by comparing standard deviations for each row.

scheduling of reinforcement: (Skinner) the manner in which the reward is given, as at fixed intervals, for amount done, intermittently, and so on.

schema (plural schemata): a logically organized plan or outline.

schizo-: Greek combining form meaning *cut off, split.*

schizogenesis: in histology, the multiplication of cells by fission.

schizophrenia: a severe mental disorder characterized by loss of contact with reality and profound behavioral maladjustments.

sclera: the outermost membrane covering the eyeball.

sclerosis: hardening of living tissues (such as the walls of blood vessels).

screen memory: protective recollection of a pleasant experience rather than of the disruptive recollection which is concealed or repressed behind it.

Seashore Measures of Musical Talents: phonograph records measuring abilities in pitch discrimination, loudness, rhythm, time, timbre, and tonal memory (1919).

secondary elaboration: in psychoanalysis, the coherence and the additive elements given to a dream narrative which distort the dream itself.

secondary goal: one which is acquired through learning, as contrasted to a primary goal which gratifies primary needs.

secondary group: in social psychology, a number of persons who have a community of interests, but who are not in face-to-face relationship (e.g., members of a political party).

secondary motives: those which are learned (e.g., wish for prestige).

secondary reinforcement: strengthening a response by use of a stimulus associated with another stimulus which has primary reinforcement value.

secondary sex character: a trait, other than genitalia, differentiating the sexes (e.g., distribution of pubic hair, voice, body build).

sector graph: syn. *sector chart;* an arrangement of scores in a circle, the circumference of which represents 100% of the scores.

secundogeniture: the status of having been the second born.

segregation: in *Gestalttheorie,* the detachment and emergence of new wholes or configurations which do not necessarily involve prior learning.

Seguin formboard: first devised for sensory-motor training of mental defectives, a board into which ten pieces are to be inserted (now included in a number of non verbal measures of intelligence).

selective perception: that which emphasizes some aspect of the situation to the neglect of others to the extent that gross distortions occur.

selective retention: in educational procedure, the gradual elimination of the uninterested and the incompetent, especially during secondary school years.

self: all that a person calls by the pronoun me or mine (William James); the mid-point of the personality (Jung); awareness of one's being and functioning.

self-abasement: extreme deference to others because of a strong attitude of inferiority.

self-abuse: masturbation.

self-accusation: morbid self-incrimination for offenses, fancied or real.

self-administering test: one which, because of its explicit instructions, may be taken without oral directions by a qualified examiner.

self-consciousness: embarrassment or lack of confidence; awareness of one's own identity as a persisting entity.

self-deception: in certain personality theories, the use of defense mechanisms (dynamisms) to protect against unconscious and repressed motives (e.g., rationalization, projection, and so on).

self-demand scheduling: (Spitz) the arrangement of feeding times when the infant seems to be hungry, not when a rigorous schedule permits feeding.

self-love: narcissism.

self-psychology: syn. *personalistic psychology;* a systematic presentation of facts and theories which are based upon the concept of a self or of selfhood as the focus (M. W. Calkins).

self-report inventory: a list of items to be checked honestly by the testee, even though the pattern of responses may indicate deviation from the normal or the desired personality organization.

sella turcica: a small depression in the floor of the skull that contains the pituitary gland.

semantics: the study of the uses and the meanings attached to words and other signs used in communication or in thinking; the correct and the fallacious ways of using and understanding symbols.

semen: male germ cells; spermatozoa and the associated fluids.

semi-: Latin prefix meaning *one-half.*

semicircular canals: three bony canals, lying at right angles to one another, in the inner ear.

semi-interquartile range: half the distance between the 25 %-ile and the 75 %-ile used as a measure of the dispersion of scores about a midpoint; Q.

senescence: old age.

senile: mental and physical deterioration in advanced age.

senium: a state of general debility in old age.

sensation: immediate awareness when a receptor is stimulated.

sensation-type: (Jung) one of the four function-types in which a low threshold exists for responsiveness to sensory stimulation.

sense-organ: the receptor and all accessory apparatus (e.g., the organ of Corti and all other parts of the ear).

sense unit: (Fechner) each just noticeable difference in stimulus intensity considered as a separate unit of experience.

sensorimotor: activity considered as involving neural connections between a receptor and an effector.

sensorium: those parts of the cerebrum which mediate sensory processes.

sensory acuity: said of the relative excitability of the receptors in any given modality (e.g., visual or auditory acuity or threshold).

sensory nerve: a nerve fiber which connects a receptor to the brain or to the spinal cord; an afferent nerve.

sentence-completion test: (Ebbinghaus) a sentence which becomes meaningful when the correct word or phrase has been supplied by the testee; as a projective technique, a means of inferring basic dynamics of the personality from the way fragments like "My father————," etc., etc., are completed.

sentiment: (MgDougall) a more or less consistent mode of affective response to any given stimulus.

separation anxiety: in psychoanalysis, the infant's vague and persistent apprehension of loss of its mother.

sequela (plural **sequelae**): pathological aftereffects of a disease or a psychic trauma.

serial learning: a rote process in which the learner must anticipate the next item in a series (as, say, verbatim learning of a series of nonsense syllables).

set: a readiness to respond to certain situations and not to others; a preparation for selection of certain stimuli and for a particular type of response.

seven liberal arts: the medieval curriculum, which consisted of the trivium—grammar, rhetoric, and dialectic; and the quadrivium—arithmetic, geometry, astronomy, and music.

sex education: scientific enlightenment of pupils about the total processes involved in reproduction and associated activities.

sex hygiene: the study of objective, wholesome attitudes towards reproduction, together with knowledge about venereal diseases.

sex-linked character: an inherited trait or character which is more frequently found in one sex than in the other (e.g., hemophilia, color blindness).

sex role: the behavior imposed upon the different sexes in various cultures (e.g., femininity in both men and women among the Arapesh).

sexual cell: an ovum or a spermatozoon.

sexual intercourse: copulation.

sexual perversion: any deviation in sex behavior of which the social group disapproves.

sexual selection: in Darwinism, the choise of a mate on the basis of special attractiveness (e.g., bright feathers, quality of song).

sexual trauma: an extremely disturbing episode, often occurring in childhood, which relates to sex and which has influence upon later adjustments.

s-factors: in Spearman's theory of intelligence, those psychoneural elements which account for successes in specific tasks, as contrasted to the general (g-factor) basic to all related performances.

shade: any color which, on the Titchener color pyramid, lies below the midline in the white-black axis and varies from mid-gray to black in brilliance.

shadow: in Jung's theory, an archetype consisting of instinctual drives inherited from subhuman ancestors and giving rise to a sense of guilt or of evil spirits.

shaman: in cultural anthropology, the medicine man of the tribe or one who holds communion with supernatural powers and practices magic.

sham feeding: with laboratory dogs, administering food which, because of a fistula in the throat, enters the mouth but not the stomach of the animal.

sham rage-reaction: the behavior of a dog or a cat in which the cortex has been operated upon, the response to many stimuli being somewhat like a normal rage reaction.

sharpening: the distortions occurring as a rumor is transmitted from person to person, whereby the details become more and more precise with the retelling.

Sheldon typology: a doctrine of constitutional types based upon classifications of the relative degrees of ectomorphy (cerebrotonia), mesomorphy (somatonia), and endomorphy (viscerotonia).

shell shock: a term used during World War I to refer to a disorder caused by prolonged effects of heavy shells or by neurotic predisposition.

Shipley Test: a measure of deterioration yielding a conceptual quotient (CQ) as a ratio between retention and abstract reasoning.

shock therapy: the use of convulsant drugs or electric current to induce seizures in the mental patient.

short-answer test: loosely, any objective examination; a measure designed to elicit short, concise responses.

short-circuiting: as a result of learning, the gradual elimination of superfluous responses, particularly in motor skills e.g., typing).

short-exposure apparatus: syn. *tachistoscope, metronoscope;* a device for brief viewing to letters, symbols, words, or short sentences, used in measuring span of apprehension or in improving habits in silent reading.

shut-in personality: one that is withdrawn, uncommunicative, and asocial.

sibling (sib):   a brother or sister who is not a twin.

sibling rivalry: a tension-provoking situation arising from unfavorable comparisons among children within the family constellation.

sight method: in teaching children to read, the procedure of word, phrase, or sentence recognition rather than of letter or syllable analysis.

sigma (σ):   1/1,000 of a second; the standard deviation.

sigma score: syn. *standard score;* a test score expressed in terms of the standard deviation of the distribution; a score indicating the position of a raw score with the mean arbitrarily set at 50 and the standard-deviation units as 1/10.

sign learning: (Tolman) an acquired expectancy that a sign or stimulus will be followed by a significate (or other stimulus) if the familiar sequence of behavior is carried out.

significance: in statistical analyses of data, the probability that in the universal array of scores the obtained score would occur beyond chance.

similarities test: a measure of ability to choose among any given array of items (words, numbers, and so on) those which are like the standard.

simulation: feigning of a disorder; malingering.

sinistral: pertaining to the left side or left hand.

sinistro-:   Latin combining form meaning *left.*

sinistrocerebral behavior: that which is dominated or mediated by the left hemisphere of the cerebrum.

sinus: a cavity within the body.

sitology: dietetics.

sitophobia: aversion towards food.

situation: a pattern of stimuli.

situational-analysis method: observations of the individual's responses to situations, usually in real life, not laboratory, circumstances.

situationism: (G. Murphy) the principle that as situations change there are changes in roles, and hence alterations in personality.

size-age confusion: overexpectations by adults when the child is large for its chronological age.

size constancy: the tendency to perceive familiar objects as of constant size, whether they be in the immediate foreground or in the remote background.

size-weight illusion: the tendency to believe that a light object of large size is heavier than a small object actually heavier in weight.

skeletal musculature: the striped muscles which are attached to and move the bones.

skepticism: in philosophy, the doctrine that all knowledge is basically uncertain or questionable.

skewness: the degree to which a frequency distribution of scores bunches up on one side of the mean and tails out on the other side.

skiascope: a device for observing light and shadows on the retina.

skill: the degree of excellence in the performance of motor acts.

Skinner box: apparatus requiring the confined animal to learn an instrumental act (e.g., pressing a bar) to obtain the reward (typically, food pellets).

skipping: by reason of superior achievement, omitting one or more school grades.

sleeper: alterations taking place after an opinion pool has been taken and vitiating the dependability of the announced results.

sleeping sickness: syn. *encephalitis lethargica;* a grave disorder marked by tremors, lethargy, weakness, and physical dilapidation.

sleepwalking: syn. *somnambulism;* trance-like behavior while the individual appears to be sound asleep.

slip: syn. *purposive accident;* in psychoanalysis, an unconsciously directed word, phrase, spelling, which, not consciously intended, expresses the real attitude.

slow learner: a pupil who cannot keep up with age mates in mastery of the curriculum but who is not a mental defective; a retardate.

smooth muscle: syn. *unstriped* or *unstriated muscle;* contractive tissue mediated by the autonomic nervous system (e.g., muscles of viscera).

smoothing: in statistics, the application of formulas to remove irregularities from the array of data, without losing any essential characteristics of the data.

Snellen chart or scale: a graded series of types printed on a white cardboard and used as a measure of visual acuity.

snow-blindness: a retinal pathology, usually temporary, as a result of prolonged exposure to very bright light, the visual field being tinged with a reddish hue.

social age: the development of a person expressed in terms of age at which any given series of social adjustments are typical.

social anthropology: study of the customs prevalent in preliterate social groups.

social attitude: an opinion or a readiness for action on an issue or a choice.

social class: status based upon similarities of an arbitrary type. such as family, income, or affiliations and often grouped as upper-upper, lower-upper; upper, middle, and lower-middle; and upper and lower-lower-class.

social climate: the characteristic procedures, beliefs, and outlooks of a group of persons, sometimes classified as authoritarian, laissez faire, or democratic.

social contract: (Hobbes) the tacit agreement whereby men, who are by nature self-seeking and ruthless, assign to the monarch the power to curb each of them and thereby avoid incessant hostilities.

social decrement: the loss in quality of behavior as a result of a co-acting group, even though the amount of output may be increased.

social distance: pertaining to the relative strength of opposition or prejudice held against minority groups.

Social Distance Scale: a list of minority groups to be rated on seven degrees of relative intimacy to which the testee would admit them.

social dynamics: (Comte) the conditions which relate to social progress.

social facilitation: enhancement of behavior by the presence of co-acting or observing groups.

social increment: enhancement of output when other persons are present, as compared with output when working alone.

social intelligence: ability to work in harmony with others, to give and accept directions tactfully, in a democratic manner.

Social Intelligence Test: an attempt to measure such social abilities as humor, memory for names and faces; common sense; everyday social observations, and recognition of mental states in others (Moss, 1927).

social psychology: that branch of general psychology which deals with behavior as it relates to other persons.

social sciences: syn. *human relations;* all the sciences which pertain to group activities (e.g., history, economics, psychology, sociology, political sciences, etc.).

social statistics: (Comte) the conditions which relate to social equilibrium.

social status: the relative position of the individual in the group hierarchy or "pecking order."

socialization: the processes whereby the child learns or introjects the folkways and the mores of the group.

socialized or adapted communication: (Piaget) that in which the other person's point of view and interests are fully taken into account.

socio-economic status: the relative position of a person evaluated from the standpoints of income, family background, occupation, and memberships.

sociogram: a chart depicting the interplay of attraction and rejection among the members of a social group (Moreno).

sociology: the science dealing with social groups and institutions —their origins, their characteristics, and their persistence.

sociometry: measurements of acceptance-antagonism, attitudes, feelings, and other quantitative aspects of individuals studied as members of a social group.

sociopathic personality disorder: any deviation from community norms which is considered to be objectionable or criminal.

socius: (H. S. Sullivan) the personality as defined in terms of its formation as a social product.

sodomy: insertion of the penis into the anus.

solipsism: the hypothetical, metaphysical point of view that ultimately no knowledge can be certain except a conviction that the knower alone has existence.

soma: the body.

somato-: Greek combining form meaning *body*.

somatogenic: of bodily origin.

somatoplasm: the totality of all cells, with the exception of germ cells.

somatopsychic delusion: an unfounded belief pertaining to one's own body.

somatosplanchnic: pertaining to the body and to the visceral organs.

somatotonia: (Sheldon) a temperament characterized by liking for adventure and risk and for vigorous physical endeavors.

somatotype: (Sheldon) "the pathway through which the individual will travel under normal circumstances" and which may be patterned as ectomorphic, mesomorphic, or endomorphic, and the gradations among them.

somesthesia: syn. *common sensibility;* the totality of vague, general cutaneous sensations, and of sensations from receptors in muscles and viscera, as well as from many other indefinite sensory data.

somnambulism: sleep-walking.

somniloquism: talking in sleep.

sonance: fusion of pitches which are arranged in succession, as in a tune.

sone: a subjective unit in judgments of intensity of sound.

sonometer: apparatus consisting of strings or wires which, when plucked, furnish stimuli for study of elementary auditory experiences.

soothsayer: one who, allegedly, has supernatural powers to foretell the future.

sophism: an argument based upon a subtle fallacy.

soporific drug: one that induces sleep (e.g., a barbiturate).

s-o-r: (Woodworth) stimulus-organism-response.

sorting test: a measure of intactness of conceptual thinking, in which the testee is required to arrange objects in simple and in abstract categories (e.g., the Vigotsky blocks).

soul: in rational psychology, the divine principle or immortal nature of man.

soul image: in Jung's psychology, the deepest part of the unconscious and comprised of the animus (male aspect) and the anima (female aspect).

sound cage: apparatus for determining ability to locate auditory stimuli and to measure the degrees of accuracy and error in the different planes.

sound perimetry: locating the spatial aspects of a field in various parts of which the individual hears auditory stimuli and tries to indicate their precise source.

sound spectroscope: apparatus which transforms sound waves into a visible form.

sour: one of the basic gustatory qualities; an acid or tart quality of taste.

sour-grapes mechanism: (Aesop's fable of the fox and the grapes) a form of self-deception in which the individual tries to make himself believe that he does not want that which he actually does want.

space perception: awareness of relative positions, distances, and so on, in any sense modality; awareness of the extent of any given stimulus.

spaced learning periods: repetitions at intervals, with interpolated rest periods or other activities, of the material to be learned, rather than learning by concentrated practice.

span: the number of separate items that can be perceived at one time; the length of time that a child is able to hold attention upon an activity.

spasm: an involuntary contraction of muscles.

spasmophemia: disorder in the rhythm of speech caused by spasms in the muscles involved (e.g., stuttering, stammering).

spastic: one who, owing to brain lesions, lacks normal coördinations and suffers from tonic spasms of large skeletal muscles (usually).

spastic gait: jerky manner of locomotion, with the legs held closely together and the toes dragged along.

spay: to render the female animal incapable of bearing young.

Spearman footrule correlation: a measure of the degree of relationship between two arrays of scores, calculated by the formula — $R = 6\Sigma G/(N^2 - 1)$, where G is the positive differences in rank and N is the number of cases.

Spearman-Brown prophecy formula: an equation for estimating the way a test would be affected by the addition or the subtraction of items.

special abilities test: a measure of proficiency in one or more specific tasks (e.g., clerical or mechanical work).

special aptitudes test: one which measures a person's likelihood of success, usually after training, in such fields as music, art, clerical tasks, mechanical work, and the like, as contrasted with his general intelligence.

special education: attention to the handicapped (usually) in learning the standard curriculum of the school.

species: in biology, a class immediately below a genus or sub-genus and above a subspecies; in logic, the class to which the term belongs, the term in question to be distinguished from all other members of the genus by a differentia.

specific energies doctrine: (Johannes Müller) the theory that each sensory nerve fiber transmits a different type of nervous energy and that the nerve fibers, therefore, mediate the sensory experience.

specificity: in Pavlovian conditioning, the stage in the conditioning of the reflex in which one, and only one, conditioned stimulus elicits the response (as compared to the irradiation during the early stages of the conditioning).

specious present: (William James) the mid-interval between the preceding and the next transitive or substantive state in the stream of thought.

specter (spectre): in occultism, a ghost or phantom.

spectral hues: colors observed when a prism fragments white light; the range of hues from red through bluish green.

spectrometer: apparatus used to identify the spectral hues.

spectroscopy: the measuring of wavelengths; the determining of Fraunhofer lines in the spectrum.

spectrum: wave lengths arranged in order (the visible spectrum for the human eye, about 390 mμ to 780 mμ).

speech area: syn. *Broca's motor speech area;* the region in the third convolution of the frontal lobe (located in the left hemisphere in right-handed persons).

speech block: a tonic-clonic spasm in the muscles used in talking; stuttering.

speech disorder: any form of aphasia which affects talk or a serious defect in the quality of the voice (aphonia, dysphonia).

speed test: a measure scored by the amount done within the time limits imposed.

speed-up: any method whereby workers are required to increase output, usually without additional compensation.

spell: in occultism, a magical influence whereby supernormal effects are produced.

Spencerianism: the philosophical teachings of Herbert Spencer, who sought to rewrite philosophy from the standpoint of an adherent to Darwin's biology.

sperm: the male reproductive cell.

spermatozoa: semen; male reproductive cells.

spermo-: Greek combining form meaning *seed.*

spherical aberration of the eye: astigmatism.

sphincter: a circular band of muscle fibers closing or contracting an orifice of the body.

sphincter type: in psychoanalysis, one who is either a miser or a spendthrift as a direct result of premature and coercive bowel training in infancy.

sphygmo-: Greek combining form meaning *heart-beat, pulse.*

sphygmomanometer: apparatus for measurement of blood pressure.

sphygmometer: syn. *sphygmograph;* apparatus for recording pulse rate.

spike: In electroencephalography, a peak in the recordings of brain waves.

spinal accessory: the 11th cranial nerve.

spinal canal: the foramena in the chain of vertebrae which contain the spinal cord.

spinal column: the chain of vertebrae forming the backbone.

spinal cord: the prolonged bundle of nerve fibers situated within the spinal canal.

spinal nerves: the thirty-one pairs of nerves which emerge from the various levels of the spinal cord.

spinal reflex: a response mediated by that portion of the central nervous system lying below the medulla oblongata.

spinal roots: those portions of the spinal nerves within or immediately adjacent to the spinal cord, the motor or efferent root emerging from the ventral (front) portion, and the sensory from the posterior (rear) portion of the cord.

spine: backbone; a sharp-pointed projection on the body.

Spinozism: in philosophical psychology, a systematic exposition, in mathematical equations, of a theory (idealistic) of behavior.

spiral omnibus test: a psychological test or measure consisting of an admixture of types of items which are arranged in ascending order of difficulty.

spiritism: occultism.

spritualism: idealistic psychology; occultism.

spiro-: Latin combining form meaning *respiration.*

spirochete (spirochaete) treponema: a micro-organism causing syphilis, and when it invades the cortex of the cerebrum, paresis.

spirograph: apparatus for recording movements of the chest in respiration.

spirometer: apparatus for measuring vital capacity defined as the volume of breath exhaled after the chest has been filled completely.

splanchnic area: the viscera

splanchno-:   Greek combining form meaning *viscera.*

split personality: a descriptive term referring to the dissociation between various parts of psychic life, one often said to have amnesia for the other (e.g., Dr. Jeykll and Mr. Hyde).

spontaneity: freedom or flexibility of behavior, with no self-consciousness or embarrassment in the presence of others.

spontaneity training: (Moreno) experience in acting out conflicts pertaining to interpersonal relationships (sociodrama) or mental conflicts (psychodrama) under the guidance of skilled therapists.

spontaneous behavior: syn. *voluntary action;* responses which are self-initiated by the individual.

spontaneous recovery: the tendency of a conditioned reflex to reappear after experimental extinction, provided that a rest period has been interpolated (Pavlov).

sport: in genetics, a mutation.

spurious correlation: in statistics, an association which appears mathematically to indicate a relationship but which actually is the result of uncontrolled factors in the study.

spurt: relative increase in speed or quality of output when the task is commenced or when it nears the close or reaches the goal.

squint: in ophthalmology, strabismus, cross-eyedness.

SR Psychology: any systematic exposition of psychological facts and theories which emphasizes stimulus-response bonds; Connectionism; Watsonism; Pavlovianism.

SRA tests: psychological tests and measures copyrighted and published by Science Research Associates.

stable affects: controlled feelings and emotions; mature socialized affectivity.

stabilimeter: apparatus for measuring sway of body.

stadiometer: apparatus for measuring height when standing or sitting.

stammering: involuntary tonic spasms of speech muscles.

standard deviation: the square root of the deviations squared from the mean of the distribution (in a normal frequency distribution, the middle 68.34% of the scores); $\sigma = \sqrt{\dfrac{\Sigma d^2}{N}}$,

where d is the deviation and N the number of cases.

standard error: any one of a number of statistical procedures to indicate the difference between the obtained and the true (or theoretical) distribution of scores.

standard score: a test score expressed in terms of units of the standard deviation of all the scores on the measure.

standardization of a test or measure: the process of making explicit and repeatable the directions, arrangements, materials, and scoring procedures for any given psychological inquiry.

Stanford-Binet: the 1916 edition, the 1937 revision, or the 1961 revision of the Binet-Simon intelligence scale for use with American children; the Stanford Revision of the Binet Simon Scale.

stanines: units dividing the population into nine groups, all but stanine 1 and stanine 9 being spaced in half-sigmas, with the mean at 5. Thus:

Stanine	1	2	3	4	5	6	7	8	9
% in Stanine	4	7	12	17	20	17	12	7	4

stapes: syn. the *stirrup;* one of the small bones located within the middle ear.

startle reaction: an involved response of sudden changes in posture, muscle tensions, and autonomic balance when the individual is unexpectedly stimulated by a loud noise.

static sensibility: the adjustment of the body to gravitational pulls from sensory cues arising in the vestibular of the inner ear; also known as the vestibular or the equilibrium sense.

statistic: any variable which may be subjected to, or which results from, mathematical treatments of the data.

statistics: the application of techniques of mathematics to the treatment of data, their classification and organization, as a basis for inferences and conclusions.

status: a person's position in the social hierarchy as determined by family, wealth, occupation, title, educational level, and the like.

status epilepticus: a rapid succession of convulsive seizures, usually culminating in the death of the patient.

STDCR: in the *Guilford Inventory of Factors,* social introversion (seclusiveness), thinking introversion (reflectiveness), depression (unhappiness, depression), cycloid disposition (emotional instability), and rhathymia (carefreeness, happy-go-lucky disposition).

step interval: syn. *class interval;* a grouping of scores between a sequence of convenient units within the total array of the scores (e.g., 80-89, 90-99, etc.).

stereognosis: perception of shapes of objects by feeling of them.

stereoscope: a simple instrument used in effecting a fusion of slightly different images perceived simultaneously by the right and the left eye, respectively.

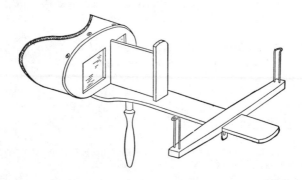

Figure 29. A hand stereoscope, used in studies of visual perception.

stereotype: an oversimplified, and usually a biased, classification of perceptual or ideational data (e.g., the stereotype of "the foreigner in the group").

stereotyped behavior: inflexible, purposeless, nonadjustive repetition of activities, words or phrases, or thoughts.

sterile: unable to procreate.

sterilization: usually, salpingectomy in women and vasectomy in men, with more drastic methods restricted to animals (e.g., castration); rendering the individual incapable of procreation.

sthenia: physical strength; muscle tonus and general physical health.

Stilling Test: a method used in detecting weaknesses in color vision.

stimulation: the arousal of a response by the application of some form of physical, chemical, or mechanical energy to a sense organ (receptor).

stimulus: any form of energy which arouses a response.

stimulus-bound response: a reaction, usually unsatisfying, which results when the person does not "go out of the field" to respond efficiently.

stimulus generalization: the elicitation of a conditioned response by stimuli like the stimulus regularly used in the conditioning process.

stimulus-response psychology: any systematic exposition of facts and principles of behavior which emphasizes the receptor-effector mechanism, with mediation by the nervous system.

stirrup: one of the small bones in the middle ear; stapes.

stochastic: with an increase in processes, events, or other data, the findings tending to resemble true probability, thus reducing the need to correct for a limited size of the sampling.

stoical attitude: unaffected by pain or pleasure.

stoichiology: that branch of biology concerned with the study of the constitution or the elements of tissues.

strabismus: cross-eyedness; squint.

stratified sampling: a random sampling of the population divided into proportional representations of each class or stratum.

stream of thought: the sequence or flow of mental contents, never twice the same at any successive moment.

strephosymbolia: the perception of the visual field as if it were reversed by a mirror.

stress interview: appraisal of the interviewee's ability to cope with attempts to induce discouragement, resentment, anger, and the like.

stressor: anything which may, or does, injure the organism.

striate body: syn. *corpus striatum;* one of the pair of large ganglia (the caudate and the lenticular nuclei) located in the cerebrum.

striped muscles: syn. *striate muscles;* the skeletal musculature.

stroboscopic effect: the illusion of movement when the light waves are periodically interrupted, as when a series of pictures is viewed in rapid succession; the Plateau effect.

stroke: a sudden seizure.

Strong Vocational Interest Blank: syn. *Strong VIB;* a self-administering series of choices among likes and dislikes for the purposes of discovering similarities or differences with interest patterns of those in representative occupational fields.

Structuralism: a system of psychology which experimentally investigates mental contents (Wundt) or the structure of the mind (Titchener).

structure: to organize more or less inchoate, amorphous material, as in a projective test (e.g., to attach meanings to inkblots).

Student: the pseudonym of W. S. Gosset, who first perfected the method of calculating *t*-ratios, a *t*-ratio being the ratio of a statistic to its standard error in small-samples analyses of scores.

studium generale: an informal organization of professors and students assembled for instruction in one of the mediaeval universities.

study: the published or verbally reported findings of an investigation.

stuporous melancholia: the most extreme form of a manic-depressive psychosis, depressed phase.

stuttering: syn. *dyslalia;* spasmosdic interruptions, blockings, and repetitions in the flow of speech.

style of life: (Adler) the manner in which a person strives to attain the goal of superiority and which determines what the individual learns, perceives, and feels, to the neglect of all else.

stylus maze: slots through which the subject in an experiment moves a stylus from the starting point to the goal, usually while blindfolded, and thereby illustrates the principles of trial-and-error learning.

sub-: Latin prefix meaning *to a lesser degree, beneath.*

subception: a preliminary, unconscious readiness for a perceptual discrimination (McCleary and Lazarus, 1949).

subconsciousness: mental activities or contents which are outside the threshold for awareness; that which is only partly conscious.

subcortical nervous system: all of the nervous system lying below the hemispheres of the cerebrum.

subculture: a grouping of persons with respect to special customs which bind them together, though they are at the same time members of the larger society of their region or nation (e.g., the Mennonites).

subjective: not directly observable by another person but accessible through the individual's own verbal report or introspection.

sublimation: in psychoanalysis, the redirection of infantile sexual aims towards activities which are socially approved.

subliminal: below the threshold for normal sensory excitation.

submissiveness: on the dominance-submission dimension of personality, as attitude of compliance, nonassertiveness, and yielding to other persons.

substitution test: a test which requires rapid substitution of letters or other symbols in accordance with a key.

subtest: a logical division of a more or less lengthy test.

subvocal behavior: implicit, or subdued, movements of the musculature involved in speech.

suggestibility: the condition of uncritical acceptance of directions or opinions given by another person.

suggestion: any form of behavior (e.g., speech, posture, gestures, etc.) by one person which induces unreflective, compliant responses in another; (self-suggestion) a mental set induced without critical analysis.

summation of stimuli: the reinforcing effects of successive stimulations, none of which by itself is adequate to produce a response but all of which, cumulatively, elicit one.

super-: Latin prefix meaning *above*.

superego: in psychoanalysis, the ideals or standards introjected from parents or parent surrogates and making up the ego-ideal and the conscience; the sum total of self-critical, self-judgmental functions, partly conscious but mainly unconscious.

superfectation: conception while already pregnant.

superhuman: behavior that exceeds the normal limits of human endeavor.

superiority feeling (or complex): (Adler) the unwarranted assumption of superiority as a means of compensating for a sense of personal inadequacy.

supernatural: not to be understood by any empirical approach; hence, miraculous or beyond the laws of nature.

supernormal intelligence: mental ability above that manifested by about 80% of the general population, as measured by standard intelligence tests, rate of progress through the curriculum, or judgments of qualified persons.

supersonic: having a wavelength of more than 30,000 double vibrations a second (for those with very keen auditory sensitivity; for normal adults, 20,000 and above.

superstition: an unfounded belief which, in folklore, may persist for a long time (e.g. the superstitions about effects of the moon upon mental patients).

supportive counseling: encouragement and positive aid to the person in difficulties, the psychoclinician temporarily taking a semidirective, advisory role.

suppression: conscious inhibition of a response.

supra-: Latin prefix meaning *above.*

suprachorioid: loose connective tissues lying between the chorioid and the sclerotic membranes of the eyeball.

supraclusion: the condition of teeth projecting beyond the normal plane.

supradrenalin: syn. *adrenaline;* the hormone from the adrenal glands.

supralabial: relating to the upper lip.

supraliminal: above the threshold, or limit, of sensitivity.

supramental: the head above the area of the chin.

suprarenal: syn. *adrenal;* one of the glands (endocrines) at the upper end of the kidneys (in human beings).

supraspinal: lying above the spinal column.

surdity: the condition of deafness, of any pronounced degree.

surrogate: anything that both stands for something else and elicits a response more or less appropriate to what it stands for (e.g., a foster parent, a cue).

surround: the environment, both actual and psychological, which elicits reactions at any given time.

survey: a tentative inquiry or a sampling (e.g., a market survey to determine attitudes toward a product).

survival value: in Darwinian theory, a trait or a behavioral characteristic which favors individual or species perpetuation in the struggle for existence.

suspicion complex: popularly, the belief that enemies are seeking to thwart or destroy the individual; a paranoidal outlook on the world.

Sydenham's chorea: syn. *St. Vitus dance;* involuntary, spasmodic twitchings.

syllogism: the formal expression of an act of deductive reasoning from a major premise, through a minor premise, to a conclusion, which may then be proved or disproved by the rules of logic.

Sylvian fissure: the large fissure, or sulcus, separating the temporal lobe from the parietal and the frontal lobes of the cerebral hemisphere.

symbiosis: the association between parasite and host; the association of two or more different species in one environment, the results usually being advantageous to each but sometimes antipathetic or harmful.

symbol: anything which stands for anything else; in psychoanalysis, anything which stands for an unconscious wish.

symbolization: in psychoanalysis, the utilization of, or seeking for, symbols to displace libidinal or latent content over to objects which may be more or less tolerated by the ego and/ or the superego of the dreamer.

symmetrophobia: dislike of symmetry.

sympathetic nervous system: one of the divisions of the autonomic nervous system, said to be functionally opposed to the parasympathetic portion of the autonomic nervous system (Cannon).

symphysodactyly: joined or fused fingers.

symptom: any observed characteristic or change indicating the presence or onset of a pathological condition.

syn-: Greek prefix meaning *with, at the same time.*

synapse: the point at which the nervous impulse passes from the axone of one neurone to the dendrite of the next.

synchronous: at the same time.

syncope: partial or complete loss of consciousness (as in a seizure).

syncretic thinking: (Piaget) the child's way of bringing together illogical data (from the adult point of view) into reasoning, without being aware of the faulty logic involved.

syncretism of perception: (Piaget) the bringing together of unlike elements (from an adult point of view) into a single act of perceiving.

syndrome: a group of symptoms.

synergy: the reinforcement of one activity by another; the normal action of the various cooperating organs of the body.

syn(a)esthesia: the concomitant association of one sensation with another that is elicited by a stimulus (e.g., colors associated with sounds).

syntality: the characteristics of individual behavior which are shared by the group as a whole in a consistent, predictable manner.

syntonia: the condition of great emotional responsiveness.

systematic psychology: the study of various formulations of facts, methods, and principles of psychology into a coherent, unified organization.

systematized delusions: fallacious beliefs which, were the premises granted, have a "private logic" or internal coherence, but which, tested by reality, have no basis whatsoever.

systolic phase: the contractive phase of heart beat.

Szondi Test: a projective technique using 48 pictures of criminals and psychiatric types to be classified as like-dislike.

t: the ratio of a score to its standard error.

tabes: syn. *tabes dorsalis, locomotor ataxia;* deterioration of the posterior columns of the spinal cord.

table: syn. *tabular arrangement;* an orderly arrangement of scores.

taboo (tabu):   that which is forbidden by the group mores.

tabophobia: syn. *ataxiophobia;* persistent and irrational fear of wasting away.

tabula rasa: (Locke) the "blank-page condition" of the mind of the infant.

tachistoscope: apparatus for rapid presentation of visual stimuli.

tachy-:   Greek combining form meaning *swift.*

tachycardia: excessively rapid heart beat.

tachylalia: syn. *tachyphemia, tachyphasia, tachyphrasia;* rapid manner of talking as if due to a "press of ideas."

tachypne(o)a: syn. *polypnea;* rapid rate of breathing.

tactile: syn. *tactual;* pertaining to the sense of touch (pressure).

tactometer: syn. (*a*)*esthesiometer;* compass-like points for determining two-point cutaneous sensitivity.

tactus: the sense of touch or pressure.

taedium vitae: neurotic boredom and indifference.

tail: either extreme of a frequency curve or distribution or the scores lying there.

talent: unusual ability, especially in one of the fields of the creative arts.

talion principle: in psychoanalysis, the exaction of retribution by the id or the superego which causes unconscious foreboding or dread as punishments for tabooed fantasies.

talipes: clubfoot; also known as cyllosis.

talipomania: gross deformity of the hand.

talisman: in folklore, a potent charm which produces supranormal effects.

tally: a method of checking items or scores (e.g.,/or/for 3 and 5, respectively).

talology: syn. *taxonomy;* classification of data.

tambor (tambour): a shallow cup with a membrane which responds to pressures, and which thus activates the stylus recording the events (e.g., changes in heart beat).

tantrum: irrational, violent anger reaction.

tanyphonia: an abnormally weak or thin voice.

taphophilia: abnormal interest in funerals and cemeteries.

taphophobia: morbid terror of being buried alive.

tapping test: a performance measure of the number of taps made per unit of time with a stylus or a measure of immediate memory span in which a cube is used to duplicate sequences of taps made by the examiner (e.g., in the Knox Cube Test).

tarantism: in folklore, an abnormal desire to dance, supposedly caused by the bite of a tarantula.

target test: syn. *aiming test; a* measure of hand-eye coordination in which the testee is required to hit a small target with a stylus.

tartar type: mongoloid imbecility.

Tartini tone: a difference tone; the third tone heard when two notes are sounded continuously.

task: any action that is assigned or is self-imposed.

taste: syn. *gustation;* the chemical sensitivity of the taste buds.

taste buds: receptors for gustatory sensations.

taste tetrahedron: (Henning) a graphic representation of the relationships among the four basic, salient taste sensations: sweet, sour, bitter, and salty.

TAT: the Murray-Morgan Thematic Apperception Test.

tau effect: misperceptions of spatial distances as a function of the time spent in observing and judging them.

tautophone: (Skinner) a reproduction of indistinct or meaningless sounds to which the testee is asked to attach coherence and/or meaning.

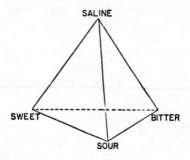

Figure 30. Henning's taste tetrahedron.

taxis: syn. *tropism;* (Verworn) a simple reaction by a plant or a protozoon.

taxonomy: syn. *taxology;* the orderly classification of data or specimens.

Taylorism: the use of motion studies and other procedures to speed up output and to reduce costs.

Tay-Sachs disease: amaurotic family idocy; congenital blindness with mental deficiency.

TE: trial and error.

techno-: Greek combining form meaning *art or skill.*

technocracy: the management of the group by qualified engineers or by the methods of engineers.

technology: the practical applications of science.

technopsychology: syn. *psychotechnology;* psychology and its methods applied to business and industry.

tecnoctonia: infanticide.

tecnology: child study.

tectorial membrane: syn. *tectorium;* the membraneous tissue of the organ of Corti.

tegument: syn. *integument;* any enveloping membrane.

tele: the attraction or the aversion existing between two persons.

tele-: Greek combining form meaning *distant.*

telegnosis: clairvoyance.

telegony: in folklore, the influence of a father upon children born subsequently by other fathers to the woman in the case.

telekinesis: in occultism, the movement of objects effected by paranormal means.

telencephalon: the forebrain.

telenergy: in occultism, the paranormal force employed by the medium to move objects.

teleology: the doctrine that natural processes are intelligently and purposefully directed towards ends.

telepathy: in parapsychology, thought transference.

telephone theory: (Rutherford) the view that tonal analysis occurs in the brain, not in the inner ear.

telesteroscope: lenses which enhance the high-relief effect.

telesthesia: in occultism, the psychic equivalent of a sensation, but without the mediation of any known sense organ or receptor.

teletactor: apparatus, used in education of the deaf, which converts sound waves into tactile stimulus patterns.

teletherapy: in occultism, bringing help to an ill person through psychic influences emanating from a medium some distance away.

telic: that which is purposefully directed towards ends.

telic continuum: the J-curve-type behavior when institutional pressures are strong, most persons then conforming, with few dissenters.

telodendron: the terminal process of a dendrite.

telophase: the stage of mitosis at which two separate cells, each with a nucleus, are formed.

temperament: in ancient psychology, the result of interbalances among the four humors; now, the enduring quality of affective functions and/or constitutional determinants.

temperature sense: responses mediated by warmth and cold receptors.

temperature spots: receptors for warmth and cold.

temporal lobe: that part of the cerebrum just below the fissure of Sylvius and in front of the occipital lobe.

tendon: a fibrous cord attaching a muscle to a bone.

tendon reflex: a muscular contraction elicited by a sharp tap on a tendon.

teniophobia (taeniophobia): obsessive fear of acquiring tapeworms.

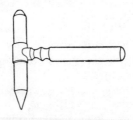

Figure 31. A temperature cylinder used in studies of sensations of warmth and cold spots.

Tenon's capsule: the connective tissues of the eyeball.

tension: the degree of tautness in a muscle or muscle group; also, the behavioral effects of worry, excitement, strain, or frustration.

tension-relaxation: in Wundt's tridimensional theory of feelings, the dimension of strain vs. ease.

tensor: a ligament or tendon that causes a muscular contraction.

tenth nerve: the pneumogastric (or vagus).

teratology: the study of monsters and of persons with gross congenital deformities.

tergum: the back.

term: a substantive word, phrase, or symbol.

terminal arborization: tree-like branching at the end of a nerve fiber.

terminal lag: persistence of physiological activities in the receptor or sense organ after the stimulus has ceased to be operative.

test: any technique for validating or invalidating an hypothesis; in mental measurement, any task (or series of tasks) that yields a score which may be compared with scores made by other individuals.

test age: the score on any given test interpreted by reference to a table of age norms, thus indicating the chronological age at which the average person achieves a similar score.

test battery: a group of tests administered seriatim in order to obtain a total, or average, score which may indicate a person's fitness or aptitude (e.g., for pilot training) or achievement (e.g., college entrance tests).

test ceiling: the highest level of difficulty represented by the items comprising a test or measure.

test floor: the easiest items which, presumably, all who take the test are able to pass and for which, on many tests, credit is allotted without administering them.

test item: any single statement, problem, or other exercise included in a psychological test or measure.

testectomy: syn. *orchidectomy;* surgical excision of the testes.

testee: syn. *subject;* the individual who is, or was, tested.

testes (singular testis): the male sex organs enclosed in the scrotum.

testosterone: male sex hormone.

tetrad equation: (Spearman) intercorrelations among a set of four tests for the purpose of locating presence or absence of a single common factor.

texis: child bearing.

TF test: a true-false test.

thalamus: syn. *optic thalamus;* a large subdivision of the diencephalon, which is said to mediate pain sensations and affective responses and to transmit to the cerebral cortex nervous impulses from various sense organs.

thanatos instinct (or principle): in psychoanalysis, a complex pattern of instinctual tendencies leading to self-destruction and death (as the antithesis of the eros instinct); the death wish or nirvana principle.

thaumaturgy: in folklore, the use of magic or suprahuman powers.

thebaism: opium addiction.

theelin: a hormone from the ovary.

theism: monotheism; belief in one, supreme God.

Thematic Apperception Test (TAT): the Murray-Morgan projective technique consisting of a series of pictures which elicit fantasies or stories expressive of the presses and the needs of the teller.

theory: a coherent explanation or unifying principle which has undergone some validation and which may be applied to many data, but which does not have the status of a law (though having more validity than an hypothesis).

theotherapy: historically, the cure of disease through mediation by the gods.

therapeutic: palliative or curative.

therapy: any procedure which serves to ease, to palliate, or to cure a disorder or personality maladjustment and which is administered by a professionally qualified expert.

thermal sensation: a response to stimulation of warmth spots in the skin; also, the sensation of heat when warmth, cold, and pain spots are stimulated simultaneously (Altruz).

thermalgesia: anomalous pain when a stimulus for warmth is applied to the skin.

therman(a)esthesia: insensitivity to warmth or heat.

thermesthesiometer: apparatus for measuring sensitivity to warmth and heat.

thermo-: Greek combining form meaning *heat.*

thermoreceptor: a warmth spot (and by extension a cold spot) in the skin.

thermotherapy: the treatment of disorders by artificially raising the body temperature.

-thermy: Greek combining form meaning *the production of heat* (as in diathermy).

thero-: Greek combining form meaning *wild animal.*

therology: the science dealing with mammals.

theromorphy: in folklore, a reversion to the form, or some aspect thereof, of a lower animal, with the attributes possessed by the animal.

thesis: an extended treatise; a proposition to be defended by argument or evidence.

thigmesthesia: sensitivity to touch or pressure; aphia; haptic sensivity.

thigmo-: Greek combining form meaning *touch.*

thighmoan (a)esthesia: insensitivity to touch or pressure.

thigmohyper(a) esthesia: intense sensitivity to pressure or touch, as of the mere weight of clothing on the body.

thinking: a broad term variously defined as phantasy, reasoning, creativity, as-if behavior (Vaihinger), implicit speech, ideational activity, problem solving, judging, planning and the like; (behavioristically) activity in response to a situation not objectively present to sense organs.

thirst: syn. *diposia, dipsia;* dryness of mouth; need for water.

thoracicolumbar portion of the autonomic nervous system: syn. *sympathetic portion;* that part of the autonomic nervous system (especially the ganglia) in the region of the chest and trunk.

thorax: the chest.

Thorndike theory of intelligence: (as opposed to Spearman's *g* factor) the doctrine that intelligence actually consists of specific abilities.

thought reading: inferences about a person's thoughts by observing facial expressions, sensing minimal muscular movements, or (in occultism) having supranormal powers.

thought transference: in occultism, communication without the use of any procedures known to science.

threat: any situation real or imagined, present or anticipated, which arouses fears and tensions.

threshold: syn *limen,* the point at which a sense organ just barely responds to a stimulus and below or above which no response is elicited.

thrombosis: the stoppage of a blood vessel by a clot (thrombus).

throw-back: syn. *atavism;* reversion to a lower form of organism (e.g., in folklore, the pointed ear or Darwinian tubercle).

Thurstone Attitude Scales: syn. *Thurstone-type attitude scales;* statements for which score values have been equated by the method of equal-appearing intervals by many judges 'and which, therefore, appraise the strength of attitudes towards any given issue (e.g., Thurstone-Chave Scale for Measuring Attitude toward the Church, 1929).

Thurstone Temperament Schedule: a personality inventory, developed by factor analysis, to appraise status on seven traits (1950).

Thurstone Test of Mental Alertness: a short measure, of the spiral-omnibus type, which has been used to select higher-level personnel (1952).

thymia: feelings, emotions, moods, and temperaments considered together.

-thymia: Greek combining form meaning the *affective condition.*

thymogenic: a disorder having its origins in feelings, emotions, and desires.

thymus: a gland of uncertain functions lying in the upper part of the thorax, and usually atrophying at the time of puberty.

thyroid: syn. *thyreoid* (preferred by some); an endocrine gland, shield-shaped, lying below the pharynx and on each side of the windpipe.

thyroidism: the morbid conditions associated with thyroid dysfunctions (e.g., cretinism and myxedema with underfunctioning, and exothalmic goiter with hypertrophy of the thyroid).

tic: a habit spasm (e.g., facial grimaces) or twitchings in small groups of muscles.

tickle: a complex, spasmodic reaction, usually pleasurable, when certain cutaneous regions are stimulated by stroking or unexpected pressures.

timbre: the overtones which accompany the fundamental tone; hence the qualitative aspects of an auditory sensation whereby different instruments and voices are recognized by differences in resonance.

time-limit test: syn. *speed test;* a series of items, often relatively easy, taken under such time limits that no one could do all of them, individual differences being therefore determined by the number correctly finished.

time-power test: a measure in which the items are usually arranged in degree of difficulty and for which time limits are also imposed.

time-sampling: observations, usually at randomized intervals and for brief periods, of an individual's behavior or performance (often facilitated by check lists or recording devices).

time sense: syn. *time perception;* proficiency in judging the extent of periods of time or in fractionating temporal intervals (the score being corrected for guessing).

tinnitus aurium: syn. *akoasm;* a ringing in the ears; a subjective auditory sensation.

tint: the result of mixing white with a primary or an intermediate color (Hering).

tissue: a collection of living cells which perform some physiological function (e.g., nerve tissue, muscle tissue).

tolerance: the heightened resistance of the body to drugs as a function of prolonged addiction; in social psychology, the ability to suffer, to put up with, to live happily among, persons of radically divergent outlooks or ethnic backgrounds.

tonal attributes: (Titchener) the pitch, the intensity, the duration, and the extensity (volume) of a tone (or noise).

tonal gap (island, lacuna): an area in the range of auditory stimuli of varying frequencies where the person hears nothing. (Some writers speak of the tonal island as an area of auditory sensitivity where elsewhere deafness exists.)

tone: the sensation elicited by sound waves of regular vibration rates; also the characteristic degree of muscular contraction of the body and the affective quality of an experience.

tonic spasm: sudden and intense contraction of a muscle.

tonicity: the normal amount of contraction within a muscle or group of muscles.

tontriphobia: morbid fear of thunder.

tonus: in physiology, the amount of contraction in a muscle or a muscle group; by some writers also, the amount of mental energy or drive.

tool subjects: those branches of the curriculum which must be mastered before advanced studies may be undertaken (e.g., reading, writing, arithmetic).

topesthesia: locomotion mediated by the sense of touch only.

topoalgia: a referred or anomalous pain.

topological psychology: (Lewin) the systematic exposition of facts and principles based upon concepts drawn from geometry and vectors.

toponarcosis: syn. *topo-anesthesia;* localized region of insensitivity.

toponymics: in cultural anthropology, the study of names of persons and localities.

torsion: a twisting movement of the body.

totalitarian group: one which does not countenance dissenters or minorities.

totem: in cultural anthropology, any object that symbolizes the gods of the tribe and that brings the tribe into personal relationships with them.

totemic principle: in cultural anthropology, the magical powers attributed to the animal or the object venerated as a totem.

touch: popularly, cutaneous sensitivity.

touch spot: a small area that is hypersensitive (compared to surrounding areas) to light pressure.

toxanemia: syn. *toxemia;* poisonous substances in the bloodstream.

toxic: poisonous.

toxicopathy: any disorder caused by poison; a toxic psychosis.

toxiphobia: morbid fear of being poisoned.

trace reflex: in classical conditioning, the establishment of a CR by presenting the new stimulus a brief interval before the adequate stimulus.

tracheophyma: a goiter.

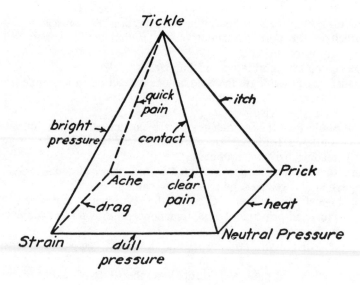

Figure 31a. Titchener's touch pyramid.

tract: a bundle of nerve fibers; a system of related parts (e.g., the alimentary tract).

trade test: a brief measure of a prospective employee's mastery of the skills required for a job; a worksample test.

traditional: in cultural anthropology, that which is orally transmitted from generation to generation; pertaining to long-established folkways and mores.

train: to impart skills (as distinct from "to educate"); a sequence of related responses (as in an action train).

trait: any distinctive physical or psychological characteristic of an individual or a group which may be shared (a common trait) or be unique.

trait-complex: in cultural anthropology, any related group of characteristics, modes of behavior, or systems of beliefs which prevail within the group.

trance: a sleeplike condition.

trans-: Latin prefix meaning *across*.

transactional psychology: the systematic exposition of facts and principles which emphasize the interpersonal relationships or the exchanges which take place in behavior.

transcendence: in philosophy, that which exceeds the limits of human understanding.

transcendentalism: (Kant) the doctrine that innate knowledge of time and space exists a priori; hence, that empirical studies of perceptual organization are fruitless.

transcortical: relating to nerve fibers which connect various parts of the cerebral cortex.

transect: to cut tissues across the longer of the two axes.

transfer by generalization: the gains in skills or understandings which may be carried over to a new assignment because of the broad principles which have been adduced by the learner in previous experiences.

transfer of training: improvement in an unpracticed function which results from previous learning (said to take place because of identical elements or because of the generalizations which have been made by the learner).

transference: in psychoanalysis, the displacement of the libido from some infantile outlet to another object or person (especially to the analyst, who may receive both positive and negative transference).

transformism: syn. *evolution;* the gradual changes in a species as a result of the impact of the environment upon survival.

transient disorders: those which arise from great environmental stress (e.g., in wartimes) and disappear as the situation becomes normal once again.

transmutation: converting raw scores on various tests into their equivalents as defined by a table of test norms in order to combine or compare scores.

transposition: in Gestalt psychology, the transfer of a previously achieved configuration or set of relationships to a new situation; also the shifting of a like or an aversion from its original direction to another one which is illogical or absurd.

transverse: lying at right angles to the medial or longitudinal axis of the body or the organ in question.

transvestism: the wearing of clothes and the use of mannerisms associated with the opposite sex.

trapezium: a transverse bundle of nerve fibers in the pons Varolii.

trauma (plural traumata): a blow or physical injury; also an upsetting experience.

traumatic disorder: a psychosis caused by a head injury, or either a psychosis or a neurosis caused by undue stress or tensions.

tremograph: apparatus for recording involuntary shaking in a finger, a limb, or the entire body.

tremolo: a rapid fluttering in a tone.

tremor: a trembling or shaking.

trephan: syn. *trephine;* to make a small incision in the skull, thus exposing part of the brain.

trial-and-error: (Thorndike) the gradual reduction in those responses which bring annoyance (disuse) and the tendency to repeat those which bring a reward (use), as the basic explanatory principle in the learning process.

tribadism: homosexuality among women.

trichromatism: in the Young-Helmholtz theory of color, normal ability to distinguish among colors, their hues, saturations, and brilliance differences.

tridimensional theory of feelings: Wundt's famous analysis into the following dimensions: pleasantness-unpleasantness, excitement-calm, strain-relaxation.

trigeminal: the 5th cranial nerve.

trigger: to release a response, the vigor of which has no direct relation to the strength of the stimulus.

triskaidekaphobia: superstitious attitudes towards the number 13.

tristemania: psychotic depression of melancholia.

tritanopia: blue-blindness.

trochlear: the 4th cranial nerve.

trophic functions: those pertaining to nutrition.

tropism: (Loeb) forced movements elicited in single-cell organisms either towards or away from the stimulus, and by extension similar types of forced movements in multicellular organisms.

tropometer: a device for measuring the rate and the extent of oscillation of the eyeball.

truant: one who has unexcused absences from school, but who, under attendance laws, should be there.

true-false test: a list of statements, often teacher-made, to be marked right or wrong, thus serving as a measure of achievement.

T-score: syn. *McCall score;* one that occurs on a 100-unit scale, each unit being 0.1 sigma of the distribution and the mean being set at 50, with the standard deviation being 10.

t-test: a determination of whether an obtained difference between scores meets the criteria established by Grosset ("Student").

tumescence: the swelling of genitalia.

tunnel vision: absence or restriction of peripheral vision.

twilight seizures: transient convulsive disorders and lapses of consciousness.

twilight vision: syn. *scotopic vision;* visual sensitivity under dim light; possibly, visual sensitivities mediated by the rods.

two-point threshold: syn. *threshold of just-noticeable differences;* the minimal distance for accurate report on whether two points, or one, is applied to contiguous areas on the skin.

tympanum: eardrum.

type: popularly, all the qualitative and the quantitative differences which set one group of individuals apart from other groups; also an individual who is a representative of the group to which he or she belongs.

typology: the doctrine that all persons may be fitted into a few clearly defined and differentiated bisocial or psychological categories (e.g., the current usage of psychiatric labels whereby to "type" persons or ethnic groups).

ulcer: the product of acid irritants upon mucous membranes causing a destruction of epithelial tissues and resultant damage; a condition said to ensue from hyperacidity caused by prolonged emotional strain, particularly in cases of peptic ulcer.

ultraviolet: light waves immediately outside the visible spectrum at the violet end; light waves below about 390 millimicrons in length.

ululation: psychotic howling or animal-like screeches.

uncinate gyrus or convolution: a part of the hippocampal gyrus containing the centers for olfaction.

unconditioned stimulus: one which elicits an unlearned response (e.g., food in the mouth of a hungry Pavlovian dog).

unconscious mind: in psychoanalysis, a dynamic and complex formation of a functional antagonism of a large part of the mind which is outside the field of awareness and the relatively small part which is directly accessible to consciousness; the totality of mental life which was never in consciousness at all or, once conscious, has been repressed into the unconscious (UCS). In analytical psychology (Jung), the unconscious mind includes not only the personal unconscious but also a racial unconsciousness made up of the archetypes or memory reverberations of a phylogenetic nature.

unconscious motivation: motives that cannot be fully intellectualized or unverbalized directions to behavior sequences; automatic behavior, such as reflective actions, habitual performances, or unintentional responses; in the psychoanalytic sense, the dynamic forces which impel the individual to actions the meaning and purpose of which lie outside the field of ego direction or awareness.

uncontrolled variables: factors which disrupt the experiment because they cannot be controlled, counteracted, measured, or anticipated.

undoing: in psychoanalysis, the mechanism or unconscious effort to abolish a tension, through a symbolic act, which is unacceptable to the ego or the superego (e.g., Lady Macbeth's compulsive handwashing); an act of trying to expiate for a repressed feeling of guilt or anxiety.

uniaural: pertaining to auditory sensitivity in but one ear.

unicellular: single-cell organism; protozoa (single-cell animal organisms) and protophyta (single-cell plants).

unilateral: pertaining to either the right or the left side of the body.

unimodal: a frequency curve or distribution with but one mode or high point.

uniocular: syn. *monocular;* pertaining to visual sensitivity in but one eye.

unit character: in Mendel's theory of heredity, any trait or characteristic, which transmitted in antagonistic pairs, either does or does not fully appear in the offspring.

universe: in statistics, all conceivable scores or data pertaining to the quantification; when the experimenter must be content with a sampling of the data, the totality in terms of which statistical corrections must be calculated (e.g., a standard error).

unpleasantness: awareness of a need for abient (withdrawal) behavior; a pervasive hedonic tone of rejection of whatever is productive of the feeling.

unproductive mania: excitement without flight of ideas.

unsocialized: not having acquired the folkways and the mores of the group.

unspaced practice: continuous repetitions of the materials to be learned without any interpolated activities or rest periods.

uraniscolalia: the speech of one hampered by a cleft palate.

uranism: a homosexual who rejects association with the opposite sex.

urethal character or personality: in psychoanalysis, one who has never completely outgrown childish erotic pleasure in the function of urinating.

urge: any strong motive which is in large part unconscious or unverbalized.

urning: a homosexual.

urogenital: pertaining to the organs concerned with reproduction and with voidance of urine.

utricle: a part of a membranous sac in the inner ear into which the semicircular canals lead; an organ in the inner ear which, with the saccule, mediates sensitivity regarding the position of the head.

uxorious: the condition of being neurotically or erotically fond of the wife.

vagus (penumogastric) nerve: the 10th cranial nerve.

valence: in Lewin's psychology, the positive-negative values of objects or situations; that quality of a situation which elicits approach or avoidance behavior.

validity: the degree to which a psychological test or measure actually predicts the criterion or whatever it is intended to measure. Validation is the process of improving the predictive value of a test or measure.

validity coefficient: quantitative scores being available on both the test or measure and the criterion, a coefficient of relationship between the test-measure scores and the criterion scores (e.g., the Binet Scale and a group test of intelligence).

value: the personal estimation of the quality of a situation; the score obtained on a test or measure; the degree of brilliance possessed by a hue.

value categories (Spranger, trans. 1928): theoretical, economic, aesthetic, social, political, and religious (mystical).

variable: a statistic representing the mathematical status of a performance; a score which may assume different mathematical values as conditions or cases are altered.

variable error: in psychophysics, the variation in quantitative results or scores which ensues when the experiment is repeated, caused by altered conditions, changes in method, or unintentional departures from strict control over the conditions.

variability: the dispersion of scores obtained by psychological tests, measures, or experiments; a characteristic spread of scores that is conveniently indicated by the standard deviation.

variance: in statistics, the standard deviation squared; the second moment about the mean of the scores; σ^2; the arithmetic mean of the deviations from the mean squared.

variate: the mathematical value assigned to a unit of performance.

varied-response stage: the initial exploratory or flexible behavior of performance when the individual is confronted by new choices in goal-directed activity.

vasomotor: nerve fibers, extending from the medulla oblongata, spinal cord, and autonomic nervous system, which contract (vasoconstrictors) and dilate (vasodilators) the muscle walls of blood vessels.

vasoreflex: contraction and dilation of the walls of blood vessels (the intima).

vector: in Lewinian psychology, a magnitude or force which may be represented by parallel lines (as in approach-approach or in avoidance-avoidance conflicts) or by divergent lines (as in approach-avoidance conflicts); a symbol indicating the translation of a point from one place to another in psychological space.

vegetative nervous system: traditional label for what is now referred to as the autonomic nervous system.

vehemence: neurotic or psychotic impetuosity and fury.

velleity: a condition of minimal volition or drive in making choices.

velum: syn. *soft palate.*

ventilate: the process of complete expression of the source for a mental conflict hitherto repressed from consciousness.

ventosity: neurotic or psychotic egocentricism and vanity.

ventral: designating that portion of the body or an organ which is anterior; the antonym of dorsal or posterior as applied to the body or an organ.

ventral median fissure: a pronounced recession in the central anterior aspect of the spinal cord.

ventricle: the cavity of an organ, as the cerebral ventricles containing a serous fluid which, if produced in abnormal amounts in early life may induce a condition known as hydrocephaly.

verbal report: a record of the mental concomitants of any behavior; a term preferred by some to the older word introspection.

verbal summator: syn. *tautaphone;* apparatus for successive repetitions of auditory stimuli (often meaningless sounds) until the listener reports that meaningful material is heard (Skinner).

verbal test: a psychological examination, individual or group, which presupposes a familiarity with the vernacular, written, printed, or spoken; any psychological test which would impose unfair handicaps upon an illiterate or non-English-speaking individual.

Figure 32. Sanford's vernier chronoscope.

verbigeration: psychotic incoherence and unintelligibility in use of the vernacular.

verification: the fourth stage in creative thinking, in which the illumination is tested realistically.

vernacular: one's mother tongue; the language an individual acquires from the earliest years of life.

vernier chronoscope: two pendulums which swing at different intervals, because of a small difference in length, and which, as measured by the number of swings to bring them into coincidence, indicate the reaction time between the release of the first and the second, the unit being usually 1/50 second.

veronalism: the condition of intoxication resulting from use of veronal (trade name for a barbiturate); mental confusion and ataxia induced by a hypnotic barbiturate.

vertebra: one of the bony structures composing the spine.

vertebrate: any animal having a backbone or spinal column, all such animals belonging to the division called Vertebrata.

vertigo: an attack of dizziness; a syncope or fainting spell.

vesania: psychosis.

vesicle: a membraneous cavity within the body.

vestibule: the utricle and the saccule, two bulb-shaped organs in the inner ear lying between the cochlea and the semicircular canals.

vestibular sensitivity: sensory cues which supply awareness of static orientation and body posture; proprioception from the inner ear furnishing cues for orientation with respect to gravity.

vestigial organ: one which has been outmoded in the evolution of the species but which is still present in the anatomy.

vibrato: syn. *tremolo*.

vibration sensation: sensitivity to alternating pressures brought into contact with a surface of the body.

vicarious experience: any experience received through fantasy, instruction, and the like, rather than through actual life relationships.

vicarious trial and error: ideational activity taking place before an overt choice is made in a learning situation; *VTE*. (Muenzinger, 1938).

Vigotsky Test: small blocks to be sorted in such a way as to indicate ability to form concepts; a measure of deterioration in the schizophrenic's ability to form abstract concepts in a sorting test modified from the Vigotsky by Hanfmann and Kasanin (1942).

Vineland Social Maturity Scale: a standardized developmental schedule, from birth to 25 years of age, indicating an individual's level of ability in taking care of needs and accepting responsibility for behavior, personal and social (Doll, 1936 *et seq.*).

violet: the hue experienced when the normal retina is stimulated by light waves about 433 millimicrons in length; the hues experienced at the upper end of the spectrum.

virago: a woman with aggressive, masculine tendencies.

virile member: syn. *penis.*

virtue: a trait of personality highly valued from an ethical or theological standpoint. Plato mentioned wisdom, temperance, courage, and justice as the four cardinal virtues.

vis-à-vis: face to face, as in an individual psychological test.

viscera: the organs within the cavities of the trunk of the body, such as intestines, liver, stomach, and so on; large internal organs.

visceral sensitivity: the sensations arising from stimulation, largely of interoceptors and sometimes of nociceptors, which give the individual awareness of hunger, pain, repletion, and the like.

viscerotonia: "The personality seems to center around the viscera. The digestive tract is king, and its welfare appears to define the primary purpose of life." (Sheldon, 1944).

visibility: the range of sensitivity to sight under such conditions as atmosphere, light, visual acuity, and so on, which determine whether visibility be reported as high or low or normal.

visibility curve: a curve which expresses the degree of visibility as a function of the wave length, with a wave length of 555 millimicrons as an arbitrary standard of reference.

visible spectrum: the relatively small range of light waves which arouse sensations of hues; the range from slightly below 400 millimicrons (violet) to slightly more than 700 millimicrons (red) in length.

vision: syn. *sight.* Vision is either monocular (one eye) or binocular (both eyes).

visionary: a daydreamer; in parapsychology, one who is gifted with prophetic insights.

visual field: the entire range of visual sensitivity at any given moment; the focus and the peripheral aspects of what is seen when the eyeballs are stationary.

visual purple: a substance in the rods of the human retina which bleaches on exposure to light and is said to function in twilight vision.

visual type: a person who has unusual ability to revive visual images of former experiences.

vita: a concisely expressed life history, usually as a prefatory section of a doctoral thesis.

vital capacity: a function measured by the number of cubic inches of air that an individual can exhale after a full inspiration.

vital statistics: recorded data pertaining to marriages, birth, deaths, health; demography.

vitalism: in philosophical biology, the doctrine that life processes are entirely different from physical forces.

vitascope: syn. *stroboscope.*

vitreous humor: the jelly-like substance within the posterior chamber of the eyeball.

vivid image: syn. *eidetic image.*

vocabulary: the total number of words which a person is able to use in speech or writing or to comprehend.

vocabulary test: a sampling of the total vocabulary of an individual, as in an intelligence test.

vocal cords: the pairs of folds of mucous membranes in the larynx concerned with speech. The vocal cords and all other organs involved in speech are called the vocal apparatus.

vocational guidance: the appraisal of aptitudes by tests, measures, interviews, and the like, to furnish information about patterns of interests, job opportunities, and potentialities for success in various types of positions.

volar surface: palm of hand or sole of foot.

volition: syn. *will.*

volley theory of hearing: repeated discharge of the nervous impulse over the auditory nerve fibers, the more intense the sound waves, the more fibers and the more volleys being involved. (Wever and Bray, 1930 *et seq.*).

volume: a tonal attribute of spaciousness, low tones being sensed as large or massive and high tones as small, thin (Stumpf, 1890).

voluntarianism: in philosophical psychology, the doctrine that freedom of choice is the predominant characteristic of the person.

voluntary: pertaining to an operant response; consciously, intentfully initiated.

von Kries theory of vision: the theory that rods mediate achromatic vision and cones chromatic vision; the duplicity theory of vision (Johann von Kries, 1895).

Vorstellung: the presentation of an idea to consciousness by way of memory or imagination; the reproduction of content once experienced through perceptual processes or the act of memory or imagination.

voyeur: in psychopathology, an individual who achieves sexual pleasure from watching members of the opposite sex undress; popularly called a peeping Tom.

wanderlust (nomadism):   irresistible impulse to travel purposelessly, as in senile dementia or in promptings by neurotic fantasion.

want: syn. *need.*

warmth: one of the four elementary cutaneous sensitivities.

warmth spot: a minute point on a cutaneous area which, when stimulated by a temperature cylinder above skin temperature, elicits a sensation of warmth.

warming-up period: some preliminary experience with a motor or physical task before the measurement of performance is initiated.

Wassermann test: a serological and spinal-fluid examination to determine presence or absence of syphilitic infection, the scores being expressed as plus or minus.

watch-tick test: a crude measure of auditory acuity in terms of the distance from which whispered digits or words can be just barely heard and repeated accurately.

waterfall illusion: an optical phenomenon usually demonstrated by fixating upon moving horizontal lines against a stationary background of horizontal lines, the latter appearing to move in the opposite direction (Helmholtz, 1866.)

weaning: in psychoanalysis, the breaking of ties which hitherto had afforded the individual ego-strength; emancipation from a state of dependency upon others.

Weber's law: a famous principle which states that for detection of just-noticeable-differences between pairs of stimuli, the stimuli must be increased or decreased in a definite ratio (Weber, 1834).

Wechsler Adult Intelligence Scale: a widely used measure of verbal and nonverbal intelligence, the content being more suitable for use with adults than in the previous Binet-type individual intelligence scales (also known as the Wechsler-Bellevue Intelligence Scale) (1939 *et seq.*).

Wechsler Intelligence Scale for Children: an adaptation of the Adult Scale (used with persons from 10 to 60) for use with children about 5 to 15 years of age; a downward extension of the Wechsler-Bellevue (WISC, 1949 *et seq.*).

weight experiment: in psychophysics, the procedure of judging the least noticeable difference between pairs of weights concealed from view behind a curtain.

weighted score: one which is assigned an arbitrary value greater than that given to other scores on subtests. It is also possible to weight scores in terms of statistical analyses of how well they predict the criterion.

weight-height tables: array of data giving the average height and and the average weight for successive school grades or age levels.

Weismannianism (Weismannism): in biology, the doctrine of the continuity of the germ plasm and of the impossibility that acquired characteristics may be transmitted by heredity (1809).

Wernicke area: a center in the posterior region of the superior temporal gyrus which mediates awareness of heard language; a brain center discovered by Karl Wernicke (1848-1905) impairments of which make it impossible to comprehend speech.

w-factor: Spearman's label for a trait of persistence, goalstriving, freedom from distractions; readiness to forego immediate goals in order to work for a major remote end.

whisper test: a rough measure of auditory acuity, the score expressed as the distance from which a whisper can be just noticeably detected and the content repeated.

white matter: those parts of the nervous system which are covered by a whitish, fatty substance or medullary covering known as the substance of Schwann.

whole method: the procedure in which materials to be learned, either by rote or for reproduction of meaning, are not broken into small units but are studied *in toto.*

whole-part-whole method: a procedure in teaching beginners to read, the first emphasis being upon sentences, phrases, and word recognition; then upon word analysis; and, finally, upon units of thought in the material.

Wiggly Block Test: a performance measure of proficiency in fitting nine pieces together into a block (O'Connor, 1928).

will: a broad concept, usually normative or ethical in connotation, designating persistence in voluntary choice or a direction of behavior toward remote, highly-valued goals.

Will Temperament Test: a measure of such traits as persistence, flexibility, speed of decision, and emotional control as revealed through handwriting (June Downey, 1923).

wish: a symbolically represented mode of eliminating a want; in psychoanalysis, the dynamic processes, usually unconscious, which lead to attempts at tension-reducing behavior.

wish-fulfillment: the symbolic representation, usually in fantasy, which, if reached, would palliate or eliminate psychic tensions; the functions of daydreams or nocturnal dreams, in psychoanalysis, are principally attempts to fulfill wishes frustrated by reality.

witchcraft: a delusional folk-belief that some persons, who actually may be mental defectives or psychotics, have voluntarily or against their will been possessed by evil spirits.

withdrawing reaction: in psychoanalysis, any behavior which, defensive in nature, either consciously or unconsciously affords some protection to the ego or the superego from reality.

withdrawal symptoms: such general reactions as schizoid (asocial) behavior; tendency to criticize others; over-response to flattery and hypersensitivity to criticism; and avoidance of competitive situations; in narcotic addicts, such symptoms as cramps, tremors, chills, and the like, following sudden deprivation.

Wonderlic Personnel Test: a 12-minute screening measure of intelligence used in selecting personnel for high-level industrial positions (1945).

Woodworth Personal Data Sheet: one of the first questionnaires for self-appraisal intended to reveal the presence or the absence of neurotic symptoms, designed (1917) by R. S. Woodworth for use with soldiers.

word association test: an attempt to explore the thought processes by making a record of sequential free associations (Galton, 1879), one word suggesting another and so on; or a list of words as stimuli which are to be responded to by the individual (Jung, 1910), who thus reveals "emotional complexes" and personal idiosyncracies.

world blindness (alexia): because of cerebral anomaly, an inability to perceive words as meaningful expressions in written or printed material.

word-fluency factor: a primary mental ability measurable by speed tests in finding rhymes and in anagrams (L. L. and T. G. Thurstone, 1941 *et seq.*).

word salad: incoherent, unintelligible speech; verbigeration; neologistic talk.

word-span test: a measure of the number of words, usually unrelated monosyllables, which, after one oral or visual presentation, can be reproduced verbatim.

work curve: a graphic representation of increments and decrements in output, physical or mental, during successive units of time.

work sample: a unit of performance, more or less typical of the whole task, which serves as a feasible measure on the basis of which to predict personal efficiency on a job or aptitude for satsifactory performance.

World Test: a series of miniature objects with which the individual may build a community, furnish a home, or represent a neighborhood, thus, presumably, bringing into expression conflictual tensions (C. Bühler, 1941).

worry: a dysphoric condition in which plans are reformulated but no action taken; a condition of pervasive anxiety and foreboding which is disruptive and maladjustive.

Wundt phonometer: apparatus for measuring auditory acuity by determining thresholds for sensitivity to small balls dropped from varying heights onto an ebony block.

Wundt's tridimensional theory of feelings: the famous doctrine that affective states are analyzable into the following continua or dimensions: pleasantness-unpleasantness, excitement-calm, and tension-relaxation.

Würzburg School: (so-named for the university); a group founded

by Oswald Külpe (c. 1900) which investigated su
as determining tendencies, imageless thought, mental s
associative functions, and systematic experimental intro
tions, all of which attracted much interest in the United St
of America.

xanthic: yellow.

xanthopsia: a pathological condition in which visual sensations seem to be yellowish in hue.

x-axis: the abscissa or horizontal line in a graph or Cartesian coordinate.

x-chromosome: the chromosome which, supposedly, when paired with another x chromosome in the zygote determines that the sex will be a female human being.

X-O Test: a cross-out measure of emotionality and interests developed by Pressey (1919).

xenoglossia: in parapsychology, the miraculous ability to understand and to use a language hitherto unknown by the psychic.

xenophobia: morbid dread of strangers or of unfamiliar customs.

y-axis: the ordinate or vertical line on a graph or Cartesian coordinate.

y-chromosome: the rudimentary chromosome which supposedly determines that the zygote develop into a male human being.

yellow: the sensation resulting from retinal stimulation in the normal human eye by light waves of approximately 575 millimicrons.

yellow spot (macula lutea): a pigmented area of the retina, about 1.1 millimeters in radius, within which lies the fovea centralis or center of keenest vision.

Yerkes-Bridges-Hartwick Scale (also known as the Yerkes-Bridges Scale): a point-scale adaptation of the Binet technique for measuring intelligence (1915); one of the first scales to determine mental age from a table of points.

Yerkes discrimination apparatus: a box in which the rat has to choose between two or more doors, only one of which leads to food, the discriminations usually having to be made on the basis of differences in illumination.

heory of color vision: a theory which posits
ndent processes in the retina, or in contiguous
ach being aroused by light waves, respectively, for
..ue, and green. The theory states that all other color
..eriences are analyzable into various combinations of these
..ree basic components.

..th: a loose term designating the interval between puberty and
young adulthood; roughly, the years between age 12 and
age 20.

zero correlation: a lack of any association between two distributions of scores.

Zöllner illusion: parallel lines which appear to slant because they are crossed by short diagonal lines.

zoöphilia: irrational affection for lower animals.

zoöphobia: morbid fear of lower animals, usually those of a harmless type.

Zeigarnik effect: the superiority of recall of unfinished tasks as compared to completed tasks.

z-scores: standard scores in which deviations of raw scores from the mean are expressed as multiples of the standard deviation in a plus-minus direction. ($z = x/\sigma.$)

Zuñi: Indians of New Mexico who are described as noncompetitive and as lacking interest in prestige or status values; hence, as a type of well-adjusted persons.

zygote: a cell resulting from the union of two gametes.

Zyve Test (Stanford Scientific Aptitude Test): a prognostic test developed to select research investigators (1927).